AMERICAN DREAM CARS

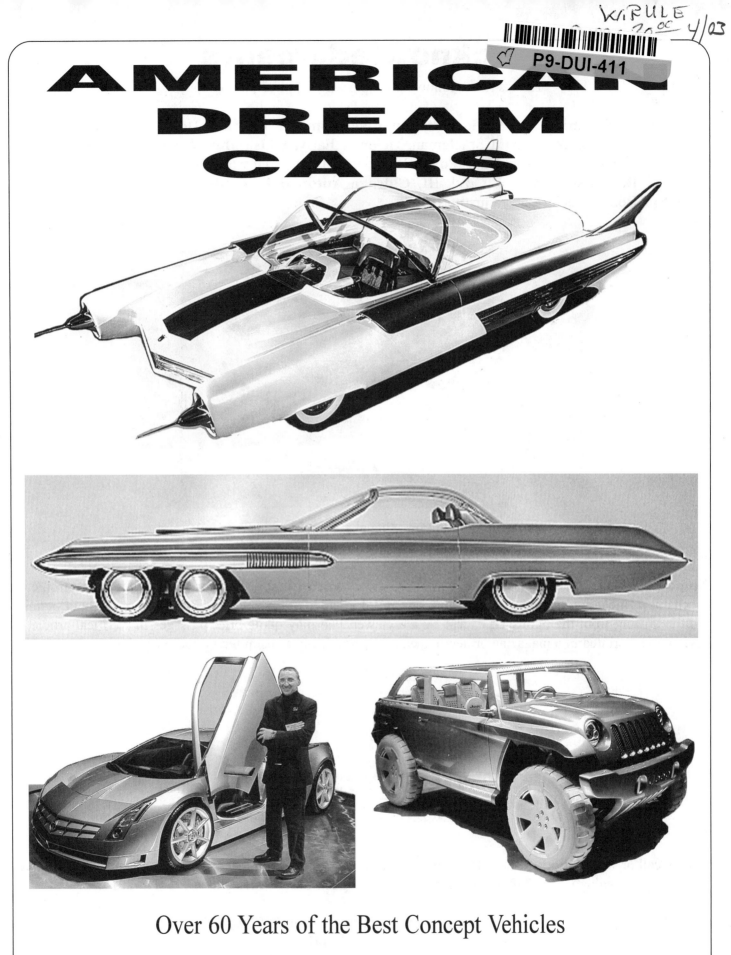

Over 60 Years of the Best Concept Vehicles

Mitchel J. Frumkin and Phil Hall

Acknowledgments

Thanks to the following people who supplied photography:

Mark Patrick, **The National Automotive History Collection, Detroit Library**; Tom Poliak; Richard Spielgman; Helen J. Early, **Oldsmobile History Center**; David Livingston; Gary Povalish; George Drolet; Howard S. Solotroff; Ray Barnowski; Jerry H. Cizek III, **Chicago Automobile Trade Association**; Jim Benjaminson, Larry Gustin, **Buick**.

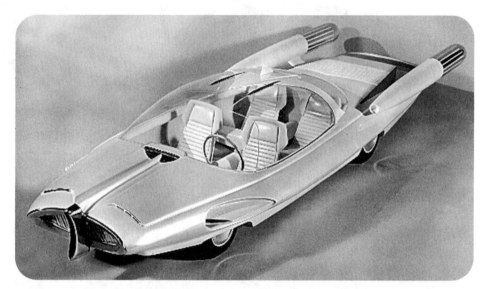

Published By:

krause publications

700 East State Street • Iola, WI 54990-0001
715/445-2214 • FAX: 715/445-4087   www.krause.com

Please call or write for our free catalog of publications. Our toll-free number to place an order or obtain a free catalog is 800-258-0929 or please use our regular business telephone 715-445-2214.

Library of Congress Catalog Number: 2002105753
ISBN: 0-87349-491-1

Photos featured on the front cover are: 2002 Dodge Razor, 1956 Buick Centurion, and 1994 Ford Power Stroke; **back cover:** 1959 Firebird III, 1999 GTO, and 1969 AMX/2; **Acknowledgments:** 1958 Ford X-2000; **Contents:** 1956 Oldsmobile Golden Rocket.

Contents

Introduction

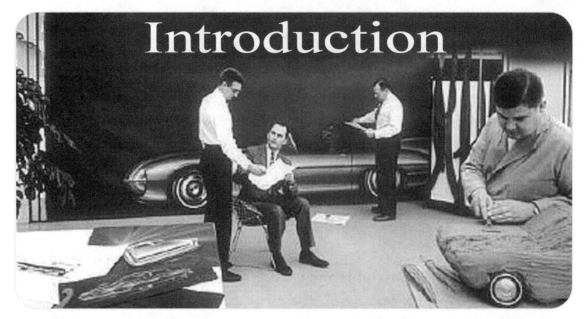

American Dream Cars is an attempt to corral as many dream, concept, and show cars as possible from the domestic automobile manufacturers. While hundreds are covered in this volume, many more dazzled and sometimes dumfounded the public over the past nearly 65 years.

Classifying and assigning a year on such a rowdy bunch of vehicles certainly is fodder for a healthy debate. Briefly, what we have attempted to do is show cars and trucks that the manufacturers displayed to the public in some fashion. They may have been seen at auto shows, trade shows, racing events, special manufacturer shows, or through the media.

As for years, it is difficult at best to come up with years for a group of vehicles that for the most part had no years assigned. While production vehicles usually have model years, dream/concept/show cars can cause confusion. They may first be shown late in one year, then appear at shows the next year and in some cases be shown for several years. Some were redone and shown off and on. Some are brought out of storage and appear several years later.

The authors generally tried to assign the model year when the vehicles were first displayed. Secondary level auto shows often have concept cars that are two to several years old, so the reader may have seen the concept car years after the one listed in this volume.

Names of the vehicles can be another area of controversy. Some have been shown under different brands. General Motors was great for showing cars under the GM banner, but having them in a Chevrolet, Pontiac, etc. exhibit. Exceptions are numerous.

Sometimes the names of the vehicles themselves are unclear. They could be listed under different names during their show lives. Also colors and equipment at any given time does not mean the vehicles stayed that way. You may see a listing for a red vehicle, but when you saw it, or the photo you've seen, shows a blue color.

Attempts have been made wherever possible to document the changes, but there is no way hundreds of vehicles can be detailed at all stages in the space available.

The vehicles themselves provide a wide variety of formats. Most are full-sized, but not all have drive trains, or even interiors. Those without engines are called rollers, for that's all they did. Some started as rollers, but eventually got power. Some were made in several versions and not all alike.

In some cases, the dream/concept cars shown are scale models. We have tried to point out those that were not full sized. In some cases, budgetary considerations eliminated the chance of a full mock-up or runner. The key, like all of the vehicles in this book, is that the vehicles were shown to the public.

In the process of design (pre-computer), a number of scale models are constructed before the full-sized clay was built. The authors have tried to stay away from such pre-production vehicles that were not displayed to the public. Of course, a few may have got by.

While the title of this book is *American Dream Cars*, not all of these vehicles are domestically sourced. The key element is that they were initiated by manufacturers from the United States. Some were built in Europe, especially in the shops specializing in coach work in Italy. Some were based on vehicles from overseas, like the Metropolitan. Ford Motor Company, with extensive facilities in Europe and eventual control of Ghia, fielded a bunch of cars that were shown in both Europe and North America. Some never left Europe, but were publicized by Ford here. In a few cases, Italian builders constructed cars based on U.S. chassis and drivetrains to get the attention of the domestic manufacturers. A few are covered and so mentioned.

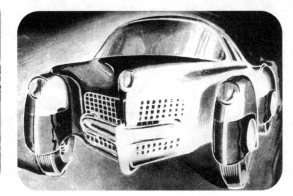

Why include dream cars, show cars, and concept cars in a volume when there is a great variance in the amount of original styling? Generally dream cars were products of the 1940s and 1950s, using a term Harley Earl of General Motors, coined. They were not based on production cars, but rather an original styling. We start with the 1938 Buick Y-Job and follow Chrysler, Ford, and independent makes as they show their ideas of the future.

Non-production dream cars dropped in number by the 1960s and many show cars, based on specially trimmed or modified production vehicles, took over the turntables at auto shows. Of course, there are exceptions and some pretty interesting ones, too, like the Chevrolet Mako Shark and Ford Mustang II.

Gradually the term concept car replaced the dream car tag. Idea car was another term, too. The onslaught of federal safety, emission and fuel economy standards in the late 1960s tied up budgets and some of the show cars of the 1970s were hardly modified at all. If you ignore these vehicles, there would be quite a gap between the 1960s and the 1980s.

With the advent of the 1980s, non-production concept cars that attempted to depict the future (much like those of the 1950s) returned. Not all concept cars just concentrated on styling. Fuel economy concerns, the future of the piston engine, and a rapidly expanding electronic universe made competition among the manufacturers for the most advanced concept vehicle a real race.

The flame that was relit in the 1980s is a five alarm fire today. With trucks taking half the new vehicle market, their population among concept vehicles has increased accordingly. Sport utility vehicles, pickups, crossovers, activity vehicles all are well represented in each round of new concept car introductions.

Show cars still exist today, but their importance has been, in most cases, overshadowed by the concepts. Many such vehicles are shown each November at the Specialty Equipment Manufacturers Association. (SEMA) show and a few are covered here.

Race cars from the manufacturers are generally not covered, but in some cases they were also displayed at shows and represent another phase of the concept spectrum.

After going over this book, considering the wide range of the subject, readers may have corrections or additional information. It is possible that this book will be updated down the road and the authors would appreciate all assistance in making such a volume a better one.

What is the purpose of a dream car? Show car? Concept car?

The manufacturers would like you to feel that they have a vision for the future and if you buy a vehicle from them, now or later, that you are making a good investment. They want their production products to attract buyers who saw a really neat vehicle they created.

For the authors, who experienced the excitement of the dream cars when they first came out in the 1950s, dream cars were appropriately named. Though short of their motoring years and traveling on bicycles, dream cars fostered dreams of what vehicles would be and created enough interest that following automotive history and looking for more dream cars became a lifetime vocation. In this book are hundreds of chances to dream, relive memories, and just get lost in what can be a wonderful, wacky, and in between world of automobiles, trucks, and vehicles.

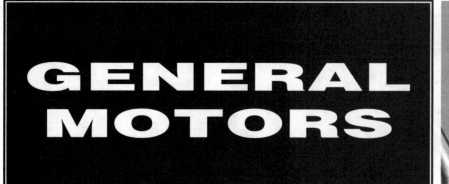

GENERAL MOTORS

Harley Earl

General Motors played a pivotal role in the design, development, and promotion of the dream car and continued its leading role right up through today where its concept vehicles are among the leaders of the industry.

Several factors played into GM's leadership role:

First and perhaps foremost was the vision of its head stylist Harley Earl, who more or less launched the dream car syndrome with the 1939 Buick Y-Job, then followed it up with a fleet of vehicles, like the GM LeSabre, Chevrolet Motorama Corvette, and a series of turbine-powered Firebirds.

Providing a stage for many of the dream cars of the 1950s were GM Motoramas, which showcased the latest dream cars from the various divisions and the corporation itself.

Succeeding Earl was William Mitchell, who shared Earl's love of style, but took it in new directions, supervising such creations at the Chevrolet Sting Ray, Shark, Mako Shark II and Buick Riviera Silver Arrows.

Having a virtually unlimited budget, compared to the competition, also fostered boldness in GM styling studies and concept cars (as dream cars were later called). Future leaders like Chuck Jordan carried the torch for new concepts as corporate philosophy permitted.

Like its competitors, GM reverted to show cars in the 1960s and especially in the 1970s. These were modified (sometimes barely) versions of production cars, so that there was something different on the turntables at auto shows.

Concept cars that shared little to nothing with production cars returned in the 1980s with the Aero series and similarly styled machines again trying to predict the future, much the way the dream cars did in the 1950s.

Although GM's 1955 L'Universelle van was a bold attempt to look at trucks of the future, it wasn't until the 1980s, when signs that recreational trucks were taking over part of the market from cars, that truck concept vehicles would start to be included in the new offerings on a regular basis. Today, trucks and cars divide the concept vehicle ranks at GM and elsewhere.

While General Motors' styling leadership was unquestioned during most of the 1950s, it would not always remain that way. GM concepts of the 1980s and first half of the 1990s were on par with the domestic competition. Chrysler Corporation began to take over the leading role. When the Dodge Viper and Plymouth Prowler were converted from concept to limited production vehicles in the 1990s, just like the 1953 Motorama Corvette, perhaps the time for GM had passed. Witness the Pontiac Aztek concept making production and it's even hard to debate.

Much of Chrysler's drive in styling was the work of Bob Lutz. When he and much of the soul left Chrysler after the takeover by Daimler-Benz of Germany, much of the leadership was gone, witness the Dodge Super 8 concept car.

Lutz landed as the new product czar at GM and suddenly the excitement and possible leadership is back. The quickly minted Pontiac Solstice of 2002 is exhibit A.

While styling leadership provides fodder for interesting debate, one factor in GM cars is that many were innovative in driveline development as well. Some were even raced. Bill Mitchell's Stingray was raced for two seasons before it became a show/concept car.

Zora Arkus-Duntov, the genius behind Corvette development, backed performance testing of the CERV-1 and various versions of Corvette concepts. Earl's turbine-powered Firebirds (I-III) were runners and were tested at speed.

While GM had no monopoly in running dream/concept cars, it certainly added to a display when you could claim that the Olds Aerotech held a world's record more than 250 mph.

This book covers concept cars through 2002. By all indication, those that follow will be even more interesting than what we've seen at General Motors.

William Mitchell

1951 LeSabre

One of two competing dream cars that started under Buick guidance, but went their separate ways was the General Motors LeSabre, first shown to the public in 1951. Though the LeSabre name would be picked up by Buick for 1959 and used to date and the side styling clearly had the Buick sweep, used in the 1950s, this example was the project of Harley Earl, head of GM Styling. It was not a Buick. In essence it was a replacement for the Buick Y-Job he used as his personal car and calling card for most of the 1940s. The XP-8 early in its development, the LeSabre became a competitor with the XP-9 (later Buick XP-300) under Buick General Manager Harlow Curtice. When he left the division to head General Motors, he kept the LeSabre alive and new Buick General Manager Ivan Wiles did the same with the XP-300. Both were shown in 1951.

Unlike the XP-300, the LeSabre went on to be used for Earl's new ride. It was based on the same basic chassis and aluminum supercharged, dual fuel V-8 and the XP-300, but differed in many ways, from rubber-based front suspension to a body that used cast magnesium body panels in many places.

Earl used aviation as an inspiration for many facets of his work and the LeSabre was a showcase.

The name came from the Air Force Sabre jet fighters, the front jet-like intake held two headlights, the rear fins hinted at P-38 induced Cadillac fins, and rear nozzle also was jet inspired. The interior instruments said aircraft in style and in the inclusion of an altimeter. Fuel tanks for gasoline and alcohol were in the rear fenders and limited trunk space.

As with any Earl creation, the longer you look, the more details you find. A clay version of the LeSabre appeared in print in fall of 1950. The real thing was displayed for the press in July of 1951.

A facelift of sorts was done for the 1953 return of the GM Motorama. Side vents up front helped overheating problems, as did exit vents in the front fenders, hidden behind ribbed panels beneath the chrome sweep. Also the rear wheel skirts were booted for an open look. As with the Y-Job, mechanical changes were made during Earl's travels with the LeSabre. Reportedly he could claim the majority of the 45,000 miles on the car, a figure few concept cars of today can hope to approach.

1954 XP-21 Firebird

Combining his love of aircraft and automotive design, Harley Earl came up with one of the most futuristic dream cars of all times, the XP-21 Firebird, which bowed at the 1954 General Motors Motorama.

Earl admitted influence from the Douglas Skyray delta wing fighter in coming up with a single passenger gas turbine powered experimental car.

With a jet-like nose, open front wheels, miniature wing, and vertical tail fin, the Firebird looked ready to take off. The driver was enclosed in cockpit, also like a jet fighter. Not just for looks, the jet theme was carried out with a Whirlfire GT-302 Turbo-power gas turbine, rated at 370 horsepower.

Though a large exhaust at the back looked like that of a jet, the rear wheels of the 2,500 pound car were driven by the turbine.

With an overall length of 222.7 inches and width of 80 inches, the fiberglass bodied XP-21 was only 41 inches high at the top of the cockpit.

At the trailing edges of the sings, brake panels would open up to assist the central-mounted drum brakes. Torsion bars assisted the front suspension and leafs the back.

Called the XP-21 at the start, the car became known as the Firebird I after subsequent versions of the Firebird came out for future years.

1956 Firebird II

For want of a better term, the Firebird II dream car, which was a highlight of General Motors' 1956 Motorama, was the family Firebird. A four-seater with a titanium body, it not only showed off its Whirlfire GT-304 gas turbine powerplant, it was also instrumental in GM's plan for a controlled access electronic highway. Such a roadway would have wires imbedded that vehicles made for it would pickup the signal and be able to run by automatic control. The unfulfilled plan still has its advocates to this day.

Still carrying a rear stabilizer fin, like the initial Firebird, the II added dual air intakes in front and pods behind the rear wheels. With four passenger seating, the engine was mounted up front. Access was almost conventional, compared to the first Firebird, with doors on each side and hatches in the roof. Wheels were kind of open, winglets and fins were found front and back.

Motoramas and Firebirds took 1957 and 1958 off, but both would return for 1959.

GM President Harlow Curtice waves from the Firebird II.

1959 Firebird III

Playing a starring role in GM's revived Motorama for 1959 was the third edition of the Firebird gas turbine series of dream cars.

The two-passenger Firebird III featured a double bubble cockpit, winglets seemingly everywhere and a toned down powerplant guided by an aircraft-inspired control system. Stretching 248.2 inches, the fiberglass bodied III was the longest Firebird yet. Wheelbase was less than half of the length at 119 inches.

Power came from two sources, a Whirlfire GT-305 gas turbine, rated at 225 horsepower and a two-cylinder 10-horsepower gasoline engine, which ran the accessories.

Access was a GM designer's delight with a combination of flip-up doors and cockpit bubbles.

Perhaps the most technically interesting feature was the Unicontrol, a console mounted knob of sorts that took care of the steering, acceleration, and braking, all with a twist of the wrist. It was useable by both driver and passenger, bringing up all sorts of interesting possibilities.

The Firebird III sat on a frame, with packages front and rear connected by a sturdy spine. An air-oil suspension connected the solid front and rear axles to the chassis. Firebird III was the last of three such designs in the 1950s, but not the last Firebird dream car.

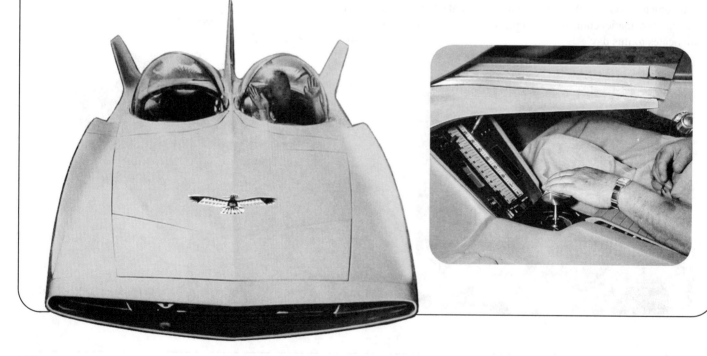

1964 Firebird IV

One of several cars General Motors showcased at its Futurama at the 1964 New York World's Fair was the Firebird IV.

Still not in the Pontiac camp, this GM dream car featured very futuristic styling like the first three Firebird designs, but not the gas turbine power.

It was intended to further showcase a programmed guidance system for electronically controlled highways of the future.

The driver was to use hand grips in the armrests. Shrouded wheels, flush glass, and fastback styling all contributed to the aerodynamics.

You weren't supposed to ask what powered the IV. It had no driveline.

1964 Runabout

Another 1964 Futurama resident was the Runabout, a three-wheeled shopper/commuter with a built-in shopping cart. Aerodynamically similar to the Firebird IV, it featured passenger access through the sliding canopy.

Driver equipment was sparse and a rear safety "Kangaroo Pocket" for the kids got you to and from the mall, along with your stash for the day. A roller, as they say, the Runabout had no known driveline.

GM

1964 GM-X Stiletto

Third of the three GM dream cars on display at the 1964 Futurama at the New York World's Fair was the GM-X, also known as the Stiletto.

Returning to jet-fighter themes of the 1950s Firebirds, the GM-X featured a pointed nose, fuselage-styled side panels, access from the rear, and a cockpit-like passenger compartment for two, complete with an aircraft influenced instrument panel and hand controls. Toggle switches were everywhere, along with lots of colored lights.

Fair folks were duly impressed, even though like the other two dream cars, drivelines were not included.

1972 ESV

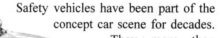

Safety vehicles have been part of the concept car scene for decades.

They more than likely are shown to please the government instead of the buying public.

Such was the case of General Motors' ESV (Experimental Safety Vehicle) which was shown to the public before being turned over to the U.S. Department of Transportation in 1972.

Based on the full-sized GM car of the period, it was designed to be crashed into a wall at 50 mph. Its objective was to protect unbelted test dummies in a 30-mph barrier crash, without special safety devices. Air cushions were to be utilized.

The car lacked front A-pillars for better vision and less chance of being impacted by occupants in a crash. The front bumper and body crush area more or less gave a preview of the bumper-regulated cars of 1973 and beyond.

Trunk lid side access was also used, so people would not stand behind the car when loading and unloading.

1969 Commuter Series

512 Electric

512
Gasoline-Electric

512 Gasoline

Delta 511 Gasoline

Future transportation needs could dictate miniature vehicles that address potential problems of fuel availability, urban crowding or clean air legislation.

In the pre-energy crisis year of 1969, the General Motors Engineering staff released a quartet of micro-commuter vehicles for press and public evaluation. Each took a somewhat different approach to minimal consumer needs.

The Delta 511 was a three-wheeled gasoline-powered two seater with a bit of the old dream car styling. A canopy lifts for access to the passenger compartment. Power comes from an Opel rear engine with an automatic transmission. A top speed of 80 mph was claimed, as was 30 mph in city traffic.

The other three were in the more compact 512 series, an elec-

tric, gas-electric, and open cockpit gas version.

The electric utilizes a Delco-Remy motor, lead-acid batteries, and has a built-in battery charger. A 58-mile range at 25 mph was claimed. A 12-hp gas engine, linked to an electric motor powered the hybrid, which was capable of operating both as a hybrid or electric.

The gas vehicle operated on a 12-hp engine alone. A variable ratio belt automatically guided the power. With a four-gallon tank, a range of 280 miles was touted or 70 miles per gallon.

Top speed of 45 mph was claimed. With cries today for high miles per gallon CAFÉ regulations from some quarters, perhaps these vehicles from a third of a century ago still may come to portend the future.

GM

1981 Aero X

An early entrant in General Motors Aero series of concept cars in the early 1980s was the fiberglass bodied Aero X, a four-door sedan which set themes for the group.

Included in its features were flush glass, flush door handles, sloping hood with special headlights, ground level air intake for the radiator, flush wheelcovers, and air-cheating rear view mirrors.

Future aero designs would appear under both the GM and individual brand banners.

1982 Aero 2000

General Motors followed up its Aero X four-door with a two-door version in 1982, the Aero 2000. The General turned out a number of Aero concepts in the period.

Probably the most notable feature of the 2000 was a console mounted control stick that took care of breaking, acceleration and steering, reachable by both driver and front seat passenger.

A similar control was a focal point on the 1959 Firebird III turbine dream car.

An early example of a head-up display projected instrumentation on the windshield for the driver. Video and navigation screens added to the display and information coming from the rather plain dashboard.

The four seat interior was accessed from sliding large doors on either side. Voice control took care of window settings, air conditioning, and heating.

Moveable wheel skirts aided in steering clearances and gave an assist to the aerodynamics, which were the theme of the car.

1984 Project Saturn

Dropping hints for its upcoming Saturn program, General Motors released photos of a concept four-door sedan around the start of 1984.

Called Project Saturn, it was conventionally styled and sized close to the Chevrolet Cavalier. Information distributed called for the car to be slightly smaller than the Cavalier and weigh 600 pounds less.

It noted plans called for the sedan, a coupe, and a SUV. A projection of 45 miles per gallon for the sedan was given.

GM did launch the Saturn brand for 1990, but the SUV did not make the lineup until 2002.

1988 Aero 2004

Centerpiece of General Motors' World of Motion display at the EPCOT Center at Walt Disney World starting in 1988 was Aero 2004, latest in the Aero series of concept cars from the General.

Featuring a pointed nose, adjustable rear spoiler, upward pivoting doors, removable roof panels, rear radiator, and even a digital license plate, it was a rather compact package at only 172.5 inches long, on a 104.5-inch wheelbase.

Height was a low 44.1 inches, but not as low as some of GM's 1950s dream cars.

1988 Lean Machine

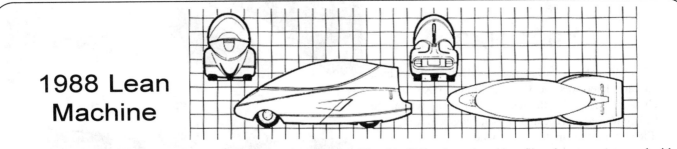

In an update of an earlier GM concept vehicle, the Lean Machine was also on display at Walt Disney World's EPCOT Center as part of the World of Motion.

Resembling an enclosed motorcycle with training wheels, the Lean Machine was actually a three wheeler.

The rider/driver is enclosed in a fiberglass passenger pod with steering, braking, and throttle controls integrated into the handle bars.

A two cylinder, liquid cooled four cycle engine, producing 38 horsepower, is located in the rear and supplies its power to a constantly variable automatic transmission via a cog belt. Wheelbase is 71 inches, overall length 122 inches and curb weight just 400 pounds, about that of a small motorcycle. A 0-60 mph run in 6.8 seconds was claimed. Its drag coefficient was a low .15.

Like the earlier model, its unique feature is to let the passenger pod lean into the turn while the rear power pack remains level…thus the name.

GM

1990 Impact

If ever a name was the opposite of a product's performance in the new car market, it was the Impact concept from General Motors. The battery-powered electric two-seater eventually reached production as the EV1 and was turned out in small numbers.

The Impact was announced in 1990 and was the result of a major development program drawing several GM groups.

A 2,550-pound coupe with a range of 120 miles and governed top speed of 75 mph, it was powered by a pack of 32 lead-acid 10-volt batteries. Most of them were in the central tunnel and some behind the passenger seats.

Two 57-horsepower electric motors, one in each front wheel, provided the motivation. The body was fiberglass and its lines could be considered aerodynamic.

After a number of delays, the EV1, was produced in Gen 1 form, with production starting in 1996 and finishing in 1997.

The cars were leased through Saturn dealers, not sold. A second batch of Gen II cars were completed by 1999. Getting them all in consumer hands took some time. Changes in battery systems and charging requirements were among the differences. Cars catching fire were among the problems.

1991 HX3

Utilizing technology that made production status about a decade later was the General Motors HX3 concept vehicle. Looking like the the minivan of the future, the HX3 combined electric and gasoline engine power.

Electric motors in the front wheels received power from a pack of 32 lead-acid batteries. When the level of charge got low, a three-cylinder gasoline engine fired up automatically and recharged them, running at a constant speed. The aerodynamically efficient (.258 Cd) body featured rear fender skirts, flush glass enclosed a lounge-type interior capable of holding five passengers and their luggage. A 120-

inch wheelbase and 184.2-inch overall length was not greatly different from contemporary minivans. Low resistance Goodyear tires worked with body styling to keep demands down on the HX3's mechanicals.

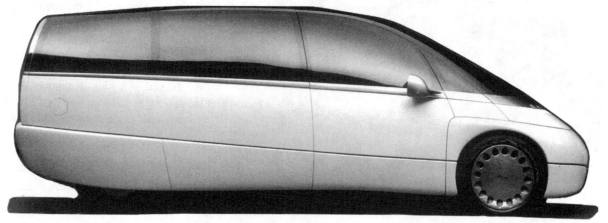

> *"Concept cars that look like bubble-topped motorcycles have been done. We wanted to take a shot at designing a fuel-efficient vehicle with real passenger car utility and comfort,"* Gary W. Dickinson, GM Technical Staffs Group

1992 Ultralite

The federal government was convinced that 100 mpg cars could easily be built, if only the domestic auto manufacturers would make the effort. Such an effort, to produce a 100 mpg car that people actually would want to buy, was the goal of General Motors.

A result was the Ultralite, a 1,400-pound four-passenger sedan that GM claimed could attain the fabled 100 miles per gallon goal while at a constant 50 mph on the highway. Powered by a rear-mounted GM's 1.5 liter, three-cylinder, two-stroke engine, the Ultralite achieved both an 80 mph figure in the EPA's highway test cycle, but could also claim a 0-60 run of 7.8 seconds.

Top speed claimed was 135 mph. All components of the Ultralite contributed to economy and efficiency. Both body and structure were carbon-fiber.

Side doors rose for access to both the front and back seats.

Window area gave an open feeling. High-intensity fiber-optic headlights and LED taillights were joined by fluorescent tube backup lights.

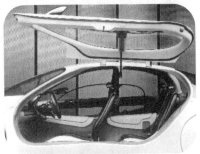

Ultralite caught both critics and car buffs by surprise. Sure, there were shortcuts like manual steering and a five-gallon fuel tank, but it was an attractive package.

To date, the government has yet to call for an 80-100 mpg vehicle to be produced.

2000 Precept

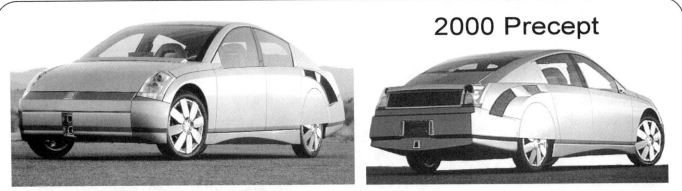

As part of the federal government's Partnership for a New Generation of Vehicle's program, General Motors built the Precipt concept vehicle, which featured a parallel hybrid propulsion system. That meant a small diesel engine driving the rear wheels and electric motors propelling the front.

The goal was to achieve 80 miles per gallon with an intermediate-sized sedan which offered acceptable comfort and performance.

An Izuzu 54-horsepower turbocharged, intercooled diesel in the rear helped with acceleration and hill climbing, while the electric unit taking power from the battery pack handled most of the motivation chores. A controller doled out the work assignments. A modified Opel transmission with a computer controlled clutch took care of forward speeds and reversing of the electric motor also reversed the car. Bragging a low .163 Cd, the outside looked similar to many concept vehicles, except for the rear where the air management for the radiator resulted in several vents of various sizes. Inside seating and electronics were all state of the art, not bare bones like might be imagined for an ultra-high efficiency machine.

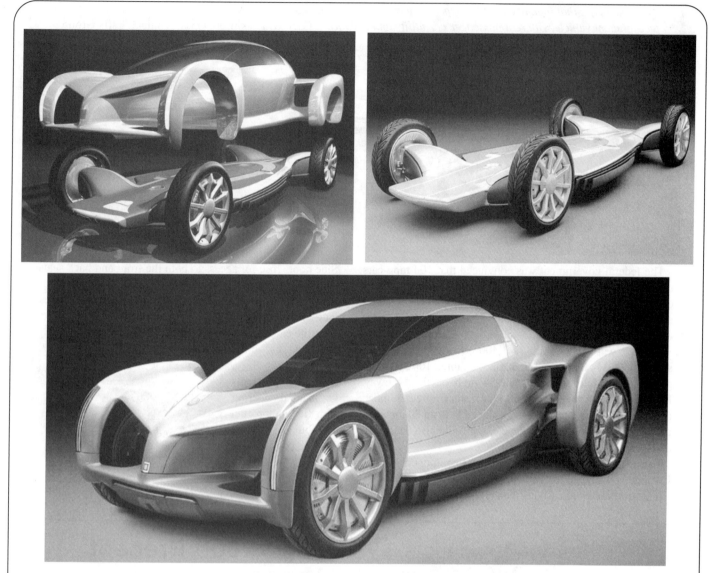

2002 AUTOnomy

An attempt to reinvent the automobile as we know it today has been made by General Motors. Shown at the 2002 North American International Auto Show in Detroit, the AUTOnomy starts with a chassis which contains all the propulsion elements. It is self contained, with a fuel cell, electric drive motors in the front wheels and drive-by-wire controls. Looking like a stylized skateboard, the chassis can be used to mount any one of several bodies, from the sports car body (called 2020) shown here to a sedan or wagon.

Even a single seat racing body could be mounted. Bodies connect to the chassis with several attachment points and a docking connection takes care of electrical connections for the braking, steering, drive power, and accessories. The car body would be freed of many of the parts it used to carry, giving designers a free reign to explore new packaging and styling. GM is claiming such a chassis design could last 20 years and could be feasible by 2020.

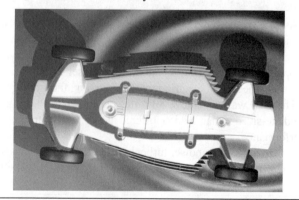

BUICK

1939 Y-Job

The Buick Y-Job is generally considered to have put dream or concept cars on the map. Shepherded by GM Styling boss Harley Earl, it was intended to show what futuristic cars GM and Buick could design, but it was also conceived of as classy personal transportation for Earl. It would serve both purposes well. Earl fought to get respect for styling at GM, helping getting the name of his department changed from Art and Colour to GM Styling. He had a good relationship with Buick general manager Harlow Curtice and convinced him that a style exercise shown in public could compliment Buick's current cars and build interest in the future.

The Y-job was started in 1938, using a current chassis and Buick 320-cubic inch straight 8. A convertible with only a bench front seat, it featured a horizontal grille with small vertical bars (which would become a Buick trademark to this day), hidden headlights, smoothed in fenders with ribbed trim, no running boards, a boat tail-like trunk, gun sight hood ornament. Its low overall height of 58-inches was helped and accented by its 13-inch wheels. The top folded into a compartment ahead of the trunk.

While it doesn't look all that radical now, in 1939 it stood apart from the crowd, as it was intended. The Y-Job was shown to the public after its completion, but not like the concept cars of today. Its main purpose was the personal transportation of Earl. He reportedly drove it regularly from 1940 until well past the war, when it was replaced by the 1951 LeSabre dream car.

Many mechanical upgrades were made during the 50,000 or so miles that Earl drove it. The Y-Job was not the first such cars of the future to be regularly driven, but its image was likely the most lasting.

It surely inspired a horde of 1950s GM dream cars and those that tried to out dazzle them.

Buick

1951 XP-300

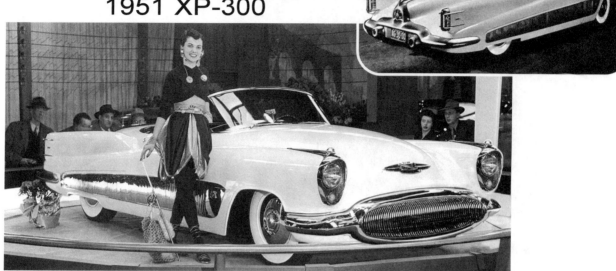

One of the two 1951 dream cars to come from the (more or less) friendly competition between GM Styling boss Harley Earl and Buick chief engineer Charles Chayne was the XP-9, which later became known as Buick XP-300. The other was the XP-8, known as the General Motors LeSabre.

Chayne and Earl each had their idea for a new dream car to replace 1939 Buick Y-Job. Division General Manager Harlow Curtice authorized the competing cars of the future in the 1940s and the race was on. Chayne set the chassis and driveline parameters for the two-seaters. A steel frame with an aluminum supercharged 215 cubic inch V-8 that ran on gasoline or methanol and produced 330 horsepower would be used for both.

The XP-300 used a torsion bar front suspension and de Dion independent rear, with Dynaflow automatic attached. It had an aluminum body, its two fuel tanks behind the seats and a split trunk. The concave grille in the front bumper, 1953-style headlight bezels and wraparound windshield all were direct sights to future production models. Almost solid chrome side sculpturing also previewed the future, perhaps inspiring the 1958 Buicks.

A rear jet-like exhaust contained a backup light. Chayne was a sports car/racing fan and the interior was very basic. A console contained gauges and other controls. A complicated hydraulic system powered the top, windows, seats, and jacking system. It was trouble prone in road use. Wheelbase was 115-inches, one less than the LeSabre and overall length was 192.5 inches, about eight shy of the LeSabre.

There was no GM Motorama in 1951, but the XP-300 was shown, before completion, at the 1951 Chicago Auto Show. It was runable later and shown to the press in October that year.

Its popularity led it to be included in the next Motorama, which was held in 1953.

1952 Skylark

Mid-year in 1952, Buick released a pre-production show car, the Skylark, that would preview the 1953 Skylark convertible. It featured many of the styling facets that not only were mirrored on the Skylark, but also would appear on other Buicks for years to come.

Most prominent were the fully cutout rear wheel openings and downswept door line, some three inches lower than the standard belt line at its lowest point. The elegant sweep of chrome on the side would continue through the 1958 models in various forms. Chrome wire wheels were shown off by the wheel openings.

Seats were lowered to fit the new bodywork and were finished in Helsinki red leather.

The body was Olympic white. Mounted on the Roadmaster chassis, it was powered by the 170 horsepower, 320 cubic inch straight eight.

When the mid-year Skylark bowed for 1953, power came from the new 322 cube V-8, rated at 188 hp.

The 1953 production version also featured new grille and rear fender styling, but kept the non-wraparound windshield, unlike its Oldsmobile Fiesta and Cadillac Eldorado counterparts.

1953 Wildcat

Plastic-bodied sports cars were the mainstay of General Motors' dream-car brigade for 1953. Buick's entry on the show circuit was the Wildcat, which gave more than a hint of the all-new 1954 models, including the Panoramic windshield. Only the Chevrolet Corvette made production status, a story in itself. While earlier dream cars featured special chassis and advanced engine designs, the Skylark was a test of fiberglass use and more a styling study than an engineering exercise.

The new V-8 was mounted on a shortened 114-inch wheelbase production chassis. There were front hood scoops flanking the hood ornament and portholes were mounted atop the front fend-ers. The front wheel covers were stationary and provided air vents for the brakes.

Skirted rear wheel openings contrasted with the open wheels on the Skylark and louvering added an extra, and possibly exces-sive, touch. Taillights harkened back to the 1949 models instead of forward, like other features on the car.

Wildcat nomenclature began a long run with Buick, not only in future dream cars, but production vehicles as well, starting mid-year in 1962. An updated 1954 version of the Wildcat featured full rear wheel openings, eliminating the skirts and louvers, and a removable hardtop.

1954 Wildcat II

Among the most radical of General Motors' mid-1950s dream cars was the Wildcat II, which bore little similar-ity to the original Wildcat, save being a Buick.

A basic plastic bodied, 100-inch wheel-base two-seater like the Corvette, was modified big time with a new front end featuring open fenders, free-standing headlights, chromed and louvered fend-er liner, and chromed suspension pieces. While we're on the chrome, wire wheels added to the glitter.

Buick's trademark portholes rode atop the sculptured hood. Twin spotlights flanked the Panoramic windshield.

Rear fenderlines and taillights followed the theme of the 1954 Skylark production car and chromed twin exhaust stacks exited the body.

Power came from the 322 CID V-8 which was topped by four carbure-tors. Individual front seats highlighted the well-styled interior.

While the Wildcat name would return again and again, actual produc-tion of a sports car from Buick would never materialize. The ill-fated Reatta of 1988 would be as close as it would come.

"My primary purpose for 28 years has been to lengthen and lower the American automobiles," Harley Earl

Buick

1954 Landau

Not all GM dream cars of the period were attempts at sports cars. Buick's Landau, shown in 1954, featured special bodywork on a Roadmaster 127-inch wheelbase chassis.

Buick was one of three GM makes that were all-new that year, highlighted by the Panoramic wraparound windshield. Among Landau features was special thin pillar sedan bodywork with the rear portion of the roof open, like a convertible. Much of the bodywork and trim below the beltline was from the production version.

Configured like a limousine, the front driver compartment of black leather contrasted with the saddle-toned rear passenger compartment that featured an armrest bar. The padded rear deck, which held the rear top when retracted, was held down by twin leather straps.

1955 Wildcat III

Making its third appearance on a Buick dream car in as many model years was the Wildcat nameplate, this time designated the III. Still in fiberglass, the Wildcat III was the first with a back seat. Though this was still not a big car with an overall length of 190 inches, styling previewed the 1957 models, at least from the side.

Frontal lines were rather subdued with absence of a hood ornament, portholes, or scoops.

The cowl air inlet was a bit exaggerated however. There was no rear bumper per se, but a pair of "Dagmars," named for the actress of such proportions, was beneath the small taillights.

A pair of bucket-type seats and a sculptured bench in the back aimed at the mass standard passenger car market, as opposed to the sports car folk. A rating of 280 horsepower was claimed from the four-carbed V-8.

1956 Centurion

All kinds of futuristic stuff could be found on the 1956 Buick Centurion. The fiberglass body featured a pointed nose with an indented grille and low level headlight pods, while the rear displayed a canted fin arrangement not unlike the 1959 production Buicks.

Aside from the transparent roof, the outstanding feature was a television camera mounted in the rear, over the jet-like bullet. This relayed a picture to the television screen on the dashboard and replaced the rear view mirror.

A dial in the center of the steering wheel handled gear selection for the Dynaflow automatic transmission.

Side trim and two toning reflected the 1956 production Buick and the tastes of the time. Front bucket seats and a contoured rear seat made this a four-passenger cruiser.

The Centurion name was a takeoff on the high performance Century line. It appeared many years later, in 1971, only after a battle for rights to it with an ambulance/hearse manufacturer.

1958 Lido

Italian coachbuilders and designers were no longer as involved in dream cars from U.S. manufacturers later in the 1950s.

The manufacturers were turning to in house and domestic builders for their latest attention-getters.

To attract their own attention, the Italian custom builders tried their hand at their own dream cars, based in U.S. chassis and mechanicals.

An example of this was the Buick Lido Coupe, shown by Pininfarina in 1958.

While attractive in appearance, it did not generate much attention or give clues to Buick's future styling.

1958 Wells Fargo

A popular attraction on the auto show circuit in 1958 was the Wells Fargo Buick. Based on the television show sponsored by Buick at the time, "Tales of Wells Fargo," it was a production-limited convertible, modified for star Dale Robertson with a western theme.

The rear chrome spear was replaced with a better looking walnut wood panel and appropriate lettering. Inside was plenty of armament, including a gun rack with rifles and pistol holsters holding same on the doors. Upholstery and floor covering used cowhide. A steer design was incorporated into the hood emblem.

Those who saw the Wells Fargo at shows were given a postcard of the car and Robertson.

When the show season ended, Robertson was given the car, just in time for its styling to be eclipsed by the all-new 1959 Buicks.

1959 Texas

To call attention to the all-new 1959 styling in general and station wagons in particular, Buick put the Texas wagon on the circuit that year.

Special badging and interior were part of the attraction, but most unusual was the metal sunroof over the front seat, a feature popular in imports at the time.

This scene, complete with an appropriate cowgirl, was not from Houston but rather at the Chicago Auto Show.

Buick

1964
Wildcat Sprint

After years of bouncing around on dream cars and engines, the Wildcat made production status in the Buick line as a mid-year performance model for 1962.

With fierce sounding names part of the marketing game for fast cars in the mid-1960s, the Wildcat Sprint made the show circuit in 1964.

Based on the production Wildcat convertible, it featured a variety of styling gimmicks, including rectangular headlights, a decade or so away from general use, but popular in Europe.

1963 Riviera Silver Arrow

If any single vehicle heralded the start of the Bill Mitchell era in General Motors styling, it was the 1963 Buick Riviera. While the production model was a sensation, even more of what the talented designer could do was reflected in the Silver Arrow show car. Complete with subtle trim changes, a filled in grille, headlights in the side pods, and wide whitewall tires, the Silver Arrow at first looked like a mild custom. A closer look will reveal a chopped roof, shortened body, and special multi-hued paint, in silver of course.

Photos of the car reveal what looked like different versions with details altered.

Mitchell continued to update the Silver Arrow for a few years after its introduction.

While called the Silver Arrow I today, due to the Silver Arrow II of 1968 and III of 1972, at its introduction it was simply the Silver Arrow.

As a further note, when the production of Rivieras came to a halt in 1999 (at least for now), final copies were called and trimmed as Silver Arrows.

1969 Century Cruiser

Needing a concept vehicle for auto shows in 1969, Buick dipped into the archives, so to speak, and recycled the General Motors Firebird IV, which first appeared at the 1964 New York World's Fair.

With hardly any changes, save badging, the unpowered Century Cruiser again touted its goal as an electronic guidance system concept that could be used on the automatic superhighway of the future.

It was changed from the original gold to blue. Equipment touted in the Buick included television, stereo, game table, and refrigerator.

Recycling concept cars was not all that unusual at GM, especially in times when budgets were tight.

1972 Silver Arrow III

More changes went into the Silver Arrow III version of the Riviera that immediately meet the eye. It was an attempt to make the boat tail design of the Riviera, which bowed for 1971, more integrated.

The roof was lowered and smoothed out and contained a B pillar, as opposed to the two-door hardtop setup on the production car. Triple rectangular headlights behind a single panel flanked the grille. Taillights were flared into twin pods on the roof.

Wire wheels and other trim variations all added to a lower look, but the styling of the 1971-73 Rivieras would take several years before gathering a following in the collector car field.

By the way, the Silver Arrow III followed the original 1963 Silver Arrow (which was later called Silver Arrow I) in being shown to the public. The 1968 Riviera Silver Arrow II did not reach the public domain, being an internal GM design study.

Buick

1983 Questor

After a couple of decades of relatively little innovation in show/dream cars, the domestic manufacturers returned to vehicles (now called concept cars) that attempted to look into the future, utilizing little from production cars.

An example of this, first shown for 1983, was the Buick Questor. It had a long life on the show circuit and was shown as late as 1995, painted white as shown here. For a look at the 1983 version, topped by a red paint job, see the color section.

The two-passenger coupe highlighted the latest Delco Electronics wizardry including multiple segment controllable seating, laser entry, CRT screen, adjustable road height and enough controls in the middle of the steering wheel to control a recording studio. Exterior styling was nearly void of Buick brand cues. Mechanicals were also absent, as there was no engine or driveline.

1985 Wildcat

Buick resurrected the Wildcat name from its dream cars of the 1950s for this one, but everything else was strictly out of the future. In cooperation with PPG Industries, this two-place concept car was accessed by a huge PPG plastic canopy. Once inside, the driver was confronted with a large circular screen in the middle of the steering wheel, on which all data was displayed.

A mid-engine design, the Buick V-6 racing engine sat right behind the passenger compartment. To enhance the competition theme, it was left uncovered.

Engines were a big deal at Buick at the time, as V-6 powered cars were among the fastest in the Indy 500. One won the pole in 1985.

While next to nothing from the Wildcat translated into future product, it established Buick as a major player in the concept car game, a position it would ride into the 21st century.

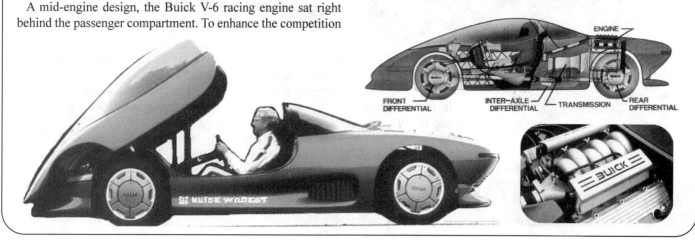

1988 Lucerne Coupe

1990 Lucerne Convertible

Flowing lines marked the Buick Lucerne coupe concept car of 1988. This was in contrast to the choppy Riviera and Regal designs that were released in the heart of General Motors' downsizing campaign.

Underneath the low, sloping hood was a traverse mounted V-8, driving the front wheels. Inside were the mandatory gadgetry including a hands-free cellular phone, silent non-key starting system and memory settings for seating, mirrors, and steering wheel. Room for four passengers with ample room removed it from the 2+2 class.

The Lucerne would have a double life in the concept car world and come back as a convertible a couple of show seasons down the road.

1989 Park Avenue Essence

Previewing production vehicles was a role the concept car would increasingly play as the 1990s progressed.

A case in point was the Park Avenue Essence that made the rounds in the 1989 show season.

Essentially it was a peak at the 1991 Park Avenue, but it was not just a fancied up production car. Front, roof, and rear details varied.

Trick stuff included a television screen for rear-seat passengers, individually adjustable climate control, navigation system, automatic wide opening doors and power footrests.

Many Buick sedan themes for the coming decade like the integrated grille were also apparent.

Buick

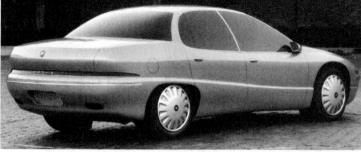

1990 Bolero

Like the Park Avenue Essence previewed an upcoming production, the Bolero was sent to prepare the masses for the 1992 Skylark. Its bold lines, especially in the greenhouse, were not nearly as foretelling as the Essence. Below the beltline there was more resemblance.

The kicked up bustle was in contrast to the smooth, sloping front, under which was a supercharged V-6, rated at 206 horsepower and, of course, spinning the front wheels. Besides styling, the Bolero was a showcase for fiber-optics with centrally located bulbs operating various lights including the trim taillights.

1992 Sceptre

A reaction to Chrysler's cab-forward design and the popularity of European imports was the mission of the Sceptre, a 1992 show season concept. With flowing lines from front to back, it carried the Buick design element signatures, most notably in the grille. A sloping windshield set the tone for the roof design. Perhaps even more unique for Buick was rear wheel drive, like the sport sedans from BMW and Mercedes-Benz.

Power came from a supercharged Buick V-6 with a styled cover and rows of fluid fillers built into the sides of the engine cover. Neither the cab-forward nor rear-wheel drive elements translated to production Buicks that followed.

1995 XP2000

Visually, the Buick XP2000 concept car could have passed for a future LeSabre, but if you thought that in 1995, you would be missing the point. It was meant to be a rolling (and auto show) billboard for the latest in electronic wizardry.

Take PCP (Personal Choice Plus) which filed all information regarding the driver, like seating, mirror, climate, sound, and security.

The driver merely touched his remote control and the car set itself up for his entry. Voice command systems for the radio, cellular phone, and climate changes were also built in. Head-up display on the windshield for key instrumentation-in color, was another facet.

Some of these items have reached production; others are still in development.

1998 Signia

Searching for the combination of sedan, minivan, and SUV, Buick broke some new ground with its Signia concept vehicle of 1998.

Starting with traditional Buick themes, like portholes in the hood and oval grille, the four-door wagon of sorts featured a removable rear greenhouse hatch and split lower tailgate with slide-out rear deck.

Inside wood trim recalled the luxury station wagons of the 1940s and brushed metal instrument surrounds gave a classy accent, yet there was navigation screen and the latest electronic features.

Television screens were mounted in the front seatbacks. Powering the front driver was the supercharged 3800 Series II V-6, rated at 240 horsepower.

No offroader, the Signia was very much on target for the crossover wagons that would become popular in the next decade.

1999 Cielo

Cielo means sky in Spanish and being able to view some while sitting in a Cielo likely ranks as the outstanding feature of many on this 1999 Buick concept car.

The retractable roof retains the side rails of a sedan, not unlike the 1950 Nash Rambler, but instead of a fabric top, the multi-piece Cielo roof retracts into the trunk area. To reflect the current market, the Cielo is a four-door model with center opening, articulated hinge units power operated, capable of opening wide to allow access for up to five passengers.

The beltline dips at the rear doors, returning to the 1950s Buick trademark. The grille also harks back to the 1930s and 40s. Both features would reappear on future concepts.

Power in the Cielo was a rather conventional 3800 Series II supercharged V-6, rated at 240 horsepower.

The automatic transmission also used throwback pushbutton controls…but it was a look to the competitors, as production Buicks did not have them. This was not the last use of the Cielo name on a Buick concept.

Buick

2000 Blackhawk

Buick pulled out all stops to answer the retro trend with the Blackhawk convertible of 2000. Parts of Buick''s past (literally) were pulled together into the concept. A 1939 Buick body and grille formed the basis of the car.

Power came from a 1970 GS Stage III 455 CID V-8, running through a modern 480LE automatic, of course driving the rear wheels. The carbon-fiber top retracts into the trunk area.

Wheelbase of 129-inches recalls the era from which the theme came. The frame was constructed for the Blackhawk.

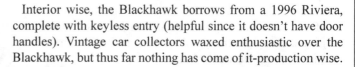

Interior wise, the Blackhawk borrows from a 1996 Riviera, complete with keyless entry (helpful since it doesn't have door handles). Vintage car collectors waxed enthusiastic over the Blackhawk, but thus far nothing has come of it-production wise.

2000 Regal Cielo

Applying the sliding roof panels of the 1999 Cielo concept car to the production 2000 Regal resulted in...the Regal Cielo, a concept shown in 2000. While the Regal GS was basically stock, its roof featured panels and a rear window that, when a button was pushed, slid neatly into a compartment just in front of the shortened trunk lid.

They moved on rails built into the roof just above the doors. Eight electric motors were involved and the whole system increased the weight just over 100 pounds. Special brakes and 17-inch wheels were about the only other changes from the standard Regal.

While interesting, the potential cost of several thousand dollars for such an option has thus far kept it from production.

2001 LaCrosse

If you liked the two previous Buick concept cars, the 1998 Signia wagon and 1999 Cielo open-roofed four-door hardtop, then you fully understood the 2000 LaCrosse, also a four-door hardtop.

Drawing on Buick themes going back to the 1939 Y-Job, it added portholes atop the front fenders to the portfolio. A side opening hood revealed a Northstar-like 4.2 liter V-8.

While it could pass for a luxury cruiser of the future, a nod to today's crossover market was a rear hatch that slid into the roof and revealed a wagon-like storage area that could be lengthened by folding down the rear seats.

Instrumentation, other than a clock, was not to be seen, unless you turned on the head-up windshield display. So popular was the LaCrosse that it was still on the auto show circuit two years later.

Buick

2001 Bengal

With a name no doubt derived from golfer Tiger Woods, who Buick sponsors on the PGA circuit, the Bengal concept car of 2001 origin explored the four-passenger roadster market. Of four-door design, the Bengal featured a modern rendition of a classic Buick grille, modest sculpturing, and combination spoiler/taillights.

Inside, the futuristic dash combined with head-up display that showed gauges on demand, voice-activated controls, and a traditional wire-mounted steering wheel.

A tonneau cover hid the rear seats when not in use and provided an area to stow your golf clubs.

Powering the front driver was a 3.4 liter V-6 connected to a six-speed automatic.

Buick needed new open cars to widen its model base and for awhile, Bengal was considered for production.

Despite the cancellation of the plan, the Bengal continued to be shown as a concept car in 2002.

1953 Orleans

At first glance, the Orleans looked like a 1953 Cadillac Coupe de Ville. However, its appearance at GM's Motorama that year was justified, as it was the first four-door hardtop shown by the corporation. Center-opening doors gave a preview of the popular body style, which debuted mid-year on production 1955 Oldsmobiles and Buicks.

The design was the brainchild of Harley Earl, chief GM designer.

Also incorporated into the Orleans was the wraparound windshield, which was also on the mid-1953 Cadillac Eldorado and other GM cars. While the Orleans didn't quite get the attention of the 1953 Cadillac LeMans dream car, it would have more effect on future Cadillacs.

1953 LeMans

Cadillac's entry in the fiberglass two-passenger sports cars in the 1953 General Motors Motorama, the LeMans, did not achieve the production status of the Chevrolet Corvette nor quite the attention of the Buick Wildcat (which followed the XP-300), but for the conservative luxury division, it was quite a splash.

Built on a 115-inch wheelbase with a hopped up 331.1-CID V-8, the LeMans drew from traditional Cadillac styling facets, like the P-38 inspired taillights, phony side scoop and heavy grille, the latter of which previewed the all-new 1954 production cars.

Returning to the rear, twin exhaust outlets provided the bulk of the bumper protection and the end of the long, long rear deck. Name wise, it wasn't quite a misnomer, as Cadillacs had done battle at the French road circuit, under the direction of Briggs Cunningham.

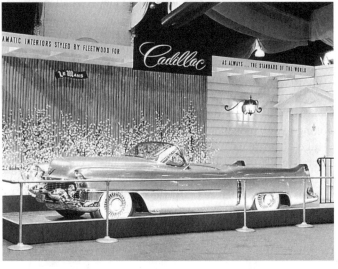

1954 LaEspada & El Camino

Using one basic two-passenger design and well-sculpted fiberglass, Cadillac released a pair of dream cars for 1954, both with Spanish names. LaEspada graced the convertible version, while El Camino meant a close coupled coupe. Both presented numerous styling clues to Cadillacs around the corner.

Harley Earl's edict that styling components should reflect light to attract the customer could be seen from countless angles.

From the quad headlights up front and the XP-21 Firebird-like fins at the rear, there was a clean break from the all-new-and heavy looking-1954 production cars.

Huge "Dagmars" flanked the simple eggcrate grille. A broad sweep of ribbed aluminum trailed the front wheel opening and the rear fins had resemblance to the 1958 models.

The wraparound Panoramic windshield swept back at a greater angle than the new cars.

Coupe doors contained frames, unlike the open window setup of the convertible. While small inside, overall length topped 200 inches. Overall height nudged past 51 inches. Power came from a Cadillac V-8.

Playing the name game, LaEspada went nowhere and El Camino migrated to Chevrolet, where it spent many years (1959-60, 1964-87) on a car-based pickup truck and later on a concept car. Two passenger production Cadillacs had to wait until the Allante in 1987. However, the new 2003 XLR is slated to come to market shortly.

Behind the wheel of the LaEspada is actor and future U.S. President Ronald Reagan.

LaEspada

El Camino

Cadillac

1954 Park Avenue

Mirroring GM's two-pronged attack in Motorama dream cars for 1954, Cadillac gave showgoers the Park Avenue four-door sedan, something closer to the customer base than the sporty LaEspada and El Camino. Using a Series Sixty chassis, GM Styling smoothed out the lines and added a few gimmicks, like triple lens taillights on each fin and stainless steel roof.

Despite showing the four-door pillarless hardtop style on the 1953 Orleans, this time thin window frames made for a more conservative appearance. Length topped 230 inches and height was a bit lower than production at just over 58 inches. Public reaction was positive and future four-door dream cars would follow. Also Park Avenue nomenclature would become a Cadillac fixture on the production vehicles and later Buicks.

1955 LaSalle II 4-Door

1955 LaSalle II Roadster

With the pending revival of the Lincoln Continental over at the Ford Motor Company, Cadillac's attempt at bringing back the LaSalle nameplate was predictable. While the Continental was a top line custom design, LaSalle was a junior nameplate to Cadillac, cancelled after the 1940 models.

For the 1955 Motorama show season, a pair of LaSalle II (the new Continental would be called the Mark II) dream cars were shown, a roadster and four-door hardtop. Basic styling was similar, but variations were quite interesting. Following the smaller theme of the original, the hardtop was mounted on a 108-inch wheelbase while the roadster had about eight inches less. Bodywork was fiberglass. Power for both came from an experimental overhead cam V-6.

Grille and front fenders borrowed from the 1940 LaSalle, but the cover back of the front wheel looked more like the upcoming 1956 Corvette. The sports car used semi-exposed wheels front and back, while the four door's wheels were more conventionally recessed into the bodywork.

It should be noted that sports cars dominated the 1953 Motorama dream cars, the LaSalle was the only one in the stable for the 1955 run.

No doubt satisfying to Harley Earl, who was instrumental in designing the original 1927 LaSalle, the LaSalle II did not lead to a revival. Rumors continued for several more years that the nameplate would return, but to date, like Rudolph Valentino, the journey back has not happened.

1955 Eldorado Brougham

Following up on the successful showing of the 1954 Park Avenue, Cadillac began preparing the way for the 1957 Eldorado Brougham with the 1955 Eldorado Brougham Motorama dream car. Not only did the steel four-door hardtop with center-opening doors preview the styling and quad headlights, it also was an attempt to downsize the Cadillac image. Overall length was 210 inches, some 17 less than the 1955 Series Sixty.

Overall height was reduced to 54.5 inches. Proportions remained very much a large car, helped by the ribbed bright panel over the rear wheel openings. More traditional-looking taillights returned.

Inside there were individual seats with the front set swiveling out to meet the passenger. Power came from an enhanced Eldorado V-8. As part of its display at the Chicago Auto Show that year, a spider-like frame was over the car to spotlight it, and frustrate photographers.

1956 Eldorado Brougham Town Car

Initial plans called for the Eldorado Brougham, which used a different body than the rest of the Cadillac line, to go into limited production in 1956. It would take another year to come about, so instead another Brougham dream car made the show circuit, the Town Car. Unlike the 1955 Eldorado Brougham and the 1957 production car, it used fiberglass body construction. It featured an open compartment in black Morocco leather for the driver and enclosed beige themed passenger abode.

Among the features awaiting the driven were radio-telephone, air conditioning controls, women's vanity, cigar humidor, thermos bottle, and glassware.

An electronic locking system both secured the doors when the vehicle was in motion and opened the center-opening doors when needed. Larger than the 1955 Brougham, it was 219.9-inches long and 55.8-inches high. Wheelbase was 129.5 inches. Save for the construction and roof design, the 1956 Town Car pretty well illustrated what was to come for 1957.

Cadillac

1959 Cyclone

Cadillac's Cyclone dream car, first shown in 1959, was full of all sorts of tricks. It also was steeped in mystery. Though it had a 325 horsepower Cadillac V-8, its connection to the division of GM is unclear. Styling brings it closer to GM's Firebird series turbine cars and the symbol on the fins is that of the original XP-21 Firebird. The multiple wings and transparent canopy that activated with the sliding doors also lean more toward the Firebirds (not Pontiacs at the time) than the luxury division. Questions are further raised as the car did not debut at GM's revived Motorama for 1959 (the first since 1956), but rather at the opening of Daytona International Speedway in Daytona Beach, Fla. Harley Earl's retirement in November of 1958 also may have played into the mix.

After Daytona, the Cyclone went on the auto show circuit. Mounted on a short 104-inch wheelbase and constructed of steel, the Cyclone sought to emulate jet aircraft, as the Firebirds before it. Two cones on the front fenders contained a type of radar, just like the fighters of the day. Headlights hid in the grille and popped to position when used. Despite the huge exhaust stacks at the back, fumes left early with mufflers in the engine compartment.

While the Cyclone drew massive attention at the shows and in the press, it led to next to nothing, as GM's dream car era, especially for Cadillac, went into hibernation. The Cyclone name moved over to Mercury where it found a home on a series of performance cars.

1959 Star Light

Pininfarina turned out a series of styling studies based on a Cadillac chassis and little else from the manufacturer. Devoid of trademark fins and egg crate grills, the cars drew some attention in the international press, but little from the intended audience, GM stylists.

After Detroit went to Italy for its early dream/show cars (for Pininfarina most notably Nash), now Italy was looking for business from Detroit.

This Star Light was shown at the Paris Auto Show in 1959. It had a single glass expanse that made up most of the roof, smooth styling, and nary a hint of Cadillac facets, save the wheel covers.

A similar Cadillac bowed two years later, the Jacqueline, named after the first lady, that could well have been the same car.

1962 Eldorado

With the dream-car era and Harley Earl's presence at GM Styling in the past, new dream cars were scarce, especially at Cadillac. This pair of convertibles made the 1962 and 1963 auto show circuits and were typical of mildly customized production cars put on display to attract auto show attendees to the Cadillac area. Other than special wheels, the open and flared rear wheel opening of the 1962 special Eldorado and the 1963 Calais are the main deviations from stock.

1963 Calais

1985 Cimarron PPG

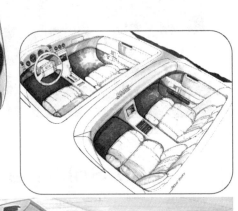

One of the catalysts of returning the domestic manufacturers to the concept car (formerly dream car) business was the pace car program sponsored by PPG Industries. These cars, originally from each of the domestic manufacturers, paced CART (Championship Auto Racing Teams) Indy Car World Series events.

The first were used in 1981 and they continued throughout the 1980s. While early examples were mildly customized production cars for the most part, by 1985 they were quite sophisticated, as shown by this Cimarron dual cowl four-door convertible.

Cadillac badly needed a boost for its small car and this special bodied custom surely didn't hurt.

Four individual seats with front and back consoles with built in televisions all belied the compact 106.2-inch wheelbase and front wheel drive 2.8 liter V-6 powerplant. Effective two-toning recalled an earlier era.

The PPG cars were not only seen at various race tracks, but many were on the auto show circuit as well.

Cadillac

1988 Voyage

Marking Cadillac's entry into the concept car sweepstakes was the Voyage, a study in aerodynamics and high tech equipment.

The four-door, four-passenger sedan was designed for stability at 200 mph and fuel efficiency, so the press release said. Door handles were replaced by remote controls and rear vision video cameras projected where the Voyage was on a screen on the instrument panel.

A hands-off cellular phone predicted the near future.

Front and rear wheels were partially covered, not unlike the 1949 Nash in styling, except that the front skirt was moveable. Overall, styling was smooth, save for the traditional Cadillac egg crate grille.

The last true non-production-based Cadillac concept/dream car was the 1959 Cyclone. The next was just around the corner.

1989 Solitiare

Following on the themes established in the 1988 Voyage, Cadillac's 1989 Solitaire concept car was a coupe, again featuring smooth lines and semi-enclosed wheels.

Perhaps the outstanding feature was the roof, a single front to back expanse of high impact safety net glass. Though it doesn't look like it, there is a back seat with access helped by a remote controlled articulated door system.

Video rear view system and hands free cellular phones were similar to those in the Voyage.

Lotus was in the GM fold at the time and helped put together the DOHC V-12 6.6-liter port injected engine. It was rated at 430 horsepower. There were MacPherson struts up front and a Corvette-like independent rear suspension with a fiberglass spring. Cast aluminum wheels were 20x7 inches.

1990 Aurora

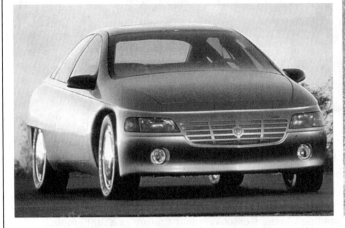

Showcasing Cadillac's answer to the luxury imports was the 1990 Aurora concept car. Styling of the six window greenhouse design, while aerodynamic, almost played second fiddle to the engineering. Four wheel drive with traction control drew power from the traverse Allante 4.5 liter V-8.

While the Aurora shown came with a TMM 700 R4 automatic, it was noted a ZF six speed manual gearbox could also be installed, something import buyers would notice. Each passenger got their own airbag.

The sunroof was adjustable in tint. A state of the art sound system, complete with CD player, ETAK navigational system and cellular phone all played to the technophile; however, there were analog gauges and a tool kit in the trunk for the European oriented.

Some of the features made it into Cadillacs, but the Aurora name drifted to Oldsmobile for a run on its luxury line.

1999 Steinmetz Catera

To infuse some pizzazz in its sagging Catera sales, Cadillac introduced its Steinmetz show car at the 1999 Chicago Auto Show. The bright orange sedan was modified by German tuner Steinmetz, which specialized in modifying Opels.

Since the Catera was an imported Opel Omega, it made sense. A supercharged version of the Catera/Opel three liter, DOHC V-6 produced 284 horsepower.

Among the features were a ground effects package, rear spoiler, 18-inch wheels, suspension tweaking, Recaro bucket seats, and aluminum pedals.

There were no plans to offer a Steinmetz edition, but the special vehicle did call attention to the Catera Sport package that was introduced at the same time.

Cadillac

1999 Evoq

Cadillac was serious about changing its image and solid proof of that was the Evoq concept sports car, shown to the public starting at the 1999 North American International Auto Show in Detroit. Featuring hard edge styling (they compared it to facets of a cut diamond), the two-place car combined a Corvette C-5 and a supercharged 4.2 liter Northstar V-8.

A Corvette-sourced four speed automatic transmission was connected to the rear differential. A rather long sports car wheelbase of 108 inches contrasted with a compact 168.5-inch overall length. Having its wheels near the corners helps account for the specs.

The two-piece retractable roof disappeared into the trunk area. Inside, a wide console separated the front bucket seats. Electronic gizmos abounded. From the start, it was stated that the Evoq was a serious candidate for production. While the name did not make the cut, the basic vehicle did.

As the XLR, it will be produced with the Corvette at GM's Bowling Green, Kentucky, plant starting as a 2003 model.

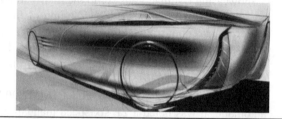

2000 Imaj

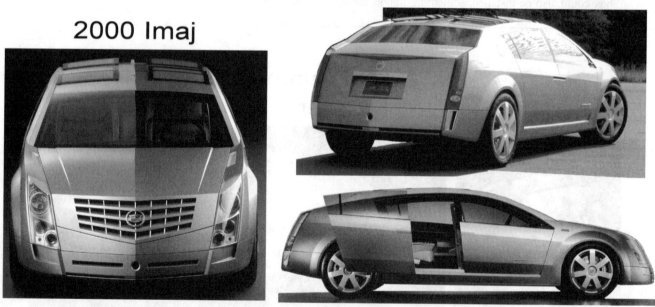

Applying the radical angled styling themes of its 1999 Evoq concept sports car to a four door sedan gave Cadillac its 2000 concept, the Imaj. While controversial, there is little question that the Imaj got spectators to take a look. Starting with an egg crate Cadillac-type grille, lines swept back to a short tail and trademark vertical taillights.

Center opening doors were not alike, as the front opened conventionally and the rear slid like those of a van.

A sunroof and four glass skylights gave the interior an open feeling. If that wasn't enough for the four inhabitants, each got a cell phone and laptop computer. The driver got to look at classy Bulgari-inspired instruments and a rear-view video screen.

Not all development money was spent on visuals, as a supercharged 4.2-liter Northstar V-8 was rated at 425 horsepower and sent its muscle to a five-speed automatic, StabiliTrak system and, eventually, all four wheels.

2000 LMP

As part of its efforts to convey a new image and compete with the European luxury brands already in racing, Cadillac took the plunge with the LMP (LeMans Prototype).

Cars were constructed by domestic builder Riley & Scott and powered by a twin-turbo version of Cadillac's Northstar four liter V-8.

Other than a new age Cadillac-type grille, the cars were not meant to resemble production or even concept Cadillacs. The European racers played by the same rules.

The LMP did attract some attention when it was displayed in shows and at tracks, but on the track, the perils of development kept success at bay.

In 2002, after many changes, the search of a major win for Cadillac is continuing.

2001 Vizon

As a continuation of Cadillac's sharp-edged styling theme of concepts from the previous two years, the Vizon cross-over vehicle was submitted for approval for the 2001 show go-round.

Seating four passengers in futuristic luxury, the Vizon had a rear cargo area and provision to use the console to carry long items such as skis. A two-way sunroof opened with the front panel able to angle upward and the rear could retract.

A naturally aspirated Northstar V-8 claimed 300 horsepower and a shift-by wire five-speed automatic transmission and a StabiliTrak controlled all wheel drive system got the power to the road, or wherever.

Not light, the Vizon weighed in at 4,870 pounds. Built on a 120-inch wheelbase, its length came out to 191.4-inches. Width was a narrow 70.9 inches.

More diamond-cut styling quests lied ahead for GM's luxury division.

Cadillac

2002 Cien

Simon Cox, GM executive director of the Advanced Design Studio in England, poses along with his award-winning Cien concept car during the 2002 Chicago Auto Show.

To celebrate its 100th anniversary, Cadillac put its new sharp angled styling on a mid-engine concept car for 2002, the Cien

Done in carbon fiber composite, the body featured scissor-style doors that pivot upward to allow access to the two-passenger interior. A removable hardtop, blue-tinted glass and a speed-sensitive rear spoiler all convey the message that the Cien can blow away any speed limit in the land. That thought was underlined by a 750-horsepower, 7.5 liter Northstar XV-12 concept engine.

With a new/old Cadillac innovation, it has Displacement on Demand, permitting the engine to run on six or all 12 cylinders. A racing type semi-automatic transmission conveys power to the rear wheels.

Inside, multiple liquid crystal displays take care of instrumentation, navigation, telematics, and rear-facing cameras. For the traditionalist, a Bulgari analog clock points at the numbers, with elegance of course.

Actually, Cadillac's 100th anniversary of production is in 2003, but that does not diminish the excitement of the Cien.

1953 Motorama Corvette

If there is one vehicle that launched dream cars into the orbit of legitimacy, it is the 1953 Chevrolet Corvette.

Introduced in January of 1953 at the GM Motorama at the Waldorf Astoria hotel in New York, the fiberglass sports car was a hit with the public from the start. What set it apart from its predecessors was that it was in mass production within six months of it debut. This link from dream to reality gave validation that these special show cars could be mined for vehicles that could make it to the road for the general public. That value still holds today with examples like the Dodge Viper, Plymouth Prowler and Chrysler Crossfire.

The basics of the Corvette are well known, full frame with Chevrolet passenger car suspension, tri-carbed Chevy six and Powerglide automatic transmission.

When production started in Flint, Mich., there were only minor trim changes, most notably the side spear was longer with the little wing reversed. A total of 300 were made. Production for 1954 shifted to St. Louis, Missouri.

The early Corvettes did not possess hard core sports car mechanicals, but it was a start and nearly 50 years later the Corvette is still with us, still fiberglass and full of true sports car performance hardware.

1954 Corvair

Following up on the successful 1953 Motorama Corvette were a trio of 1954 Corvette dream cars, the Corvair fastback coupe, Nomad station wagon and bolt-on hardtop for the production Corvette. All but the Corvair design reached production in some form. Converting the Corvette roadster to an enclosed coupe and extending the greenhouse to a four window design all gave a new look to the basic Corvette design.

A jet exhaust-like cove around the rear license plate completed the slanting rear roof design.

Three small vents in front of the front door and chrome slats behind the rear side window all gave typical GM design some interesting accents. Mechanically, it was similar to the 1954 Corvette with a Chevy six. Production was considered, but Corvette sales fell short of early expectations and ended any chance for a Corvette-based Corvair.

The nameplate did resurface as a name for the 1960-69 Chevrolet compact with the rear-mounted air-cooled six.

Chevrolet

1954 Nomad

Perhaps garnering the most attention of Chevrolet's three Motorama dream cars for 1954 was the Nomad, which looked like a Corvette station wagon.

In reality, it wasn't Corvette-based at all, but mounted on a 115-inch wheelbase Chevrolet wagon chassis. The front clip looked like standard Corvette, but was made especially to fit the width and cowl of the Nomad.

With unique frameless doors and rear window styling, the Nomad actually previewed the mid-1955 Chevrolet Bel Air Nomad in the passenger car line.

Rear end styling was a combination of future Nomad and Corvette.

Powering the Nomad, like all show and production Chevrolets for 1954, was the 235.5-CID six, with the Corvette triple carb setup and 150-horsepower rating.

Production Nomads would grace the Chevrolet passenger car line through 1957 (along with cousin Pontiac Safari), but the Nomad name would come and go for decades to come.

It was even recycled on a Chevrolet concept car in 1999.

1955 Biscayne

Chevrolet's first dream car that was not Corvette-themed came in 1955 when the Biscayne four-door hardtop made the Motorama and auto-show rounds.

With a few styling cues from the LaSalle II dream cars of the same year, the hood mounted headlights and center-opening pillarless doors gave the four-passenger design an airy feel.

Its large windshield not only wrapped around, but also went well into the roof. A cove, looking like a reverse of that on the

1956 Corvette, started in the front door and wrapped around to the rear and enclosed the taillights.

The wide-toothed grille and fenders with pods on the front end didn't quite match up with the smooth styling further back. Power came from Chevrolet's new 265-CID V-8.

Though the design didn't directly translate to the production line, like earlier Chevy dream cars, the name did, showing up as a mid-priced model for 1958 and being demoted to the bottom line for several seasons thereafter.

1956 Impala

A virtual lending library of ideas for future Chevrolets could be found in the 1956 Chevrolet Impala Motorama dream car. Built on a 116.5-inch wheelbase chassis with a 265-CID V-8, the Impala previewed the production 1958 Bel Air Impala hardtop on name, side trim and roof design with reverse-slanted C-pillar.

The fiberglass bodied coupe had room for five passengers. A Corvette-like grille and spoke wheels with knockoff hubs gave a sporty look.

The windshield design was similar to the 1955 Biscayne dream car and somewhat like that on the all-new 1959 production Chevrolets.

Rear styling also was Corvette influenced. The Impala would be Chevrolet's last Motorama dream car. The Motorama traveling transportation shows would take the next three model years off and return with production-based vehicles, at least as far as Chevrolet was concerned.

1956 Corvette SR-2

One of the earliest competition/development/show vehicles was the Corvette SR-2, constructed in 1956 off the Sebring Racer-2 chassis (thus the name).

Harley Earl supervised the design of a special body for it with a wide grille, side covers, and small single wing on the trunk. It was then given to his son Jerry to drive. However, it ended up being raced at Road America by Dick Thompson. It continued to be run in sports car road races as a development vehicle for Chevrolet driveline parts, including fuel injection.

It was considerably modified by Bill Mitchell (who would succeed Harley Earl as head of styling) for 1957 Daytona Beach speed trials duty, with a larger rear wing, trailing from a driver headrest, cones for the headlights, modified side coves (minus the scoops), and aluminum wheel covers.

An aircraft-like canopy was also designed to be used, if needed. Buck Baker drove the SR-2 to a win for the modified class in the standing start mile, at 93.047 mph, but lost out on flying mile honors to a Jaguar. The SR-2 continued to see sports car

duty, again as a development testbed, but the advent of the Corvette SS and GM taking seriously the Automobile Manufacturers Association. ban on factory involvement in racing, helped curtail any further major success.

The SR-2 continued to be shown and raced, under Mitchell's guidance, after the ban. A more-or-less replica of the SR-2 was built in 1956 for Harlow Curtice, GM president. It had a rear wing, but was a stock Corvette, mechanically.

Chevrolet

1957 Corvette Super Sport

While other experimental Corvettes of the period were constructed for racing, the 1957 Super Sport may have looked like a race car, but its primary purpose was the show circuit. Based on a production Corvette, the Super Sport featured twin cockpits, racing stripes and scoops in the rear of the cove area, similar to the SR-2 racing Corvette.

It had all the stock Corvette goodies, which meant it was an excellent performer, but its primary role was going around turntables, not race tracks.

1957 Corvette SS

Following early success with production models and the SR-2 racing version, Chevrolet was ready to take the step to the specially constructed race car, necessary to run with the best from Europe.

Under the guidance of Zora Arkus-Duntov, a tube chassis race car was constructed with the primary purpose of competition, not shows.

The Corvette SS was light weight with a magnesium body, independent rear suspension, inboard brakes, 283-CID fuel injection V-8, four-speed transmission and bodywork somewhat resembling the current Corvette of 1957.

Actually two cars were built, the looker shown here (with Duntov at the wheel) and a test mule for development.

The SS was entered at the Sebring, Florida, endurance race in March and failed to finish. A plan to build two more cars and enter the 24-hour LeMans (France) contest was quashed by the Automobile Manufacturers Association. ban on factory racing.

The SS survived for demonstration runs. The mule went on to real racing fame in Bill Mitchell's Sting Ray.

1959 Corvette XP-700

With entering competition by manufacturers banned at the time by the Automobile Manufacturers Association., it was back to show vehicles for Corvettes.

The Bill Mitchell guided XP-700 of 1959 was a styling study that the public was able to see.

A protruding grille predicted little, but the rear wraparound lines clearly were an early form of the restyling on the 1961-62 production Corvette. Exposed side exhaust carried the theme of the 1957 SS a bit further and provided a transition to the coming Shark/Mako Shark.

After the 1959 show rounds, the XP-700 was altered from the form shown here, with a longer and smaller grille, extended tail and double bubble plastic roof, complete with a periscope. Color went from red on the original to silver on the revision.

1960 Corvette XP-700: See Color Section

1959 Sting Ray

On its long road to becoming a Chevrolet show car, the Sting Ray led several lives and most of them took place on the race track. General Motors adhered to the AMA ban on factory racing, presenting a challenge to Bill Mitchell, head of the styling department. He took the Corvette SS test mule chassis, had Larry Shinoda design a body, got it cast in fiberglass and mounted, then entered it in sports car races at his own expense.

The result was tabbed the Sting Ray. Since Chevrolet could not be involved, the race car carried no Chevy nameplate in its two racing seasons. Dr. Dick Thompson and John Fitch were among the drivers of the fuel injected 283 powered machine in 1959.

Problems surfaced and the car was rebuilt for 1960 with new bodywork and mechanicals. It is shown here at Road America in the 1960 configuration (above). The Sting Ray was retired from racing after 1960.

However, Chevrolet now embraced the car and it was put on the show circuit (lower), bowing at Chicago in February of 1961. With the upcoming all-new 1963 Sting Ray production car, it was a popular attraction. Later it got a Mark IV 427 V-8 in place of the small block.

Many concept/show cars are made to look like race cars. Here is an early example of a vehicle that took the opposite route.

CORVETTE
STINGRAY
AN EXPERIMENTAL VEHICLE
TO TEST
HANDLING AND PERFORMANCE

Chevrolet

1960 CERV I

Where the CERV I fit in to the scheme of things at Chevrolet in the early 1960s is still a subject of debate some 40 years later. It was a test vehicle, a show vehicle but, strangely, not a vehicle that was raced in competition. CERV initially stood for Chevrolet Experimental Racing Vehicle. Since GM was in its anti-racing mode at the time, it later was changed to Chevrolet Engineering Research Vehicle.

Constructed to Indianapolis 500 specs (at a time when front engine roadsters ruled), it featured a rear-mounted small block 283 connected to leftover parts from Corvette SS project. Various racing venues were tested including a super speedway (Daytona), Pike's Peak, and a road course.

Ultimately, GM policies prevailed and the CERV I was never raced.

Over the years, it was fitted with different bodywork, engine combinations, and was used in several tests. It also was a popular attraction on the show circuit, but didn't make the 1961 Motorama.

Zora Arkus-Duntov, who guided Corvette and CERV I development, is shown with it here in its early bodywork.

1961 Shark/Mako Shark 1

To help entice the motoring world for the all-new 1963 Corvette Sting Ray, Chevrolet sent the Shark, designed *after* the 1963 design was finalized. Pulling cues and the bubble roof from the Corvette XP-700, the Shark featured styling cues from Bill Mitchell's racing Sting Ray, enhanced side exhaust and body tone variations, not unlike the mako shark Mitchell caught while deep-sea fishing.

Hood and side sculpturing very much previewed the 1963 product. Power started with a supercharged 327-CID small block V-8, but over the years, other engines were tried, including a big block 427.

It was mounted on a 1961-62 Corvette chassis, slightly modified. Initially it was billed as the Shark, but in its later life became the Mako Shark I, contrasting with the Mako Shark II, which would follow. Unlike the racing Sting Ray, the Shark was predominately a show car.

1961 Impala Special

General Motors Motorama shows ended their run after the 1961 version, but the emphasis on dream cars really ended after the 1956 show. The series was revived in 1959 and a few cars of the future were shown, but Chevrolets on display were production-based. An example was the 1961 Impala Special con-vertible. It featured bucket-type front seats, a special interior, modified exterior trim, and spoked wheels.

Note that it was not the Impala Super Sport (SS) mid-year option, which came with a bench front seat and different trim details. The show car did not intro-duce the 409-CID V-8 either.

1962 Monza SS & Monza GT

Auto show spectators were not the first to see a pair of Chevrolet Corvair idea cars, the Monza SS and GT. That honor went to fans at Road America (Elkhart Lake, Wis.) in 1962. The duo didn't go on the show circuit until 1963. Based on a stock Corvair rear-engine platform, the cars took the styling exercises of the division to the compact segment from the sports car Corvette, which had a bunch of dream/show/test vehicles over the past several years.

The open SS was a two-seater on a shortened 88-inch wheel-base. A cut down windshield made the SS appear even lower.

Of no less radical design was the GT, a coupe that had the body split in the middle for access. The rear half opened as well for engine access. Louvered rear windows gave a performance flavor. Both cars dropped a few hints as to what the next gen-eration 1965 Corvair would look like, especially in the cove that marked the back of the cars.

Chevrolet

1963 Monza

Super Spyder

Carrying more cues from the current production Corvair was the 1963 Monza Super Spyder, a two-passenger, shortened wheelbase show car from Chevrolet.

Exterior rear exhausts, redone front styling, cut down windshield and side windows and a sail panel for the driver, plus a single rear air inlet, not unlike a Porsche 356, marked the Super Spyder. It served both the race track exhibition and auto show schedules.

1964 Toronado

Designated for duty at the 1964 New York World's Fair was a customized version of the 1964 Chevrolet Impala convertible, the Toronado.

Rectangular headlights, chopped windshield, special wheels, side-exiting exhaust and special interior marked the show car.

Since the body style was in its final year, there was no follow up. However, the Toronado nameplate was grabbed by Oldsmobile for its 1966 front drive personal luxury car, where it garnered far more attention.

1964 Super Nova

Debuting at the New York Auto Show and later on view at the New York World's Fair was the Super Nova, a show car that combined the design of the basic compact Chevy II and sportiness of the Corvair Monza.

As it turned out, it would have provided competition for Ford's Mustang, soon to be released. However, the Mustang was in production and the Super Nova was a proposal-one that was turned down by GM brass.

As it turned out, the Super Nova laid the groundwork for the GM F-cars, which turned out to be the 1967 Chevrolet Camaro and Pontiac Firebird. It featured seating for four, bucket seats, a console, clean exterior styling, and rear-roof sail panels, which made the production 1966-67 Chevelles.

1965 Concours

Full-sized cars were gradually losing favor with young buyers as the 1960s progressed and the action in muscle and performance cars would be in the intermediate and smaller models.

However, in 1965, Chevrolet fielded the Concours convertible at the auto shows. It featured variations on the all-new Impala convertible like hidden headlights, subdued bumpers, special wheels and bucket seat stuffed interior.

It also provided a showcase for Chevy's new Mark IV 396-CID V-8, offered for the first time in its big cars that year. As for the Concours name, it made production status, not on a convertible but on a Chevelle station wagon in 1967 and other models from time to time.

Chevrolet

1965
Mako Shark II

Having multiple identities over its lifespan was what many consider the best looking Corvette idea car of all time, the 1965 Mark Shark II.

Led by chief stylist William L. Mitchell, the design team created coupe that turned out to foretell the 1968 production Corvette quite accurately. With a pop-up front clip and roof panel, the Marko Shark II styling featured enhanced fenderlines for the wheels and a nearly flat, slatted rear window.

Early, it was called the Mako Shark, but before its appearance, a decision was made to call the Shark the Mako Shark I and this new one, Mako Shark II. Side exhausts were on the early show model, which did not have a driveline. When the 427 was installed, the side exhaust was omitted. Both running and non-running versions can be seen here.

It was not the end for the vehicle however, as in 1969 it was rebodied and became the Manta Ray show vehicle.

Chevrolet

1965 Turbo Titan III

In the mid-1960s, there were several attempts to mate the gas turbine with heavy duty trucks. By far the most attractive and futuristic was the Turbo Titan III, shown by Chevrolet in 1965. An entirely new body covered the turbine.

Headlights popped out of the doors in the intake pods. Side windows flipped up. Chevrolet even stylized a trailer to go with the tractor.

The turbine never made mass production in big trucks and even cab styling has yet to attain the flowing line of this nearly 40-year old truck.

1965 El Camino Surfer

Just the thing to haul around surfboards was the 1965 El Camino Surfer, which made its debut in winter at the Chicago Auto Show-quite far from the nearest surf. With top and windshield header removed, mahogany side and tailgate trim, special wheels and trimmed out bed, the Surfer showed Chevrolet's imagination using its production vehicles.

As part of the display it was pulling a Chevy-powered racing boat.

The 396 Mark IV engine in the Surfer was likely up to the task.

1967 Camaro Waikiki : See Color Section

1967
Dream Camper II

Outfitted trucks were not all that common as show vehicles in the 1960s, but today are approaching half of the concept vehicles at auto shows.

In 1967, a Chevy Van 108 was shown with a fiberglass bubble roof with plexiglass front section, fold-out "balcony bedroom," and interior with refrigerator, stove, sink, and drawers.

It was not so much a glimpse of the future but rather an answer to the Volkswagen Camper, which was popular at the time.

1967 Astro I

With the Corvair phenomenon winding down, the Chevrolet Astro I would be the last major concept car based on the rear engine compact. With an 88-inch wheelbase and mid mounted air-cooled six, having one overhead cam per bank, the Astro I was not unlike the 1962 Monza GT. Both did not have doors, per se, but roof panels that split and flipped up to allow access to the two-person passenger compartment.

On the Astro, a hatch lifted behind the windshield. The seat rose to meet the passengers, then descended and reclined to allow the low roof to close. A periscope rear view mirror looked over the blind rear quarters. Astro I bowed at the 1967 New York Auto Show.

The Corvair died part way through the 1969 model run, but the Astro name would have a long life at Chevrolet, first on concept cars and later on an ageless rear wheel drive minivan.

Chevrolet

1968 Astro-Vette

Looking fast was what the Astro-Vette, first shown in 1968, was all about. Using the all-new 1968 Corvette chassis and basic body as a structure, Astro-Vette was a show car, not a go car.

While Corvette engineers were working with mid-engine, four-wheel drive prototypes, the motoring public was fed this sleek fiberglass open roadster. Huge painted flags on the front, abbreviated windshield, sleek airfoil/rollbar, rear skirts, implied ventwork, extended tail and flush wheels all gave the impression of speed capability.

No known speed runs were made.

1968 XP-880 Astro II

Following the mid-engine, Corvair-based Astro I was the Astro II, but there were several steps before this mid-engine machine became a show car. It started life as Chevrolet's XP-880 mid-engine research vehicle. Using a Chevrolet 427-CID V-8, Pontiac Tempest transaxle, rear mounted radiator and backbone frame, it was part of the division's exploring a mid-engine design for the next Corvette. It was not, however, the favored design of Corvette godfather Zora Arkus-Duntov.

After testing was completed, GM brass determined a show car was needed for the New York Auto Show. A new fiberglass body, with doors, was mounted on the chassis, a new interior designed and a name added, Astro II. When the car was shown to the public, it was already a dead end, but there would be more mid-engine Corvette prototype/show cars to come.

1968 Camaro Caribe

Combining a Camaro convertible with a small pickup truck was the premise of the Camaro Caribe, shown in 1968. Dropping an open pickup bed in a passenger car is not new, even an open one, but it sure attracted its share of "what ifs" at the time. Chopping down the windshield, installing a rollbar/airfoil combo behind the front seats, adding special trim, wheels, reflective tires and interior enhanced this show car.

1969 Astro III

Demonstrating a revived interest in the gas turbine, General Motors Astro III hit the show circuit for 1969-and well beyond, more often than not in a Chevrolet display. Though there was not a Chevrolet badge on the vehicle, the division handled the bulk of the publicity and transport.

An Allison turbine was located in the rear with a compact two-passenger compartment just ahead of it. Not unlike the belly tanker hot rods of the 1950s, the rear wheels were mounted in twin pods, fastened by a small wing. A pair of wheels up front were close together, making it look like a three-wheeler.

A canopy lifted to provide access to the aircraft inspired interior. Wheelbase was 94 inches while overall height just nudged past the 40-inch mark.

Astro III was the third in a series of Astro concept cars for Chevrolet, but not the last.

Chevrolet

1969/70 Manta Ray

After its show days were over, the 1965 Mako Shark II was driven awhile by Bill Mitchell. Then it was decided, since it looked so much like a production 1968 Corvette, the car would be restyled and shown again, this time as the Manta Ray. Changes to the roof and rear styling, plus the return of side exhausts, gave the Manta Ray a lower, wider look.

Power was updated to a ZL-1 aluminum 427-CID big block from the iron 427 and it was ready for its second life as an exhibition vehicle at race tracks and show car.

The shaded paint was more subdued than on the II.

It was the end of an era in a way, as future Corvette concept cars would explore other engine and chassis designs than the production cars had.

1970 Corvette XP-882

Zora Arkus-Duntov's idea of what the mid-engine Corvette of the future was supposed to be was the Corvette XP-882. In intra-Chevrolet competition with the XP-880, the 882 was drawn from the little shown CERV II test vehicle, which was mid-engine and four wheel drive.

Though not raced, the CERV-II (Chevrolet Engineering Research Vehicle), provided performance data. That crude package was put into passenger car form with the 882. Like the XP-880, it featured an automatic transmission, unlike the 880, the radiator was up front. Built by 1969, two prototypes had 400-CID small block V-8s and Turbo Hydra-Matic transmissions. Height was just 42 inches. GM politics, off and on racing/performance guilt pangs, and budget considerations killed the program.

Instead of wasting away, one of the prototypes was refurbished and put on display at the 1970 New York Auto Show to counteract the expected appearances of the DeTomaso mid-engine Pantera Ford would be marketing in the U.S. and the American Motors AMX/3, said to be ramping up to production.

The show biz decision was so fast for the metallic silver XP-882 that the GM bureaucracy didn't get a chance to put a new name to committee. As a result, the XP-882 tag was used at the show. The car was simply labeled a prototype.

1972 Camaro Berlinetta

Bill Mitchell had a 1970-1/2 Camaro he dubbed the Z28 Berlinetta. For 1972, it was updated with a soft, sloping front end and rectangular headlights. It was a proposal for the bumper-regulated 1973 and 1974 model years.

As it turned out, the frontal styling was close to the 1978 Camaros. For 1979, the Berlinetta name, tossed around for several years, was used to replace the Type LT designation. After Mitchell retired, the Berlinetta was put on the show circuit and was widely displayed in 1977.

1972 Reynolds Corvette

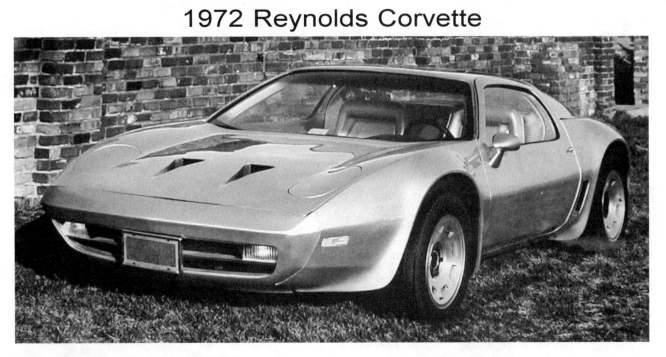

Body work was the story of the XP-895 Corvette project, or rather projects. Updating the mid-engine XP-882, new rounded bodywork was designed for the two working chassis.

One was done in steel, the other, in cooperation with Reynolds Metals Co. was in lighter weight aluminum. Reynolds sponsored the aluminum car, which was put on display by Chevrolet in 1972. As it turned out, the Reynolds body display was not long-lived. The XP-882 chassis would have yet another assignment at Chevrolet.

Chevrolet

1972 Corvette 2-Rotor

Though eventually billed as a Corvette, the 2-Rotor concept car was more of a prototype for the projected Chevrolet Monza 2+2 Wankel-powered subcompact and a replacement for the Opel GT.

General Motors bought into the Wankel rotary engine program big time in 1970 and envisioned the radical powerplant as a companion car to the Vega. The 2-Rotor was built in Italy by Pininfarina and based on a shortened Porsche 914 chassis.

It was built in 1972, but not shown to the public until 1973, along with the Corvette 4-Rotor. Corvette's entry into proposed uses for the Wankel did not come until after the 2-Rotor was under construction.

1973 Corvette 4-Rotor

When Chevrolet Engineering became convinced that joining the Wankel program to the mid-engine Corvette was the only way to reach production, work was started on the Corvette 4-Rotor, using a namesake version of the engine. For a chassis, the tried and true XP-882 was called on. It most recently had seen duty under the XP-895 Reynolds/steel body concept car. Sleek new bodywork, complete with gullwing, bifold combo doors belied what pieces had been there before.

It was decided to show both the 4-Rotor and the 2-Rotor, built by Pininfarina, in 1973 in Paris, before the domestic folk got to take a peek. Despite the high hopes, the Wankel winging went nowhere, thanks to development problems. When the Monza 2+2 and its siblings went on sale in 1975, conventional piston engines were found under the hood.

Eventually, the Japanese Mazda found success with the Wankel.

Chevrolet

1973 XP-898

Well disguised is the Vega heritage of the Chevrolet XP-898 coupe. What looked like an attempt at a Vega-based two-passenger sports car was touted more for its construction than configuration.

Using plastic basic structure, the XP-882 had urethane injected sandwich construction with suspension pieces attached to it. Crashworthiness was a major configuration, considering the upcoming bumper standards from the feds. Not only was it light, but the XP-898 was also small, with a 90-inch wheelbase and 166-inch overall length. Vega-based running gear was used.

1976 Monza Super Spyder II

Following up on the 1962 Corvair Monza Super Spyder was the 1976 Monza Super Spyder II, based on the production Monza 2+2 hatchback. Far less exotic, it used a basic Monza body with aerodynamic enhancements mike a sloped nose (containing a florescent headlight system), flared wheel openings and revised rear end treatment.

Power came from a Cosworth modified Vega four with sidedraft Weber carbs, attached to a Borg-Warner five-speed manual gearbox. It would be awhile before ground-up concept cars would again be common for General Motors makes.

Chevrolet

1977 Corvette Mulsanne

Show-and-go duties were assigned the Corvette Mulsanne, first seen in 1977 and for a long time thereafter. Powered by a 350-CID LT1, it featured a modified front end with covered headlights, periscope rear view mirror, and subtle reworking of the other body panels.

Named after the long straight on the LeMans (France) track, it saw duty as a pace car for the Sports Car Club of America's Canadian-American (Can Am) Challenge Series.

It was also a popular attraction at car shows and Corvette-related gatherings.

1978 Malibu Black Sterling

Keeping buyers' attention for its newly downsized intermediates was a chore four GM divisions faced for model year 1978.

Part of the plan was displaying a slightly customized Black Sterling version of the Malibu at auto shows.

Two-tone paint, rear spoiler, special wheels, and modified interior were attractions. It took awhile for younger buyers to warm up to the Malibu coupes, but after production of the rear-wheel-drive two-doors ceased in 1981, they went on to become popular street machine material.

1979 Camaro Ultra Z

At a time when the future of domestic V-8 engines was very much in question, it was refreshing to see Chevy put together a special performance experimental/show version of its Camaro.

The Ultra Z looked the role with a whale tail rear spoiler, two-tone paint, appropriate lettering, and an assortment of hood and fender vents. A T-top completed the exterior gingerbread.

All of the above contributed to its success as a show car in 1979 and 1980, but under the hood is where the real action was.

An aluminum 350-CID V-8 was accompanied by fuel injection and a turbocharger.

An automatic transmission was up to the torque demands of the powerplant.

1981
660 Turbo Citation

Determined to make its front-wheel drive Citation a performance addition to the pack, Chevrolet showed the 660 Turbo Citation in 1981. Mechanically, its claim to fame was a turbocharger boosting its 2.8 liter V-6 from 110 to 170 net horses.

Fiberglass body add-ons, trick wheels, appropriate lettering and a black-out grille all explored what a front wheel drive domestic performance car might look like. It would take the market nearly 20 years to take to the idea.

If nothing else, the 660 called attention to the new X-11 performance option for the Citation hatchback.

1981 Turbo Vette III

Chevrolet did a series of turbocharged Corvettes in the late 1970s and early 1980s, exploring the advantages of the exhaust-driven turbocharger to extract performance from smaller displacement engines.

For 1981, the experimental Turbo Vette III was on stage. It featured a throttle body fuel injection setup on an aluminum 350-CID V-8 and Garrett Air Research turbocharger. A boost of 30 percent in output was claimed. Graphics carried the exterior treatment with multi-hued blue striping on a pearlescent white coupe body. Nearing the end of its production run, the last Corvette of the third generation was the 1982 model.

1982 TPC

Not all concept cars probed the aerodynamics and performance horizons of the future. In the early 1980s, several looked at how small a package could be used to provide transportation in the possibly fuel-starved years ahead. One such example was the Chevrolet TPC (Two Passenger Commuter), which made the auto show circuit in 1982.

Developed by General Motors Advanced Product and Manufacturing Engineering, it featured minimal body bulk, a .8 liter three-cylinder engine and five-speed manual transmission. Having only a four-gallon tank, it was said to provide a range of from 270 to 380 miles, depending on the traffic or highway cycles of the EPA test. Miles per gallon claims ranged from 68 to 95. It weighed in at only 1,070 pounds and had overall length of 128.4 inches.

Thus far, Chevrolets this small have yet to be produced.

Chevrolet

1983 Aero 2002

Claimed to have the lowest aerodynamic drag coefficient (Cd) of any car of its size ever tested by General Motors, was the Chevrolet Aero 2002, shown in 1983. The four-passenger Citation concept had a Cd of .14 and required only 2.1 horsepower to overcome wind resistance at 50 mph.

If the body were used on a Citation chassis, it was said to be capable of 65 miles per gallon at highway speeds.

A 68 degree windshield rake, enclosed underbody, flush glass all around and enclosed wheels were part of the slippery package.

Chevy later noted that the Aero 2002 was only a mockup and didn't have a full interior or driveline.

1984 Citation IV

Following up on the Aero 2002 was the 1984 Citation IV concept car. It explored the combination of outstanding aerodynamics and transportation needs and unlike the 2002, had body interior and a driveline. Claiming a Cd of .265, it was noted to be superior to the all-new 1984 Corvette's .341.

Wheels were more exposed, wipers and exterior rear view mirrors added to drag, but this was a useable vehicle.

Power came from a fuel injected 2.8 liter V-6.

Front suspension was a variation on the Corvette single-leaf composite fiberglass spring used in the rear. There was room for four passengers on the trim bucket seats. Wheelbase was a bit shy of 103 inches and overall length was 183.1 inches.

1984 ASC Lumina El Camino

American Sunroof Corp. (ASC) was doing convertible conversions and other projects for Chevrolet at the time and it was looking for more work.

Front wheel drive pickups were on the market in 1984 when this Lumina El Camino proposal was fielded. The rear wheel drive El Camino was in production at the time and would be into 1987.

This concept failed to translate to a production model.

1983 Corvette GTP

Unveiled June 1, 1983 at the Detroit Grand Prix, the Corvette GTP was a clear indication Chevrolet and General Motors were officially back in auto racing. Actually, the GTP had little in common with the Corvette, as it was a pure race car, utilizing a Lola chassis with a mid-mounted 209-CID turbocharged V-6 engine.

It conformed to International Motor Sports Association. (IMSA) Camel GT Series rules and was intended for both show and competition, not unlike the 1957 Corvette SS, when Chevy was also in racing.

The fiberglass body was similar to other GTP racers at the time more than the Corvette.

Racing development of the GTP was turned over to Rick Hendrick and other examples were constructed. Despite many changes, the Corvette GTP did not garner much success for Chevrolet.

Chevrolet

1985 Camaro GTZ

Smoothing out the aerodynamics of the contemporary Camaro made for quite an attractive show vehicle in 1985. The GTZ, done in yellow and black, used enhancements from front to back.

Starting with the nose, the new front clip (held on with hood pins) enclosed the headlights, altered the grille opening, picked up two rows of louvers in the hood and gracefully merged with the ground effects bodywork. A spoilered tail, winged rear valence panel, and flush taillights brought up the rear.

A racing type fuel filler and small scoops in front of each wheel complimented the changes. Inside was a black leather interior with yellow striping.

It appeared during Chevy's racing V-6 development period and thus had an aluminum 4.3-liter version with fuel injection. A five-speed gearbox helped spin the rear wheels.

1985 Eurosport RS

A pre-production show car making the rounds in 1985 was Chevrolet's Eurosport RS. A Celebrity four-door sedan with the Eurosport option was fancied up with a blackout grille, ground effects bodywork, front air dam, headlight covers and rear spoiler. Wider 225/50VR-16 tires and a 3.3 liter V-6 with fuel injection were among the mechanical features. Many of the pieces showed up on the mid-1987 Eurosport VR option for the production Celebrity four-door sedan and wagons.

1985 Twin Turbo S-10

Performance vehicles that get their first public showing at the Specialty Equipment Manufacturers Association. (SEMA) show each fall in Las Vegas would become increasingly common. Shown in 1985 was the Twin Turbo S-10, a pickup truck with fiberglass rear window surround deck pieces. Dual turbochargers boosted its fuel injected 2.8 liter V-6.

Wheels were from a Camaro Z28.

Chevrolet

1986 Corvette Indy

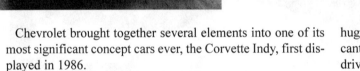

Chevrolet brought together several elements into one of its most significant concept cars ever, the Corvette Indy, first displayed in 1986.

Combining its Ilmor-sourced Indy 2.65 liter Indy V-8, its experience in mid-engine Corvette prototypes and aerodynamically bold recent concepts like the Citation IV, the Corvette Indy again pointed to a possible design for a future Corvette. The twin turbocharged, double overhead cam V-8 was mounted transversely and visible through the rear window. The package was sleek, featured a transparent roof and huge side scoops for the engine. Perhaps even more significant were features like drive by wire controls, four wheel drive, four-wheel steering, traction control, active suspension, and anti-lock brakes.

A cathode ray tube and dedicated rear camera provide vision arrears. Each door housed climate and radio controls. While we are still waiting for the first mid-engine Corvette, many of the Corvette Indy features have made production status. After a long absence, Chevy has even returned to have its name on an Indy engine.

1987 Aero 2003A

The lowest coefficient of drag of any vehicle on the planet, .166, was claimed for the Chevrolet Aero 2003A, which was among the concept cars shown in 1987.

It was an update on the 1984 Citation IV concept with enhanced wheel skirting, hidden wipers, inside mirror, hydraulic height adjustment system, and smoothed underside.

Power remained from a 2.8 liter, fuel- injected V-6.

Chevrolet

1987 Express

More than just another aerodynamic concept vehicle, the Chevrolet Express, initially shown in 1987, was the latest iteration of General Motors' long-running experimentation with the gas turbine.

Powered by a mid-mounted GM AGT-5 turbine, the Express was designed to be capable of running at a constant 150 miles per hour. Not a toy for the hot rodder, it was to be part of a system of federal limited access highways where high speed travel was the norm.

The four passenger, two-door car was accessed with a hatch raising the roof. Cd was an amazing .195. Ground effects built into the carbon-fiber body, covered wheels and engine location were all part of the speed package.

Electronic gadgetry abounded including drive-by-wire controls, instrumentation and three dash-mounted screens and cameras replacing mirrors.

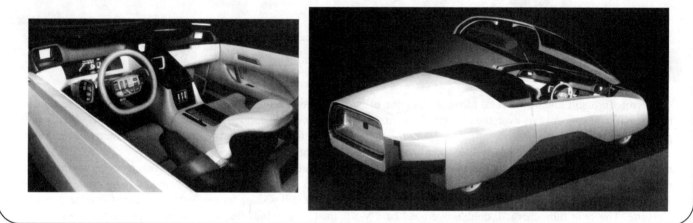

1987 ASC Corvette Geneve

Designed by ASC, Inc. in cooperation with the General Motors design staff, the Corvette Geneve, first displayed in 1987, embodied subtle modifications to the Corvette Roadster. Ground effects body work and dual rear spoilers took cues from the Corvette Indy concept car.

The sloped nose and raised tail added sleekness.

Taillights were flush mounted, exterior mirrors were redesigned and a hard tonneau cover was behind the redesigned interior. Sculptured leather seats and redone console marked the changes.

A Corvette 5.7 liter V-8 and automatic transmission were stock.

Combining high tech wizardry with an off-road SUV is all the rage today, but was a bit unusual in 1987 when this Blazer XT-1 concept truck was on the turntables. With a 103-inch wheelbase and overall length a shade under 170 inches, this compact package was stuffed with electronic and mechanical marvels.

A self-sensing four-wheel drive selected its own combination of front- and rear-wheel traction.

There were four-wheel steering, drive-by-wire controls, four corner leveling, adjustable ride height, electronic traction control, and a multi-function reconfigureable color CRT instrumentation.

The XT-I was mounted on a separate chassis and powered by Chevy's Vortec 4.3 liter V-6. Tinted glass abounded from the large windshield to the rear hatch.

1988 Venture

Standing out after a bunch of two-door Chevrolet concepts was the Venture of 1988. The four-door sedan featured a glass covered roof with lift-off panels front and rear, wind-cheating frontal styling, and creature comforts aplenty. With bucket seats for four, the front seats featured 15-way power adjustment and a lower back massage setting.

Automatic fold-away side and lower bolsters aided entry. A transverse composite leaf suspension was computer controlled for ride and handling.

Four-door concepts would become increasingly popular, but the Venture name wouldn't be on them, as Chevrolet relegated it to its minivan line in the next decade.

Chevrolet

1989 PPG XT-2

Billed as an IROC Camaro with a pickup bed powered by a 360-hp V-6, the PPG XT-2 of 1989 filled dual roles as a concept vehicle and pace truck for the CART PPG Indy Car World Series.

More than just a looker, it had a Corvette suspension and Trans Am 4.5 liter V-6, capable of 0-60 mph in six sec-onds. For its on-track duties, it featured rollbars, a fire extinguishing system, dual batteries and strobe lights. PPG Industries, sponsor of the CART series, likewise sponsored the truck.

The XT-2 was a follow-up in Chevy's concept trucks to the 1987 Blazer XT-1.

1990 CERV III

Bowing at the 1990 North American International Auto Show in Detroit, the Chevrolet CERV III (Corporate Experimental Research Vehicle) had several purposes, all of them noble. It was the third in the series of CERV mid-engine test vehicles and it was a civilized version of the 1987 Corvette Indy, also with the engine mid-ship.

The metallic blue looker was intended to be a step toward get-ting the Indy concept close to production form, meeting drive-ability, safety, and production feasibility needs. Unfortunately, the mid-engine Corvette that could be bought has yet to come to reality. A traversely mounted LT5 V-8 of ZR-1 fame was aided by twin turbochargers and able to produce 650 horse-power. A three-speed automatic transmission, working through a two-speed auxiliary, gave six speeds forward. Four-wheel steering and an active suspension were included.

The body, which could be removed for service, was a combi-nation of carbon fiber, Kevlar, and aluminum honeycomb. Side doors rose vertically, pivoting from the front fender tops.

A navigation system for the driver also displayed information on the suspension and steering.

1990 Concept Camaro IROC

Making its debut at the 1990 Los Angeles Auto Show was a pretty good and advanced preview of the all-new 1993 Camaro, the Concept Camaro IROC, as it was initially called.

Since it was designed in California, it simply became known as the California Camaro as the show season wore on. Carrying IROC-Z lettering on the side, it featured broad front and rear glass and wrap over glass panels incorporated into the gull wing doors.

It remained a 2+2, though its sleek lines easily could have been for a two-seater. Wheelbase was 104 inches, overall height just 48.75 inches, and length at 186.4.

No roaring V-8 in this one, as a DOHC V-6 provided the horses.

There was a considerable rush to get it ready and it reportedly went from scale model to runner in six months.

1990 Geo Tracker Hugger

Chevrolet's import-fighter line, Geo, wasn't immune to show vehicles, as this Geo Tracker Hugger demonstrates.

Based on the Suzuki-designed 4x4, the Hugger, it featured revised doors, roof and rear panel extensions, leather front seats, no back seat, and special wheels.

Chevrolet

1990 Geo California Concept Storm

Dressing up the new Geo Storm, sourced from Isuzu, produced the California Concept Storm for the 1990 show season.

Lowered two inches, with a revised front clip with hidden headlights, covered rear quarter windows and molded in side panels all differed from the production Storm.

Special seating and interior features were also inside the blackout greenhouse.

1991 Monte Carlo

To test the waters for a return of the Monte Carlo nameplate to the Chevy lineup of production cars, this concept vehicle was shown in 1991.

Monte Carlo was last produced as a 1988 model and, since its introduction as a 1970 model, had a long history of personal luxury and success in racing.

The Monte Carlos of yore were all rear wheel drivers, but this one was based on Lumina front-wheel-drive fixin's. It had a 3.4 liter DOHC V-6 and automatic transaxle. Styling was two-door hardtop like and quite rounded.

Engineering highlights included 18-inch wheels, electronic muffler with noise cancellation, adjustable pedals and a four-place sound/climate control system.

Monte Carlo did return to the Chevy parade as a 1995 model, based on the Lumina platform. The Lumina two-door was axed in the process.

1992 Corvette Sting Ray III

A reach for the past with an eye on the future was the goal of the Corvette Sting Ray III, which was a highlight of auto shows in 1992.

The idea was to recapture the excitement of the original Bill Mitchell Sting Ray and its followers. Using a 102-inch wheelbase, the same as the original Corvette, it stretched 1990s styling smoothly and wound up two inches shorter than the 1992 Corvette.

Power came from a modified LT1 located just ahead of the cockpit. For balance, the transmission was back by the differential.

Seats were fixed, while pedals and gauges moved to suit the driver. Carbon fiber was used for much of the body structure. Unlike some open concept cars, the Sting Ray III had its own convertible top.

1992 Sizigi Van

To distract showgoers from the controversial Lumina APV minivan with its "dustbuster" windshield, Chevrolet fielded the Sizigi APV concept in 1992.

More conventional in styling, it was stuffed with people-pleasing features like dual sunroofs, sliding table, television, VCR, credit card starting, hidden running boards and halo interior lighting. A trio of overhead consoles (one for each row of seats) contained air conditioner outlets, lights, storage and sunroof controls. Satchel pockets, which can be removed and used as briefcases, were located in the front door trim panels.

Showing you can't have too much fun in a Chevy minivan, dual speakers in the rear hatch door can be folded down when the door is raised to serenade the neighbors at picnics and tailgate parties.

1993 Highlander

If you looked under the chartreuse and purple paint and all the gingerbread of the Highlander concept at 1993 auto shows, you got a preview of the restyled 1994 Chevrolet S-10 extended cab pickup truck.

Trying to catch your eye were a moveable roll bar that made room for a roll top cover for the bed, a sliding driver side second door, a tool compartment on the left side that included an air compressor, fresh water supply for campers, a videotape and television that can be viewed from the bed, and a removable radio/tape player.

Extra lights on the rollbar helped night driving and a two inch rise in ground clearance helped navigate the back woods, or whatever.

Power was Chevy's 4.6 liter V-6, which worked through an automatic tranny. Concept trucks were very much in play at the time.

1995 Cavalier Spyder

Part of the extensive Chevrolet display at the 1995 SEMA show in Las Vegas was the Cavalier Spyder, a roadster based on the restyled 1995 Cavalier convertible.

Big wheels, ground effect bodywork, a double hooped airfoil, and tangerine paint all gave it the look needed to entice the young street machine pilot.

Chevrolet

1996
Monte Carlo SS

To bridge the huge gap between the production front wheel drive, V-6 powered Monte Carlos and the NASCAR rear wheel drive, V-8 powered creations, Chevrolet demonstrated it knew the difference when the Monte Carlo SS was unveiled at the November 1995 SEMA show in Las Vegas. To bring the lime green vehicle to life, a Camaro platform was used as a basis, and then stretched so that a then current Monte Carlo body would fit.

A 467-horsepower, 406 cubic inch enlargement of Chevy's small block V-8, Borg-Warner T-56 six speed manual gearbox and 3.45-1 axle ratio drove the wheels that were supposed to be driven, the rear ones.

Big wheels, tires, and rear-wheel flares all added to the performance car's performance. *Motor Trend* tested the SS and found 0-60 came in 4.4 seconds and the quarter was done in 12.9 seconds and 114.6 mph in the traps.

Thus far, all production Monte Carlos remain front wheel drive, V-6, etc. and all race cars remain otherwise, but with Bob Lutz at GM, anything can happen.

1998
Monte Carlo
Intimidator

To give fair warning of the restyled 2000 Monte Carlo that was around the corner, Chevrolet unleashed its Intimidator concept at appropriate 1998 venues.

With a decidedly NASCAR Winston Cup theme, it honored Chevy's top driver, Dale Earnhardt, who died in the 2001 Daytona 500. Unlike the racers, production Monte Carlos have front wheel drive and V-6 power and that is what the Intimidator had.

Performance mods upped the horsepower to 295, still well shy of the Cup cars.

Body extensions for ground effects, two-tone red and silver paint, an aluminum-faced dashboard with racing gauges, roll cage, four Recaro bucket seats and Simpson five-point belts conveyed stock car racing atmosphere. Special tires and wheels did the same.

1999 Nomad

Forty-five years after the original Nomad dream car bowed in 1954, Chevrolet recycled the name and idea of a sporty wagon in the 1999 Nomad concept, which bowed at the North American International Auto Show in January. Rear wheel drive and V-8 powered, the Nomad featured an independent rear suspension shift-by-wire transmission, retractable roof, extended load floor, and a sliding rear door on the left side.

Venetian blind-like slats in the roof slide forward to expose a 36-inch opening at the rear of the roof, not unlike the Studebaker Wagonaire of the 1960s. The tailgate folds down and slides forward to ease access to the rear compartment.

To haul all of this around with authority, small block LS-1 V-8 was called upon. The original Nomad dream car led directly to the production 1955 Chevrolet Bel Air Nomad. This Nomad concept has yet to be followed up by anything.

1999 Tonka

Among Chevrolet show vehicles at the 1998 SEMA show was the Tonka truck, based on 1999 Silverado extended cab pickup.

To resemble the sandbox version, the body was jacked up to allow 44-inch tires. A large brush guard front bar, with winch and a big tow hook, could get the Tonka through the real world sandbox. Roof lights, blacked out fender flares, a large visor and Tonka and Silverado graphics all told the world what the truck was about.

Tonka is a brand of Hasbro, Inc. and in 2002 is involved in another show truck with Ford.

Chevrolet

2000 SSR

When the SSR concept truck was on the Chevrolet stand at auto shows, many couldn't believe General Motors answered the nostalgia trend with such a meaningful package. When the specs were looked at, it was even more amazing: six liter small block V-8, full frame, and rear wheel drive.

Chevy fans became downright ecstatic when production of the SSR was announced…more or less in the form of the concept vehicle. It's hard to know where to begin in describing the features.

The retractable hardtop probably ranks right up there with the 1947-53 inspired grille, 50ish dashboard and uncluttered side and rear styling.

A hint of rear fender flares is timeless. The game began to see how much of the good stuff would stay around for production and what would be the source of the various components.

Since the 1953 Corvette, a few select dream/concept vehicles have made production status relatively unchanged.

Fifty years later, the SSR is slated to join the short list.

2000 Bruin

Bowing at the 2000 SEMA show, the Chevy Bruin medium duty pickup played to selected audiences for the next year or so

If you look close, it's not based on the Chevy Silverado but rather on the Express van. There is a growing market for medium duty crew cabs for race car haulers and recreational vehicles. Though having a pickup bed is somewhat unusual, the package, with sloping fiberglass front clip, is attractively integrated.

Befitting its 26,000-pound GVW (gross vehicle weight), the Bruin draws power from a 6.6 liter Duramax diesel, rated at 300 horsepower.

A five speed Allison automatic transmission helps spin the dual rear wheels. The five lucky folks to ride in it get a leather interior, dual sunroofs, and plenty of room.

2000 Traverse

To further confuse the blurred lines between cars and trucks, we have the Traverse, a Chevrolet cross-over vehicle of 2000 vintage.

Featuring rear tail and liftgates, like station wagons of old, the Traverse touted both off-road prowess and sedan comfort.

Based on a shortened truck platform, it had all wheel drive and rear storage.

Inside was a bevy on electronic stuff for the day's youthful buyers, including a laptop computer that connected to the Internet. There was no arguing what side of the debate the grille was on; it was strictly Chevy truck.

2001 Borrego

Calling on the four-wheel-drive expertise of its partner Subaru, Chevrolet came up with the Borrego concept, first shown in 2001. Utilizing a Subaru chassis and drivetrain, the Borrego two-door could change from a four-passenger sedan to a two-passenger pickup with open bed.

A dual cockpit design was meant to give a sense of protection in rough going. Hand-holds and gel padding were all aimed at protecting the occupants. Rally gauges let you know how fast you were going and stuff like that.

To help those in the rough, an air compressor (with a hose) and pressurized water tank were on board.

GM's Los Angeles styling studio guided the concept.

Chevrolet

2002 Bel Air

After recirculating popular names of the past like Impala and Malibu, could the Bel Air be far behind for Chevrolet? The answer could be seen at auto shows and in the media in 2002 as the Bel Air concept convertible made its bow.

The body was said to recall the classic 1955 through 1957 Chevrolets and if you look hard enough, some cues were there.

The dash was kind of like the 1955-56 models, the gas tank filler was reached through the left taillight and 1957 hints surrounded the headlights.

The grille was more a reminder of past Chevelles. Overall, the effect was quite pleasing, but not quite retro. Underneath, instead of looking back, the chassis was from the next generation small Chevy pickup, complete with an aluminum turbocharged inline five, similar to what the new trucks will have.

A rating of 315 horses, more than any stock 1955-57 Chevy, was advertised.

Taillight/gas tank filler.

OLDSMOBILE

1951 98 Holiday Palm Beach

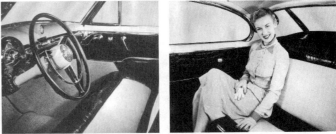

Among the show cars from General Motors was the 1951 Oldsmobile 98 Holiday Palm Beach.

It was one of several cars based on production cars with most of the changes involving special interiors. A tropical theme graced the backdrop and vehicle furnishings, which included alligator hide, green leather, and wicker accents.

Other surfaces were flax and Irish linen. Green paint and a cabana crackle tan top set off the exterior.

1953 Starfire X-P Rocket

While Buick, Cadillac and Chevrolet GM Motorama dream cars for 1953 were of the two passenger variety, Oldsmobile's card in the deck was the Starfire X-P Rocket, a four-seater, and like the others, having a fiberglass body. Its low, slab-sided lines contrasted with the mid-year Oldsmobile Fiesta production convertible, which was shown at the same time.

Done in turquoise, with turquoise and white individual seats, the Starfire previewed many coming styling features including a 1956-like grille, 1954 side trim and taillights, and the Starfire name, which would have a run on production cars, starting in 1954 and appearing off and on to 1980.

The name came from the Lockheed F-94 Starfire fighter, which was new at the time. The 1953-like dash contained five extra gauges.

Oldsmobile

"These Oldsmobile-designed experimental sports cars give our engineers and stylists a free hand in automotive design without limitations." Jack F. Wolfgram, Oldsmobile general manager

1954 F-88

Holding the distinction of being the most Corvette-like of the Oldsmobile dream cars was the F-88 of 1954.

It shared the 102-inch wheelbase and fiberglass body.

Features were very Olds-like including the wide-mouth grille, bullet taillights and sidesweep trim.

Large vertical exhaust outlets were the point of departure for gasses from the 324 cubic inch Olds Rocket V-8. It was trimmed with a single four barrel carb, had 9:1 compression, and lots of chrome under the hood. The plastic bubble headlight covers, which were similar to the 1953 Starfire, added to the dream car effect of the gold sports car.

Sadly, Oldsmobile never fielded a sports car. The role was left to Chevrolet.

1954 Cutlass

Another aircraft derived Oldsmobile dream car bowed at the 1954 General Motors Motorama, the Cutlass.

Named after the Chance-Vought F7U Navy fighter, the Cutlass name would start something at Olds that at one time would be used on nearly half its cars in production. Paired with the F-88, the more radically styled Cutlass was mounted on a 110-inch wheelbase and featured a combination of fastback and boattail roof lines with slats over the rear windows.

A stylized wide-mouth grille, flared front wheel openings, fins, and multi-plane taillights all gave the eye a virtual dance over the vehicle from feature to feature.

Competition-inspired instrumentation and swivel sets were among the highlights of the interior in the 51.5-inch high car. Power was the same as the F-88 dream car, using the newly enlarged Olds Rocket V-8.

Probably carrying less signature Oldsmobile styling elements than other 1950s dream cars from the division was the 1955 Delta, a four-passenger two-door hardtop with dimensions close to the production 88.

Body construction consisted of fiberglass below the beltline with a brushed aluminum roof. Reflecting the growing two-tone paint trend, the Delta was done in shades of blue, with a bright and big cove behind the front wheels.

Quad headlights flanked the squared off grille, while wraparound taillights abandoned the bullets in use at the time. Twin aluminum fuel tanks were inside the rear fenders.

Inside were swivel front seats and a free-standing instrument panel that was imitated in part by the 1957 model production cars.

A 250-hp Rocket V-8 with 10:1 compression served as on-road motivation.

1955 Delta

1956 Golden Rocket

For a GM division that billed itself as the home of the rocket, it was only natural to name a dream car for your trademark. The Golden Rocket of 1956 Motorama and auto show fame was, of course, gold, but that did not attract the crowds. Its horde of styling gimmicks did.

The two-passenger fiberglass sports car was startling from every direction. In front a peaked air inlet was joined by a pair of forward-thrusting fenders with rocket-like headlight projectiles. Thrust tubes marked the rear with small light-tipped fins riding the fender tops. The cozy cab had roof panels that lifted for entry. Swivel seats and a tilt steering wheel also helped the egress bit. Instruments were again in the center of the steering wheel. There was a split backlight, not unlike the 1963 Corvette.

Overall height came in under 50 inches. Power was rated at 275 horses, of course, from the Rocket V-8.

Oldsmobile

1957 F88

Even though there was no GM Motorama for 1957, Oldsmobile came up with a dream car, using a recycled Motorama name, the F-88, first shown in 1954.

Carrying out the F-88's sports car format, the 1957 F-88 appeared to be a larger car. The fish mouth grille carried bold O-L-D-S-M-O-B-I-L-E letters, while quad headlights would be on production Oldsmobiles starting in 1958.

Side trim was a non-traditional spear and quite like the 1961 Pontiacs. Small fins stopped well short of the taillights, which resembled the 1957 units turned 90 degrees. Inside, a central dome dashboard theme was similar to the first F-88.

After five straight years of dream cars, the 1957 F-88 would be the last non-production-based concept Oldsmobile for nearly three decades.

1962 X-215 Fire Rocket

Dream cars of the 1950s gave way to show cars of the 1960s for Oldsmobile.

This modified F-85 Cutlass convertible featured a fiberglass cover over the rear seats, stylized rollbar, abbreviated windshield and side windows, a different grille and other exterior modifications. Inside were special bucket seats and instrumentation.

The X-215 Fire Rocket's purpose was to publicize the 1962 turbocharged 215-hp, 215-CID Jetfire coupe.

1963 El Torero

Four slim bucket seats, special interior paneling, and a trim console through the middle were the primary features of the 1963 el Torrero show car that Oldsmobile fielded on the circuit that year.

As was quite common at the time, a production model, in this case a 98 convertible, provided the basis for the vehicle. Assisting the necessary Spanish motif was the appropriately caped model.

1964 4-4-2 Convertible

A show car version of its newly introduced 4-4-2 option for its Cutlass line was Oldsmobile's entry in the GM Futurama exhibit at the New York World's Fair in 1964.

Basically a production convertible, it featured a revised grille with rectangular headlights and bumper/grille. Special chrome wheels and two-tone paint continued the exterior mods. Inside, body-contoured astronaut seats accommodated four.

Power was listed as a 310-horsepower version of the 330 CID Jetfire Rocket V-8 and the press release noted it was the Police Apprehender option (which the 4-4-2 started with). There was also a four speed trans and dual exhausts.

The car was used on the show circuit again for 1965 and this time was to have the 400 CID V-8, four-barrel carburetion, and dual exhaust, just like the 4-4-2 for 1965.

Oldsmobile

1969 4-4-2 Apollo

Still naming specially-built cars after flying objects, the 1969 4-4-2 convertible with a one-off interior was dubbed the Apollo, after our space program adventures. The highlight was an interior with four articulated contoured bucket seats.

The stock exterior had to make do with slightly different striping and Apollo badging. The name eventually flew over to Buick and found a home on its Chevrolet Nova-based compact.

1970 Cutlass Supreme

To help celebrate its new 1970 formal roofed Cutlass Supreme, Oldsmobile put a show car of the same name out for public consumption that year.

It featured even larger sail panels for a more formal look, spoked wheels and special interior. The Cutlass Supreme was Oldsmobile's answer to the Chevrolet Monte Carlo and Pontiac Grand Prix personal luxury intermediate.

If you liked the show car in 1970, you could get more of it in 1971 when it was shown, with minor changes, as the Contessa. (See color section.)

1971 Cutlass Contessa: See Color Section

> *"We use concept cars first and foremost to educate both the buying public and ourselves."*
> David North, chief designer of the Oldsmobile II studio at GM Design Staff

1987 Aerotech Short Tail
& Aerotech Long Tail

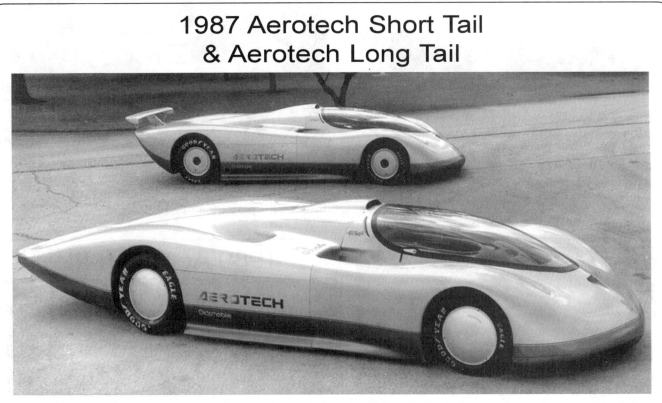

Happily, not all concept cars are made to revolve around a turntable. A few are genuine high performance vehicles.

A case, or rather cases, in point is the 1987 Oldsmobile Aerotech duo. The mission was to test aerodynamics and provide an impressive debut for the new Quad 4 double overhead cam engine about to be used in production cars. It scored well on both counts.

Two cars were constructed using carbon fiber single seat bodies on March Indy Car chassis. Engine size was reduced from the production version of 2.3 liters to 2.0.

The short tail (ST) had a turbocharger and was estimated to put out 900 horsepower.

The long tail (LT) had twin turbos and was good for 100 more horses.

Famed race driver A.J. Foyt got the nod to drive and the test was held at the Ft. Stockton, Texas. oval. On Aug. 27, 1987, Foyt took the ST to a new closed course record 257.123 mph. He then got in the LT to set a new flying mile world record of 267.399 mph.

Glory attained, the Aerotechs went on the show circuit through the next year. Quad 4 reached production status starting with the 1988 Cutlass Calais and is still with us in the 21st century.

Oldsmobile

1989 Aerotech II

Attempting to translate the sleek aerodynamics of the Aerotech record-setting concept car to a passenger friendly package was the assignment of the 1989 Aerotech II. A two-door with a glass-covered rear deck, it was only 48 inches high and described as having a bullet-like silhouette. The rear panel was split and opened from either side for access. Airbags were used for all four occupants. A color navigation monitor was programmed with compact discs and a ceiling console mounted holographic device projected a red warning icon on the rear glass when the brakes were applied. Like the first Aerotech, power came from the Quad 4, but this time it was a production-based 2.3 liter unit.

1989 Aerotech III

Perhaps stretching the Aerotech name too far was dubbing the 1990 Oldsmobile Cutlass Supreme four-door sedan the Aerotech III. Increasingly over the next decade, advance production cars were shown as concepts a season or two before their debut. Such was the case with the III.

Basking in the glory of the record-setting Aerotech of 1987, the III had a unique four-bucket seat interior, a supercharged Quad 4 engine and a rear-facing radar system for its venture on the show circuit.

It was billed as a link between a 260-mph record-smasher and a touring sedan that customers will one day drive off the showroom floor.

1989 California Trofeo

Billed a concept car by Oldsmobile, the 1989 California was more of the traditional show car mold, a production vehicle with special trim. The production Trofeo coupe picked up new aero side panels, large diameter alloy wheels, and a new set of front air scoops.

A rear spoiler provided more of a cove effect around the taillamps. Power came from a turbocharged, intercooled Quad 4, which was bolted to a five speed manual transmission.

Taking credit for the design was the GM Advanced Concept Center in Southern California, thus the name.

Oldsmobile

1990 Expression

Accurately predicting the sports activity market a decade into the future, the 1990 Oldsmobile Expression concept car was dubbed a family sports sedan. Using an elliptical profile, the fiberglass body featured smooth, unobstructed lines, front to back. On a 104.9-inch wheelbase and at just over 200 inches long, the package was well proportioned.

A 230-horsepower Quad 4 provided for power needs. Inside tech goodies included four wheel steering, traction control, on-board navigation, rain-sensing windshield wipers, and an entertainment center/tailgate combo. The latter featured a Nintendo game center, VCR, hot and cold storage areas and for after the tailgate party, a vacuum cleaner.

1991 Achieva

As part of a scheme to prepare new car buyers for its upcoming 1992 Achieva, the 1991 Achieva concept car made the scene. While its dimensions were close to the coming production car, the styling of the four-door sedan was more Audi-like than Olds.

With a red exterior below the beltline and black roof, it did garner its share of attention. The glass was flush mounted, common to concepts at the time and the door handles were missing, also not unusual. Rear seats were free standing and could recline for passenger comfort or be folded flat for storage.

Ubiquitous Quad 4 power was inserted and it was noted that a new single overhead cam version would be available in fall, just in time for the production Achieva.

1992 Anthem

"You can consider this car an advanced Cutlass Supreme, representative of design trends we'll see in the late 1990s or early 21st century," said Dennis Burke, Oldsmobile designer, when the Anthem bowed on the show circuit for 1992. With a long wheelbase and short rear overhang, it was a concession to Chrysler's upcoming cab-forward design.

Done in titanium silver with a gray and beige leather interior, Anthem styling probably served more as a preview to the Aurora line, which bowed in the spring of 1994 as a 1995 model.

Inside were the obligatory gadgetry, highlighted by a noise cancellation system and halo lights. A supercharged Quad 4 was installed, but the vehicle also was designed to handle a new two-stroke V-6, which was under development.

Oldsmobile

1993 Aerotech Aurora

Reprising its dual role as a record-breaking speed trials and concept vehicle, the 1987 Aerotech short tail returned to the spotlight in 1992 and 1993.

Replacing the two liter quad four with a four-liter Aurora DOHC V-8 (from the upcoming 1995 Aurora production car), Oldsmobile was able to crank more performance out of the aged chassis. The result was a run in December 1992 at the 7.712-mile Ft. Stockton, Texas test track that lasted around the clock for eight days.

The Aerotech Aurora V-8 broke 47 speed/endurance records in world, international and national categories. Touted most was smashing the Mercedes-Benz records for 10,000 and 25,000 kilometers.

The latter was a 158.386 mph average. Olds noted that the engine was not altered all that much for the run.

After setting the records, the Aerotech Aurora turned to the show circuit for 1993, helping prepare the way for the Aurora, which would be sold starting in spring of 1994.

1995 Antares

Intended to be a preview of the 1997 Cutlass, the 1995 Antares concept four-door ended up looking more like a downsized version of the contemporary Aurora.

The bright purple Antaraes was some 17 inches shorter than the Aurora and was powered by a V-6 version of the Olds Northstar V-8. Purple and tan leather and trim was all over the interior, which featured bright accents. There was no Oldsmobile nameplate on the exterior of the car, one of the early problems that was beginning to surface in products from the division. The name came from a constellation in the southern part of the sky. Another sign?

1997 Alero

A surprisingly youthful concept car from Oldsmobile, the Alero made the rounds in 1997.

First shown at Detroit, the coupe featured taught, upswept lines, 18/19-inch combo wheels, and a two-piece glass roof, with electrically adjustable light transmission. Inside, the four passenger coupe was attractively styled with leather seating.

Both the Alero name and general styling were used on the Achieva replacement for the 1999 model year.

Production is to continue into the 2003 model year, just short of the end of the road for Oldsmobile.

1999 Recon

Debuting at the North America International Auto Show in Detroit in 1999 was the Recon, a cross-over vehicle that, if produced, might have saved Oldsmobile from its pending demise. The tall wagon featured advanced, but non-distinctive styling, no B-pillars, two sunroofs, and Smart Trac II all wheel drive.

A 3-liter DOHC V-6, rated at 200 horsepower, motivated it. Flat panel displays, front and rear, provided both information and entertainment.

Buttons in the center console and steering wheel controlled the functions. Space age design seats with no covering or padding were said to be both comfortable and damage-proof. The polyurethane floor covering was also claimed to be very durable.

Overall, the Recon was quite compact with a wheelbase of 110.2 inches, overall length of 176.6, and width of 72.2 inches. Wheels were 19-inch aluminum with the Michelin PAX System of run-flat tires.

2000 Profile

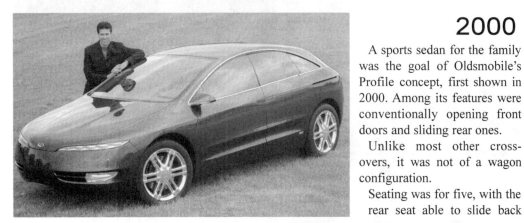

A sports sedan for the family was the goal of Oldsmobile's Profile concept, first shown in 2000. Among its features were conventionally opening front doors and sliding rear ones.

Unlike most other cross-overs, it was not of a wagon configuration.

Seating was for five, with the rear seat able to slide back and forth, and recline.

A Smart Card keyless entry system provided seat, radio, mirror, and steering wheel adjustments for the driver.

A sporty 250-horsepower 3.5 liter DOHC V-6 and automatic all-wheel-drive got it down the road. Wheelbase reached 113 inches and overall length just over 185 inches.

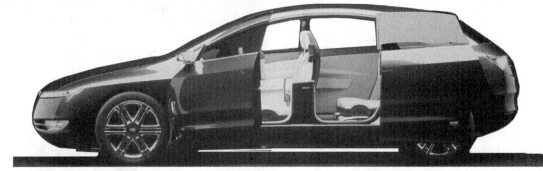

"We have designed this Profile sports sedan as a logical step for drivers looking for an innovative, refined, and sophisticated vehicle that can meet their personal and family lifestyle." Phil Zak, GM Character design manager, shown standing next to the Profile.

Oldsmobile

2000
Intrigue
OSV

2000
Alero
OSV

About a year before General Motors announced it was going to discontinue the brand, Oldsmobile launched a specialty vehicles operation to handle performance versions of its products, similar to that of other brands.

Oldsmobile Special Vehicles (OSV) had three 2000 models on display at the November 2000 SEMA show in Las Vegas, an Intrigue, an Alero, and a Silhouette.

Certainly plans called for more to come. With the impending demise, none ever reached production status. *Motor Trend* tested a 2001 OSV Intrigue and was impressed with the Aurora V-8 that replaced the supercharged V-6 in the 2000 model.

We, of course, will never know what could have been done.

2001 04

Sadly prophetic, the 04 concept car shown by Oldsmobile in 2001 went through design stage before it was announced in late 2000 that Oldsmobile would be phased out over the next few years.

As of 2002, information is that the end will come in 2004. Based on an Opel Astra chassis, the four-door open car was created by Oldsmobile and Bertone of Turin, Italy.

Aimed at the young buyer, the four passenger 04 featured a rear air foil and removable roof panels and retractable rear window.

Oldsmobile styling cues, especially at the front, were applied. An information ring with liquid crystal displays kept the driver informed.

Ten buttons on its perimeter let the driver control what had to be controlled.

A two-liter turbocharged DOHC four-cylinder engine, mated to a five-speed drove the front wheels. Overall length was a subcompact 162.2 inches. After the announcement of the Oldsmobile phaseout, the 04 lost its Oldsmobile identity in some cases.

Oldsmobile badging was not to be found and at some shows it was displayed in the General Motors section and not with the other Oldsmobiles.

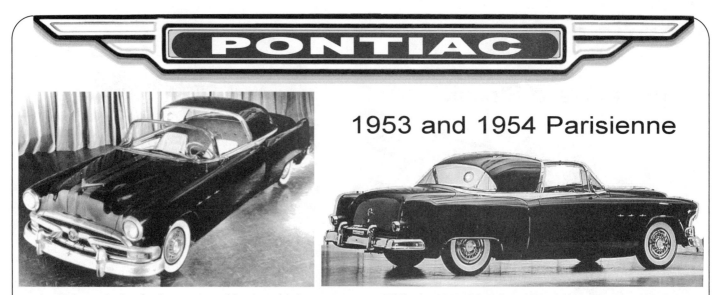

PONTIAC

1953 and 1954 Parisienne

An early example of a dream car making a multiple-year run, a common practice today, can be found in the 1953 and 1954 Parisienne.

While other GM Motorama dream cars of 1953 were one-offs, the Parisienne utilized a 1953 Pontiac production car (likely a convertible) with major body modifications. Most notable was an open front landau roof with a Panoramic wraparound windshield.

Side sculpturing was also altered with a scoop nearly the depth of the panel. Inside were bucket seats that moved for access to the rear.

While the 1953 example was black, it was redone in a lighter tone for 1954 and a 1954 grille replaced the 1953 unit. While the 1953 was a star of the Motorama, a lesser role of just auto shows awaited the 1954. Pontiac later used the Parisienne name on Canadian and eventually U.S. full-sized cars.

1954 Bonneville Special

Pontiac's Motorama star for 1954 was its first sports dream car, the Bonneville Special. Using a name that would make the production cars in 1957 and never be let go, the 100-inch wheelbase red fiberglass Bonneville had a transparent plexiglass roof with opening panels over the seats to aid access.

It looked every bit the competition car it was designed to be; however, Pontiac was a year away from having its new V-8 and the 48-inch high machine had to make do with a flathead straight eight and Hydramatic transmission, somewhat limiting potential performance. Hood lines flowed back from the open grille to two small scoops, via the traditional Pontiac silver streaks.

Defining the rear was a vertically mounted spare tire and wheel with an exposed center. Red bucket seats and full instrumentation, spread across the dash, marked the interior.

Harley J. Earl's trip to the Bonneville Salt Flats in Utah, where speed trials were held each year, was said to be the inspiration for the name.

Pontiac

1954 Strato Streak

Following other GM divisions in fielding both sports car and sedan dream cars for 1954 Motorama and auto show duties was the Strato Streak four-door sedan.

It appeared in two forms, first with a metallic green hue and later metallic red. In the latter form, it was billed as the Strato Streak II.

The fiberglass bodied vision of the future was mounted on a Star Chief 124-inch wheelbase. Notable features were center opening doors without a centerpost. Swivel front seats aided egress.

Styling was a combination of shapes that did not necessarily get along.

With a wraparound windshield, the rear backlight contrasted by being a three-piece package with body lines at the breaks.

Pontiac billed the Strato Streak as a combination of sedan and sports car, a theme that would be used on many cars for decades to come.

1955 Strato-Star

A Motorama showcase for Pontiac's new V-8 was a six passenger coupe, on display during the 1955 season. Thin roof pillars may have previewed the future, but contrasted with the heavy styling below the beltline.

Like the 1954 Bonneville Special, roof panels over the front seats raised to help access.

Barrel-sized coves behind the front wheels also contrasted with the partially enclosed rear wheels.

Small air intakes over the headlights were a variation on the theme, used in the 1955 production models.

1956 Club de Mer

Arguably Pontiac's finest styled dream car and one of the best of the 1950s was the 1956 Club de Mer, a blue fiberglass sports car that was a major star at the GM Motorama and on the auto show circuit.

Building on the theme of the 1954 Bonneville Special, the grille opening was filled with a rounded panel that held concealed headlights and the start of the silver steaks.

Again, they ended in small hood scoops. Fuselage sides continued the rounded theme and a single, center-mounted fin graced the back. Twin aircraft-type windshields broke the air for the passengers, seated in bucket seats.

Controls were console or door mounted, except for the steering wheel. Unlike the Bonneville, ample horses resided under the hood with twin four-barrel carbs kicking the Pontiac 316 CID V-8 up to 300 horsepower.

1959 Bonneville X-400

1960 Bonneville X-400

Instead of dream cars, Pontiac resorted to fielding show cars for several years, starting with the 1959 Bonneville X-400.

Based on the production Bonneville convertible, it featured concealed headlights, special interior and supercharged 389-CID V-8. The name returned for 1960, again utilizing a convertible. This time it had Lucas lamps for headlights, blue dot taillights and a special interior.

After 1960, the X-400 tag would take a year off, before beginning a run on Grand Prix-based vehicles.

Pontiac

1962 Monte Carlo

To make a high performance two-seat roadster, Pontiac shortened a Tempest compact, cutting the wheelbase from 112 to 97 inches and the overall length to 175 inches.

Cut-down windshield and side windows encircled the cockpit, which held two bucket seats and a console.

Enhancing the horses was the job assigned a supercharger, mounted on the 194.5-CID slant four (half a V-8).

A pair of raised rear panels, special headlights, trim, and racing stripes completed the package.

It was displayed at car shows and run at race courses during the 1962 season despite carrying 1961 Tempest styling.

The Monte Carlo name didn't stay at Pontiac, as Chevrolet claimed it for a line of 1970 luxury intermediates.

1962 Grand Prix X-400

Continuing the X-400 show car line after a year's absence was the Grand Prix version for 1962. Although the production Grand Prix came as a two-door hardtop only, the X-400 previewed a Grand Prix ragtop, which came along in 1967.

Again, supercharging was used, along with four side draft carburetors. Rectangular headlights with wire covers and modified trim graced the outside.

Inside were twin sticks, one for the four-speed manual gearbox and the other for an exhaust silencer.

1963 Grand Prix X-400

Appearing on both the custom and new car show circuits in 1963 was the Grand Prix X-400 convertible. It followed the format of past X-400 show cars with a supercharged, sidedraft multi-carbed V-8, trick body modifications, and special interior.

A fiberglass hood, complete with scoops, rectangular, wire-mesh covered vertical headlights, twin side scoops, full-width taillights, and a blacked out grille marked the pearlescent yellow exterior.

Thin shell bucket seats and chrome accented floor mats gave showgoers something to look at inside. The X-400 show car series, which started in 1959, would continue.

1963 Tempest Fleur de Lis

Fleur de Lis was Pontiac's salute to France, home of the famed LeMans race course and namesake of this Tempest LeMans convertible, used as a show car in 1963.

Save for the partially blacked-out grille, exterior modifications were minimal. Modified seats marked the interior.

1963 Maharani

Like the Tempest Fleur de Lis, the Maharani was a modestly modified production convertible shown in 1963.

A Bonneville convertible provided the basis and peacocks provided the feathers, which decorated the interior. Seats were redone in multi-hued leather and the tropical theme was carried out with a pearlescent turquoise paint job.

Pontiac

1965 GTO Tiger

Taking its tiger theme to the show circuit was the Pontiac's GTO Tiger convertible.

Using a basic stock production car, the interior was decked out with tiger fur (fake, hopefully) seats, and trim and tiger claw seat belts.

The car was also named the Grand Marque V by some sources.

The intermediate GTO was one of the leading muscle cars at the time and was in its second year of production.

1966 Bonneville Le Grand Conchiche

With a name almost as long as the car, the 1966 Bonneville LeGrand Conchiche made the show circuit as an attempt to show what a two-door limousine with a landau roof would look like.

Surely it answered a question few had asked.

The chauffeur's compartment featured black leather bucket seats. Spoke wheels and pearlescent paint dressed up the outside in sporty, rather than formal tones.

1966 Banshee

Pontiac would use the Banshee name many times for its concept cars and proposed production cars with the title more than once. However, since the dictionary defines it as a female spirit whose wailings forewarn of death, it somehow never made it.

A dream/concept car that never made it was the 1966 Banshee, which was to appear at the New York Auto Show.

Photos were released and the press got a glimpse of the fastback coupe with rising roof panels, but GM politics pulled the car from the show and future displays before the public ever saw it. The two seater was a prototype for Pontiac's upcoming F-car, the Firebird, which would bow for 1967.

The Banshee was also known as the XP-798 and Scorpion in its early stages.

1968 Banshee II/Fiero

Using a stock Firebird chassis and inner body panels, the Banshee II (also known as the Fiero) was shown in 1968. It had a stock driveline and 400 CID Pontiac V-8. Fiberglass body panels were attached to the innards with the result a sleek open cockpit two-seater with more in common in looks with the Corvette than the Firebird.

Low-cut windshield and side glass and an airfoil built into the leading edge of the rear deck were among the features. A stock Firebird dash was modified with extra gauges.

1969 Cirrus

To come up with show cars for its divisions at a time of budget crunches for federal safety and emission standard compliance, GM recycled some of its dream/concept cars. Such was the case with the 1969 Pontiac Cirrus.

It was redone from the 1964 GM-X which was built for the 1964 New York World's Fair.

The exaggerated fastback picked up a new nose and was said to have a Pontiac 400 CID V-8 power. The GM-X was a roller. Inside it was still like an aircraft cockpit with 21 dials and numerous control levers.

Pontiac did noting more with the Cirrus name, which eventually ended up on a line of Dodges in the 1990s.

Pontiac

1972 Edinburgh

Mildly customized for show duty in 1972 was the Pontiac Edinburgh, based on the Grand Prix SJ, which was in its last year on this body style. It featured a red, white and black scotch plaid accented interior and a black paint job with red striping. The Edinburgh was one of three basically stock Pontiac show cars that season.

1974 Banshee III

1979 Banshee

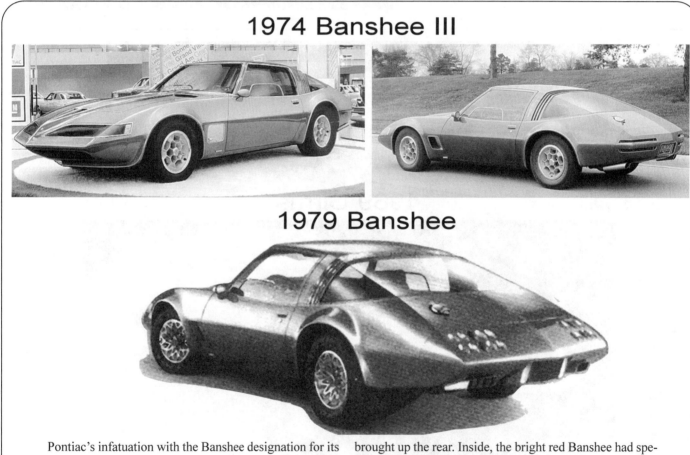

Pontiac's infatuation with the Banshee designation for its show cars continued with this Firebird-based Banshee III, on the circuit in 1974 (upper). Using a Firebird chassis, inner body panels and Super Duty 455 CID V-8, a new exterior considerably sharpened up the styling.

Headlights were behind plastic panels, large vents sat back of the front wheels and thin, wraparound taillights brought up the rear. Inside, the bright red Banshee had special bucket seats up front and a fold down bench in the rear. The dashboard was stock Firebird.

A couple of seasons later, the Banshee III was given a facelift (make that a taillift), with multiple-lensed lights, new exhaust outlets, and other minor modifications, and sent out to shows again (bottom photo).

1978-9 Trans Am Type K

Considered for limited production was the Firebird Trans Am Type K (for Kammback) two-door wagon.

A clever design, it featured a roof extended to the back bumper with a fixed back window and lift-up hatches on either side. Production 1978 Trans Am pieces abounded, but the plan was to offer another model in the Firebird line.

Pininfarina was hired two construct two prototypes and cost out the project. One was silver with red insides and the other gold with the interior done in beige.

Costs eventually outpaced reality and the Type K was never produced. However, it became a popular traveler on the show circuit, so much so that the cars were updated with 1979 front clips and kept on tour for several years.

1978 Sunbird Special

1978 Grand AM CA

A pair of mildly modified Pontiacs were displayed in the 1978 auto show season, the Sunbird Special and Grand Am CA. Both featured top openings in the oppressive non-convertible era.

The subcompact Sunbird (above) notch-back coupe got rear sale panels, slatted rear quarter windows, a sunroof, and rear spoiler.

Trans Am wheels and pearlescent white paint completed the visuals.

On the right, is the CA, which tried to capture the gingerbread on the short-run 1977 LeMans Can Am.

A rear opening hood scoop, rear fender shields and T-roof (not a LeMans option) dressed up the downsized two-door sedan.

Pontiac considered returning the Can Am to market, but decided a show car was enough.

Pontiac

1979 Grand Prix Landau

Many auto show attendees in 1979 were treated to a customized version of the Grand Prix. The rear quarter of the roof was removed and when combined with the hatch roof, it formed a Porsche Targa-like hoop over the rear seating area.

Special seats and a rose color, including the hatch panels, were part of the package.

1984 Fiero Convertible: See Color Section

1986 Trans Sport

While Chrysler Corporation was far from modest (or correct) in claiming to invent the minivan, Pontiac made a significant move toward investigating the future design and releasing it to the public. Case in point was the 1986 Trans Sport concept minivan. With a massive glass-enclosed front-passenger compartment and a gull-wing right side door, a feeling of openness (and possibly sunstroke) pervaded the black, red, and gray cladded package. It sure looked to be out of the future, compared to the production vans of 1986.

inside, electronic wizardry abounded including cathode-tube instrumentation, a computer for the front-seat passenger, television screen for the rear-area occupants, and a scanning screen replaced the rearview mirror.

Six bucket seats awaited the riders and each had individual radio controls and ear phones.

To power all this and propel the Trans Sport, too, was a 2.9 liter aluminum turbocharged V-6. Indeed a look at the future, the Trans Sport previewed several features on the production 1990 Trans Sport, which was known for having a "dustbuster" windshield, nearly as large as the concept car.

"Here at Pontiac, we looked at the Trans Sport as a unique opportunity. It was our chance to demonstrate the kind of freewheeling innovation you would expect from a totally new breed of Pontiac." Terry Henline, Pontiac Exterior Design Studio chief.

1987 Pursuit

By the late 1980s, concept cars were pretty much back to what the dream cars were in the 1950s, making serious attempts to look at future transportation and get the motoring public to do the same.

An outstanding example could be found in the 1987 Pontiac Pursuit. A four passenger coupe, it featured four-wheel steering-by wire, four wheel drive, adjustable road height, head-up instrument display on the windshield, and a steering pod instead of a wheel.

Skirts on all four corners moved with the wheels, for clearance. A light bar replaced the headlights. Front seats folded for rear seat egress and a built-in child seat could be setup and used in the back seat. Rear seat passengers also got individual color television monitors, built into the headrests.

A small two-liter four had double overhead cams, an intercooler and turbocharger, and was good for 200 horsepower, not unlike today's higher output small engines. A five-speed manual transmission metted out the horses.

Just short of 188 inches long, the Pursuit indeed was a pursuit of the future.

Pontiac

1988 Banshee

Pontiac's seemingly never-ending infatuation with the Banshee name led to this 1988 preview of the next generation Firebird. The fiberglass body was attached to a tubular frame.

Larger than the current F-bird, it was 201 inches long, 80 inches wide, and had a 105-inch wheelbase. Power came via a 4.0-liter dual overhead cam aluminum V-8 rated at a sedate (for today) 230 horsepower. It was still rear wheel drive, used a five speed manual tranny, independent rear suspension, and four-wheel disc anti-lock brakes.

Dramatic styling front and rear, flush doors, and devices for air management marked the outside.

Inside was the usual cast of tech goodies, but notable were the fixed front seats with electrically adjustable steering wheel and pedals.

While the styling cues were translated (broadly) into the design for the all-new 1993 Firebird, the Banshee name remained confined to concept cars (many of them).

1989 Stinger

Youth-oriented "activity" vehicles weren't abundant in the new vehicle market in 1989, save for the Jeep Wrangler, but Pontiac's crystal ball was working well when it came up with its 1989 concept vehicle, the Stinger.

All-wheel drive with room for four passengers and a short 164.8 inches long, the Stinger could be modified in several ways. It had a carbon-fiber body and all glass, but the windshield could be removed, including the glass panels in the doors. The latter could be replaced with a beverage cooler and a storage compartment.

The radio could be removed for outdoor use (not unlike the 1958 "Sportable" radio option), as could a stored utility seat, camping stove, picnic table, vacuum, extension cord, mess kit, tote bags, dustpan, and even a vacuum cleaner. All kinds of neat ways to store the stuff inside were part of the concept.

Pontiac would pursue the youth activity market again with concepts, but has yet to take the bold step from a production standpoint, unless you count the Aztec.

"There's an emerging interest in the young group for sport vehicles that fully express their unique lifestyles. This spirited transportation that allows one to experience life to the fullest is embodied in the 1989 Stinger." Ed Benson, director of Pontiac Market and Product Planning

Sunfire

1990 Sunfire

Some of the stages a concept car goes through before the public sees it are shown for the 1990 Pontiac Sunfire. From sketch to body construction to interior buck and testing the platform and drivetrain, it's a complicated process involving many talented people.

Their work was worthwhile in putting together the sub-compact testbed. Looking like a coupe, the Sunfire had four seats inside and four doors to get into them. The back doors were smaller and all doors opened at the center, without a centerpost. Such a style would be more common in concepts in the coming decade.

Other highlights included headlights that popped up from the cowl, no exterior door handles, full-width taillights, and a forward lifting clamshell hood. Body construction was carbon fiber. Overall length was only 179 inches with wheelbase at 109 inches, as the wheels were at the corners.

As can be seen from the platform photo, the Sunfire was a front driver, with a 2.0 liter, DOHC turbocharged four pro-ducing 190 horsepower and a five speed manual gearbox to harness it. Pontiac didn't forget the Sunfire name and used it on the replacement for the Sunbird subcompact, starting with the redesigned 1995 models.

Pontiac

1991 ProtoSport 4

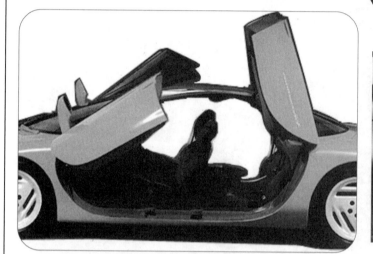

Pontiac continued its four-door theme from its 1990 Sunfire, but applied it to a larger and more powerful package when it unveiled the Protosport 4 concept for 1991.

Indeed it was the doors that were most noticeable, as they swept up and out of the way of the four passengers. They put the 4 in the name, not the powerplant, as it was a DOHC 250 horsepower V-8 and drove the rear wheels, with help from a 700-R-4 automatic.

The red carbon fiber body wrapped around white wheels, stretched 120 inches apart. The cockpit-like driver compartment (note the mockup) featured analog gauges that were reflected onto a mirror, which enlarged them.

Rear seat passengers got color television monitors that had a built in VCR. They also got air bags mounted in the headliner. Headlights and taillights were minimal in size, but not in output. Up front, high intensity discharge lights (HID) kicked out the lumens, while light-emitting diodes (LED) brought up the rear.

"We wanted a vehicle that would suit the needs of warm weather customers who want their transportation to provide a number of functions and we believe Salsa fits that bill." John G. Middlebrook, Pontiac general manger

Versatility and fun were leading features of Pontiac's Salsa concept car, which started on the show circuit for 1992 and continued for a couple of years. Designed at General Motors Advanced Concepts Center in southern California, it showed its heritage, which played well with the beach crowd.

It could be a convertible, hatchback, or panel delivery, depending on the rear roof section you attached, or unattached. The five passenger two-door was only 155.6-inches long and sat on a 98-inch wheelbase.

A front driver, it was powered by a 1.5 liter, DOHC four and came with a five-speed manual transmission. Side exhausts are white and black anodized aluminum.

1992 Salsa

Pontiac

1994 Sunfire Speedster

Pontiac fielded the first Sunfire concept car for the 1990 season. The nameplate returned on another concept four years later. Instead of a coupe, it appeared on a two passenger roadster. Further use of the Sunfire title was planned for the 1995 model year when its redesigned subcompacts would be so named, replacing the Sunbird badge.

Carrying many styling cues from the future Sunbird, the Roadster carried out a sporty theme with side exhausts, rearview mirrors on the windshield header, a built-in spoiler over the rear deck cover, hood scoop, and luxurious leather seats. There was no top to be found, hidden or otherwise. Power was ample with a supercharged DOHC 2.4-liter four rated at 241 horses, followed up by an automatic transaxle spinning the front wheels.

While the production Sunfire was considerably less dramatic, there was a convertible (four passenger) in the line from the first year.

1997 Rageous

Trying to keep track of all the gimmicks on the Rageous of 1997 can give you a headache. Pontiac seemingly emptied its gadget bin, combining the performance of a Firebird with the utility of an SUV. Luckily the Aztek wasn't finalized at the time.

Starting with the basics, it was a four-door hatchback with a 315-horsepower 350-CID small block V-8, six-speed manual gearbox, independent rear suspension, and rear wheel drive. Inside it carried four passengers, but the back seats folded down like a wagon, for storage.

The dash carried a bunch of round gauges and looked more 1950ish than anything.

Outside, a Pontiac split grille led to a ram air scoop and hidden headlights.

Side sculpturing was a combination of shapes, not all singing the same tune. Radical rearview mirrors and a rear spoiler show a jukebox influence.

Taillights were a series of tube-like units.

There have been many new SUV designs in the last couple of years, but thus far the Rageous has not led to one of them.

1998 Montana Thunder

Pontiac stylists of the late 1990s could not be accused of following the crowd. Further proof of that can be found in a concept minivan, which debuted in the 1998 season.

Based on the 1997 Trans Sport Montana-optioned van, the Thunder was covered with eye catching facets and done in bright red and black paint and trim.

A revised front clip featured larger grille openings, air scoops, hidden headlights and road lamps. The body was chopped 2.5 inches and side cladding was, well, different.

In back the rear hatch operated electrically, like the side doors, and there was a built-in bicycle rack. Taillights were slat-like lenses. A wide track effect was accented by 18-inch asymmetrical wheels and body flares. Tread was nine-plus inches wider. Special chrome encased instrumentation and three-tone leather seats filled the inside.

Power came from a massaged 225-hp V-6 and stopping came from Firebird four-wheel discs. Actually, the styling didn't fit in at all with the Montana option's western-style semi-SUV marketing. For 1999, the Trans Sport name was dropped for the van, in favor of Montana.

1999 GTO

Since its production demise in 1974 (when it was a gussied up Ventura), Pontiac has wanted to revive its famed GTO muscle car. One such vision was the GTO concept, shown in 1999.

The four-passenger coupe was designed as a rear-wheel-drive screamer with 19-inch wheels in front and 20-inch wheels in the rear.

Split grille, hood scoops, and big haunches in the rear all saluted GTOs that had been built before.

Side ribs gave the look of speed and acknowledged the future. Inside the cockpit was strictly 21st century. How fast could it go? We'll never know, as this one was a roller. There was no driveline.

Pontiac still is intent on a GTO revival, the latest possibility is an imported Holden Monaro from Australia.

Pontiac

1999 Aztec

Perhaps the most controversial concept vehicle in automotive history was shown by Pontiac in 1999, the Aztek. Radical styling is nothing new in concept vehicles, but making it to production almost unchanged after strongly mixed public reaction broke new ground. It was not a success in the market place after its introduction as a 2001 model and likely was a major factor in General Motors hiring Robert Lutz to oversee its vehicle design in 2001.

A cross-over vehicle with an innovative activity oriented interior, the Aztek was marked by exterior styling that was conflicted by a variety of lines and shapes.

"Sporty, provocative and exciting," said a press release. You be the judge which adjectives described it. Body cladding was added to the 2001 production model, but removed for 2002 to look more like the original concept Aztek. The change didn't help spur the lackluster sales.

2000 Piranha

Aiming concept vehicles squarely at the youth market (whatever it be called) was a Pontiac tradition going back decades. When the Piranha was launched for the 2000 show season, it was the latest in a long line.

Billed as an activity vehicle, the four door Piranha featured removable seating for four, an opening rear hatch, a lightweight tub in the cargo area that served as a trunk or removable cooler, and a glovebox that also could serve as a cooler. Instrumentation was minimal.

Wide track wheels measured 18 inches in front and 19 inches in the rear. A 2.2 liter supercharged four-cylinder

engine spun a five-speed automatic transaxle and then the front wheels. Styling was compact and angular, accentuated by silver and blue two-toning.

John Mack, man behind the styling of Piranha, is shown with his creation.

2001
Sunfire HO 2.4

Putting some pizzazz in its low-priced Sunfire's image was Pontiac's mission for the HO 2.4 show car, which was first seen in 2001 and continues to be displayed in 2002.

HO translates to high output, if you follow Pontiac performance history, and the 2.4 liter overhead cam four was helped in that direction by a supercharger.

Rated at 195 horsepower, literature for the car claimed it would go fast, but failed to say how fast.

Trick frontal styling, rear spoiler, lowered ride eight, 18-inch chrome wheels, four-wheel disc brakes and body enhancements including fender flares all conveyed the intentions of the manufacturer. Inside Sparco front seats, aluminum shift knob and parking brake and a fire extinguisher gave showgoers reason to look in the windows.

2001 Grand Am Hot Wheels

What better way to reach the youth market target of the Grand Am than have a promotional tie-in with a popular toy line?

Pontiac did just that with the Grand Am Hot Wheels Model, which made the rounds in 2001 and returned for 2002. Taking a four-door sedan for a start, the dress-up began. There was a new rear fascia with a large spoiler, clear taillights with red and orange bulbs, special rocker panel styling, 18x8-inch American Eagle chrome wheels, P245/40/ZR18 BF Goodrich Z-rated tires, Hot Wheels interior and exterior graphics, Ram Air hood scoops, NASCAR quick-fill recessed fuel filler cap, low restriction exhaust, metal alloy racing pedals, and performance paint stripes.

"Have you ever dreamed of bringing a Hot Wheels car to life and getting behind the wheel?" That was the question literature on the car asked.

Pontiac

2001 Rev

As a follow-up to its 2000 Piranha youth-targeted concept, Pontiac showed off the Rev for 2001.

Another small four-door with sporting aspirations, the Rev fit into the cross-over parade with its all wheel drive and 245-hp 3 liter OHC V-6. Its five speed manual transmission could be shifted automatically with a drive-by-wire "joystick."

The suspension was adjustable for height, depending on the terrain. Wheels were a combo of 19 inches in front and 20 in the rear. Fenders and rocker panels were composite. The center opening doors did so without a B-pillar, easing entry and exit situations. Cargo storage was accessed by a lift, tailgate combination.

Inside was the entertainment and information devices you could handle, plus carbon fiber dash and door panels for resistance to wear and tear.

2001 Vibe GT/R

Before production started in Fremont, California, the Pontiac Vibe was shown in a couple of forms. It appeared as the Vibe GT at auto shows in 2001, then at the GT/R, loaded with accessories from General Motors Service Parts Operations.

In the latter form, shown above, it has a rear roof spoiler, another on the rear deck, new front and rear fascias and 19-inch Montegi racing wheels. Ride height was lowered three inches.

The Vibe (and its twin the Toyota Matrix) went on sale in 2002, but the accessories on the show car have yet to come to market.

Pontiac

2002 Grand Prix G-Force

Labeling a preview of a future production vehicle a "concept" is common practice these days. Spectators at the 2002 Chicago Auto Show and selected venues thereafter got an up-close view of the next generation 2004 Pontiac Grand Prix, under the guise of the G-Force concept.

Sleeker styling, minus Pontiac's traditional body cladding, 2+2 seating, a stiffer chassis, and a 280-hp supercharged version of GM's venerable 3800 Series II V-6 all made for an impressive package. There was no word if there was to be a two-door model coming along with it.

2002 Bonneville G/XP

Billed as a "tuner" rendition of the Bonneville sedan, the G/XP debuted at the 2002 Chicago Auto Show. Aside from the elimination of body cladding, most of the modifications were of the hot-rod variety, using old-school terminology.

Today hot cars modified for performance are called tuners. Lower by 1.5 inches, the G/XP got a K&N air filter, Corsa cat-back exhaust system, and boost in supercharger pressure. An output of 270 horsepower was claimed from the 3800 Series II V-6.

Sitting on 19-inch wheels with cross-drilled and slotted brake rotors made handling and stopping of the same priority as performance.

The stealthy dark Argentinean blue paint and smoked light lenses, front and back, all added to the sought-after image.

Pontiac

2002 Solstice Roadster

A new direction for Pontiac was unveiled at the North American international Auto Show in Detroit in January of 2002.

Both a roadster and coupe were shown. Reports circulated that the concept cars took four months from idea to reality, thanks to the driving force behind major changes at General Motors, vice chairman Robert Lutz.

It was Lutz who drove the roadster onto the stage at the press preview (above). The Solstice was voted Best in Show. Billed as an affordable sports car, the Solstice featured simplicity, while previous concepts were known for gadgetry.

"Obviously, you can't say it's going to be produced before its had a chance to make the rounds," Lutz said.

Early word from the "rounds" indicates Pontiac has a winner. If Lutz's past performance at Chrysler Corporation is any indication (Dodge Viper, Plymouth Prowler), Pontiac and GM fans are in for a good ride.

2002 Solstice Coupe

Saturn

2001 CV1

Concept cars from GM's shadowy Saturn division were, and are still, quite rare. First shown at the 2000 Los Angeles Auto Show, the CV1 was an attempt to combine a wagon, SUV, and perhaps a sedan.

Under the arched A-pillar and extension was a three-door system on each side. The front doors opened conventionally, while the rear two was a kind of bifold deal, allowing access to an unusual seating arrangement.

The second row of seats was a pair of jump seats that folded down from the front seatbacks. There was also a third row of seats facing forward. LCD readouts for each wheel's tire pressure were among the interior features.

Saturn didn't follow up on the CV1 gimmicks, but did get its own SUV, the 2002 Vue.

2002 Sky

Expanding its horizons, Saturn tested the waters for a roadster/convertible with its Sky concept, on display for the 2002 show season.

Using the three-door format from its S-Series coupes, there are two doors on the driver side and one on the passenger. A fairly small package, the Sky has a 102.4-inch wheelbase, length of just 165 inches and overall weight at 2,300 pounds.

A supercharged 2.2 liter four produces 180 horsepower and a five speed manual transmission guides power to the front wheels. A removable tonneau cover converts the Sky from a two-seater to four and stows in the trunk.

The Sky could be a double preview of future Saturns, both in S-Series styling and a new open body style.

GMC

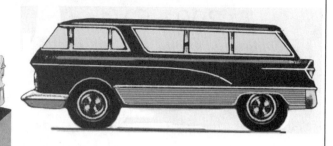

1955 L' Universelle

Combining style, utility and a look at the future, GMC previewed the van/minivan with its 1955 Motorama showing of the L'Universelle. While Volkswagen and other European manufacturers offered the small, forward control van at the time, GM dressed it up in dream car fashion and added a variety of engineering innovations.

Sporting "Dagmar" front bumpers, a wraparound windshield, aluminum cladded sides, 1955 Chevy Nomad-influenced rear styling, and an overall height about a foot lower than contemporary panels trucks, the L'Universelle was an attention-getter.

The cargo area was accessed by clamshell doors on each side. Mechanically, it featured a mid-mounted Pontiac V-8 and front-wheel drive.

Air for the radiator was drawn through a vent on the roof. A rendering of a passenger version was shown, but no examples were known to have been built.

The L'Universelle proved a preview of the domestic small vans introduced for 1961.

1988 Sierra CART/PPG

A GMC Sierra pickup truck was modified for pace car...oops...pace truck duties for the CART/PPG Indy Car World Series in 1988. It was the fifth straight year that GMC was the official truck supplier of CART (Championship Auto Racing teams).

With many CART events on road courses, modifications to the Sierra were needed. A lower ride height, revised suspension travel, reinforced frame, 16-inch Goodyear Eagle P255/50 ZR16 tires, and special stainless steel exhaust system were among the alterations.

In the looks department, changes were made both for the show and track audiences. They included glass T-top, ground effects package, walk-though passage from bed to passenger compartment, and two rear-facing jump seats.

A roll cage was also installed. The body modifications were handled by specialty builder Cars & Concepts.

1988
Sierra A/R 400

An unlikely combination of a rugged GMC Sierra pickup and Active Ride suspension from Lotus Engineering Ltd. of sports car fame produced the A/R 400, which was shown during the 1988 season.

General Motors owned Group Lotus plc. at the time and was anxious to apply its technology where it could to benefit from the investment.

The claimed result was a vehicle capable of outstanding comfort and handling through a full spectrum of conditions. The sophisticated Lotus Active Suspension System used a computer controller and hydraulic pressure system to transmit kinetic energy to the wheels when needed. Cost no doubt prevented it from seeing mass production.

The flareside body on the Sierra AAR/400 was modified to include brush guard, spoiler, roof spotlight, front winch, tow hooks, and a special paint job.

1989
Syclone

High-performance pickup trucks weren't the norm in 1989, but GMC correctly perceived a market for them in 1989 when the Syclone concept pickup was put on the show circuit.

Starting with the compact S-15, GMC raided the GM parts bin and picked a 3.8 liter turbocharged V-6 that wasn't doing anything at the time. It had last seen production status in the 1987 Buick Grand National, a legendary performance car.

Rated at 270 horsepower, it was teamed with an enhanced Turbo-Hydramatic, 3.42 rear gearing and Goodyear Eagle GT 16-inch P245/50VR tires. The combo was good for 0-60 runs under six seconds and 103 mph in the quarter.

Ground effects body work, a rear spoiler, deck cover and front air dam all added to the go-fast image. Articulated bucket seats and console dressed up the inside.

GMC claimed no production plans, but used the Syclone to test public opinion. The reaction was overwhelmingly positive, resulting in production Syclones from early 1991 through 1992.

GMC

1989 Centaur

Named for the half-man, half-horse creature of Greek mythology, the GMC Centaur concept truck attempted to blend comforts for man (and woman) and hauling ability into one aerodynamically massaged package.

Its interior had room for five in a passenger car environment and the Centaur was capable of handling 2,000 pounds of payload and had a towing capacity of 5,000 pounds. Shown in 1989, it would have been right at home in the new crossover-vehicle market a dozen years later.

The short hood covered a three liter, horizontal in-line six, attached to a five-speed automatic and four-wheel drive. A self-leveling air damper suspension, four-wheel electric steering and anti-lock brakes all contributed to car-like ride and handling.

The overall package was that of a compact S-15 pickup. Flush glass all around and a two tone silver and translucent bright metallic red paint job added to its look of the future impression.

1989 Kalahari

For a pre-production preview of its 1990 four-door Jimmy, GMC sent the Kalahari concept truck on the show circuit in 1989. Utilizing a luxury theme, it set it apart from the more mundane versions that would be at the dealers.

Light graphite pearl paint covered the ground effects panels, fender flairs, and surrounded the 17-inch Goodyear GR tires and special wheels.

A sunroof and luggage rack topped it off. Inside, cognac-tinted leather and African rose wood trim upgraded the environment, while a slide out rear platform aided loading the day's catch from your safari, or mall trip.

1990 Transcend

Exploring the open pickup truck interested GMC, at least as far as concept trucks for the 1990 season went.

Based on the full-sized Sierra pickup, it featured a retractable hardtop and a permanent arch over the rear of the passenger compartment.

The bed and cab were a single unit, like the 1961-63 unibody Fords. Two tone raspberry and magenta paint graced the outside, while raspberry and black leather and cloth trimmed the bucket seats and interior.

The console held a compact disc player and other goodies. With a lowered suspension and a bit of a rake, it was along the lines of a hot rodded truck, popular at the time.

1990 Mahalo

The attention of future younger buyers was the goal of the Mahlo, a 1990 convertible pickup concept, based on the coming 1991 Sonoma compact pickup. The three-tone paint job of a coral body, accented by a diagonal sea-spray design in seafoam green edged in white, competed with the ground effects body work, spoiler and bed cover for attention.

Custom mirrors and air dam enhanced the front bumper. The color scheme was continued into the interior.

1990 Syclone LSR

To help set the stage for the February 1991 introduction of the Syclone performance pickup, GMC built the Syclone LSR to challenge the speed record for a truck.

Using the extended cab, modified 5 liter Buick V-6 engine, and a lowered body/suspension, it was driven by Don Stringfellow to a two-way average of 204.076 mph at Bonneville Salt Flats, Utah, on Sept. 14, 1990.

With the record set, the vehicle went on display thereafter. It should be noted that the production Syclone had a conventional cab.

GMC

1991 Rio Grande

The overdue redesigns of GMC's full-sized Jimmy SUV and Suburban were revealed on the 1991 auto show schedule, thanks to the Rio Grande and Sagebrush concepts. While most Chevrolet and GMC pickups were all new years ago, the two and four-door SUVs made do with the old bodies. They would be changed for 1992 with the Rio Grande based on a new Suburban and the Sagebrush on the new Yukon, which replaced the Jimmy.

Rio Grande concept features included a big glass sunroof, body cladding, high-mounted taillights, and custom seating by Lear. The all-wheel drive, two-toned concept also had a rear vision video system, an old GM dream car gadget.

Companion Sagebrush, also a 4x4, featured many of the Rio Grande pieces, plus a special off-road grille. Rio Grande power was via a 6.5 liter turbocharged diesel V-8, while the Sagebrush made do with the 5 liter gas V-8.

1991 Sagebrush

1992 Sonoma GTX Sportside

Bringing the sportside (fender) design to the compact class was the mission of the Sonoma GTX Sportside, a concept truck of 1992.

Full-size trucks were getting new sportsides, but the compact class, which had smaller beds to begin with, lagged behind. The composite bed was similar to that on the larger Sierra pickup.

Other body tricks, including ground effects and front fender flares, completed the package.

A Syclone-like turbocharged V-6 powered the GTX.

1998 Sierra
Modern Nostalgia

To appeal to the street machine audience, GMC and new divisional sibling Pontiac displayed a pair of flamed show cars at the 1997 SEMA show. The Pontiac was a Grand Prix, while the Sierra extended cab pickup carried the colors for GMC.

Its flame paint job called attention to other modifications, including tonneau cover with built-in spoiler, trick grille, a slammed suspension, big wheels, and flared out rear-wheel opening. Putting show vehicles in the annual November Specialty Equipment Manufacturers show in Las Vegas, Nev. was a must at this stage of the 1990s. Show vehicles later appeared at auto shows, racing events and custom car shows.

2000 Terradyne

The first of a family of futuristic trucks with controversial styling, the Terradyne, came along for 2000.

It featured bold bodywork and many innovations aimed at the need of the recreational light trucker in the coming years.

The four-door pickup utilized center opening, sliding doors. The short pickup box extended could be extended from six to eight feet when extra room was needed.

A side storage system with powered access doors make enclosed storage space available on either side, while the bed can still carry open loads.

Of cab-forward design, the engine compartment still left room for a new Duramax 6.6 liter turbo diesel and a roomy passenger compartment.

A five-speed Allison automatic and four-wheel steering completed the preview of mechanical things to come from GMC.

Among the other practical facets was a 5,000 watt on-board generator driven by the engine and outlets for both 110 and 220 volts.

One could not view the Terradyne without a strong opinion of what the truck of the future should, or shouldn't look like.

"The goal was to produce a truck with the characteristics of a well-made precision tool. Visually, Terradyne expresses this philosophy through the use of exterior billet cut styling." Carl Zipfel, GMC design manager

GMC

2001 Terracross

The SUV in GMC's Terra series of concept trucks came along for 2001. The Terracross featured the same billet styling as the others, but expanded the window of package experimentation.

A three-panel glass sliding roof, Avalanche-like mid-gate that permitted it to take on pickup truck duties, and a comfortable five-passenger seating arrangement all made the vehicle as versatile as possible. Front doors opened conventionally, while rear doors were sliders.

There was no B-pillar, aiding entry. Underneath, a somewhat tame unitized body held a 3.4 liter V-6 engine, automatic, and four-wheel drive.

Wheelbase was just shy of 113 inches and overall length came to 171.9 inches.

Inside, the electric playland, common to concepts of the day, was there for entertainment and information. Not done, another Terra series GMC would be shown in 2002.

2002 Terra4

Third in the series of Terra concept vehicles from GMC was the 2002 Terra4. It fit between the 2000 Terradyne pickup and 2001 Terracross crossover wagon.

Exterior styling borrowed heavily from the Terracross. A four-door pickup with conventionally opening doors, it concentrated most of its innovations in the bed area where the sides opened for access and a retractable cover of aluminum slats allowed the truck to carry tall items.

Like the popular Chevy Avalanche, a pass-through area behind the rear seats opened up, a feature not yet in the GMC line with the Terra4 was shown. While interior accommodations for the passengers were luxurious, a hardware look with bright areas carried the truck theme.

Competing with the eye candy was a hybrid powertrain with a 5.3 liter V-8 and a 4.8 kilowatt motor/generator integrated to propel the vehicle.

GM brass noted the system would be optional starting in 2004.

Is this the last of the Terra concept series? Will future GMC trucks look similar? The questions are as old as dream cars themselves.

**2000
H2 SUV**

**2001
H2 SUT**

General Motors bought the marketing rights to AM General's civilian Hummers, but not the manufacturing operation. AM General had a history in military and government vehicles and joined the histories of Studebaker, Kaiser, and American Motors.

AMC sold AM General during one of its financial crisis. The Humvee military vehicle replaced the Jeep and its successors and AM General made a low-key effort to sell a version to the public. Humvees and Hummers used GM engines, so the relationship dated back into the 1980s.

The original Hummer, called the H1 after GM's move, had a limited market at best, but GM saw a demand for lower-priced and easier to produce versions. The first product of that philosophy was the H2, shown during the 2000 season.

Based on a Chevy truck chassis with a Hummer-like body and off the shelf GM power, the H2 was an instant hit.

In 2000, an SUV made the rounds and for 2001, a four-door pickup called the SUT (Sport Utility Truck) followed. Power came from a six-liter Vortec V-8, coupled to a five-speed automatic and, of course, four-wheel drive. Like the Chevrolet Avalanche, the SUT features a moveable rear bulkhead to convert from passenger to pickup truck duty. Angular exterior sheet metal, like the now-named H1, convey the ruggedness of the Hummer brand. The inside is filled with metal accents. Plans call for H2 SUV production to start as a 2003 model. It will be the centerpiece at a string of new exclusive Hummer dealers being built across the country. The SUT could follow.

Ford Motor Company

Ford's styling wizard, George W. Walker, and the X-1000 dream car of the future, from 1957.

When it came to dream, show and concept cars, the Ford Motor Company, like its founder Henry Ford, followed a different path. Sometimes it was ahead of the competition, sometimes behind, and sometimes off on its own path.

While General Motors and Chrysler Corporation were building pioneer dream cars in the 1930s and early 1940s, Ford was not a player. A plastic car was shown in 1941, but that was to demonstrate what could be done with Henry's beloved soybeans, not give previews of the future like the Buick Y-Job and Chrysler Thunderbolt.

Under the direction of Henry Ford II, Ford did come forth with dream cars and some great ones, too, like the Lincoln XL-500, Mercury XM-800, Turnpike Cruiser, and Lincoln Futura, styled under the direction of George Walker. However, it also wasn't afraid to show its dream cars in miniature. Ford fielded scale model dream cars from the 1953 Syrtis retractable hardtop to the 1962 Seattle-ite XXI of 1962 with many in between, and with many directed by famed stylist Alex Tremulis.

While Chrysler and GM were racing each other with gas turbine powered dream and show cars, Ford's calling seemed to be fascination with levitation. More of aircraft engineering persuasion, Ford studied the cushion of air motivation principle with its Volante scale model and such iterations as the Glideair, Levacar, and Levascooter, the latter a platform with a chair and a tiller.

Ford got back on the ground, so to speak, with the prospect of a low cost, low-powered sports car, starting with the 1962 Mustang I. That grew to the more conventional Mustang II of 1963 and it all set the stage for one of the most successful car models of all time, the 1965 Mustang, which bowed in April of 1964. While the production Mustang owed more to the Falcon than the original Mustang concept cars, it was the case of concept cars being used to set the stage for a new production vehicle.

As was the case with the competition, the 1960s were filled with modified production show cars from Ford, Lincoln and Mercury. Notable customizers like George Barris and Gene Winfield were given designs to build and build they did. Cars like the Fairlane GT A-Go-Go and Comet Escapade were some of the cars that not only made the auto shows, but were regulars on the custom car show circuit as well.

Trucks went from work vehicles to recreational play things and a good part of the transition came in the 1960s. Ford was always big in trucks and it put some out there like the Apartment van, Bronco Dune Duster, and Ranger series in the mid-1960s and would have truck show and concept vehicles on its specially built vehicle roster right into the next century.

One area where Ford differed from the other domestic manufacturers was in sourcing its concept cars from overseas. While General Motors and Chrysler (at one time) had extensive manufacturing operations overseas, they did not rely on European models and builders like Ford.

When Ford acquired Ghia of Turin, Italy, in the early 1970s, it turned the designer and custom coach builder into a virtual mass supplier of Ford concept and show cars. Indeed, it is this relationship with Ford's European operations that can cause some confusion as to which vehicles stayed in Europe and which were shown in the U.S. Since this volume tries to stick to vehicles that are related to this country, there is an area here subject to question. Some European sourced Fords never were shown in the U.S., but Ford generated extensive media coverage. Others with seemingly little interest for American drivers were brought over and shown. Others were brought here for evaluation, but it is questionable if the public ever saw them. In short, perhaps no other segment of the book caused as much confusion.

Ford returned to a healthy diet of non-production based concept cars in the 1980s, parallel, more or less, to GM and Chrysler. Again, much Ford sourcing came from Europe. Its Probe Series of the 1980s explored the latest technology in aerodynamics and power trains and its Aerostar series probed the wonders of the rear-wheel drive minivan, at a time Chrysler was peddling a bunch of front drivers.

An experiment with New Edge styling on the Synergy and a few others went nowhere, but did end up being the new religion for Cadillac and GMC.

Where Ford may have the inside track is retro. J Mays was snatched from Volkswagen after doing the New Beetle and proved he could take Ford styling on a similar trip back with modern updates. The Thunderbird concept was the first light of the new era and made production status with little change. A Sports Roadster concept shows that the history book is wide open at Ford. Another Mays-led effort was the 2001 Forty-Nine concept, drawing on a number of mid-century Ford styling themes. It did not make the production cut.

Today, Ford concept cars are truly exciting, like the Mighty Tonka F-350 and the production-promised GT40.

J. Mays

FORD

1941 Plastic Car

Automotive pioneer Henry Ford's interests also include a life-long infatuation in agriculture, This included the study of soybeans, which lead him and his company to the research and development of plastic materials.

In November 1940, FoMoCo premiered an experimental automobile of which the body was composed of 32 strips of plastic mounted on a tubular-welded steel frame. Basically the only major steel parts were the wheels and motor.

A press release from Sept. 14, 1941 mentioned that, "The plastic panels are only three-sixteenths of an inch thick, but will absorb a blow ten times as great as steel without denting."

Estimated weight of Ford's experimental plastic car was only 2,000 pounds, making it about a 1,000 pounds less than conventional steel cars.

Styling was like nothing else in Ford dealer showrooms at the time, but indicated the coming smooth, slab-side styling of the 1949 Ford, Mercury, and Lincoln.

1953 Syrtis

Historically significant, though only a 3/8-scale model, the 1953 Syrtis shows an early developmental stage in Ford's quest for a retractable hardtop roof automobile. The persistence paid off, as the dream was put into production with the introduction of the 1957 Fairlane 500 Skyliner.

Shown in the photo below from May 1953 is a group of newspapermen mesmerized by the working model of Roof-O-Matic as it went through its transformation. The rear deck and roof were electrically operated, and the rear window could be swung overhead and against the back of the front seat as a rear-seat windshield.

Ford

1954 FX-Atmos

Voted most likely to appear in a Jetson cartoon, the Ford FX-Atmos dream car was very futuristic for the early 1950s.

Space-age innovations included twin hypodermic needle antennae up front, jet tail fins, rocket-shaped taillights/exhaust ports, and the ubiquitous glass dome roof.

A Roadarscope (Ford's spelling) located in the dash told what was ahead, and the car could take over steering when set on autopilot. Hands-free driving was envisioned at the time to be possible by metal plates installed in special highways that would correspond to the vehicle, keeping it on the planned course. This would allow the driver to take a nap or play some cards, while the car did all the driving.

When inside the closed vehicle, the driver could communicate with pedestrians outside the car via microphone. Driver's seat was centrally located with two passenger seats beside and slightly behind.

Atmos was one of the first Ford idea cars that featured handgrip steering in place of a conventional steering wheel, though this concept had no engine or drivetrain.

1955 Mystere

Mystere was very jet age thinking with its huge glass bubble windshield and a planned rear-mounted gas-turbine engine. Its public debut was in late 1954, and caused a sensation wherever it was shown. From the overwhelming positive public reaction, Ford repeated the deep dip side molding on the 1955-56 Fairlane models, plus the canted fins and front fender sculpting of the 1957-58 lineup.

The roof canopy, hinged at the back, would raise-up 70 degrees when the half doors were opened. Since there were no windows to lower while driving, a scoop at the top of the windshield brought fresh air into the interior. Swivel seats up front made it easier to access the interior. It was also stated that if the car was produced, it would be equipped with air conditioning.

Along the lower rear fenders were indented chrome air inlets that supplied the engine. To start the rear gas-turbine engine, (but only theoretically, as the Mystere did not have one), the driver had to punch in a set of numbers on the push-button ignition, similar to modern telephones. Like the original VW Beetles, the spare tire and luggage would have been carried under the hood.

A wild innovation was the mid-dash airplane type steering wheel, mounted on a column that allowed it to be swung over to either front seat. This enabled the driver to become the passenger, and vice-versa, without either leaving their seat. Four-bucket seats and a console filled the interior, along with a TV and a telephone with a very long cord.

1956 Cougar

Long before Mercury branded the Cougar name on its 1967 pony car, Ford used it on a 1/8th-scale dream car model. Done as only one half of the car, it was placed next to a mirror to simulate the entire vehicle.

This far-out dream car emphasized a V-8 engine with the design of a circular radiator core.

The idea was to utilize most efficiently the circular path of the fan blade.

Painted a firebrand red, Cougar featured a divided windshield, large side exhaust stacks, (like the 1953 Syrtis), concealed headlights, and a deck-mounted spare tire.

"Dream car designs help in the search for new styling themes and often suggest ideas that can be used in the more immediate tomorrow." George W. Walker, 1957

127

Ford

3/8 Scale Dream Cars

Ford Motor Company once wrote the following description about developing dream cars:

"These are the visions of the advanced automotive stylists. To them, no concept is too fanciful for exploration. It may contain the germ of something valuable"

Scale models severed as early three-dimensional interpretation off the stylist's rendering, allowing management to judge whether to go on to a full-size prototype.

Beginning in the early 1950s, Ford exhibited a series of 3/8 scale models to the public, including the Syrtis, Cougar and X-2000 shown on previous pages. Six more far-out concept vehicles are featured on these two pages, as further examples.

Others, not pictured, are the jet-nosed Cutlass two-seat hardtop coupe, the Cavalier that had a plastic hood and aluminum body, and Bolero, which gave the impression of moving while motionless.

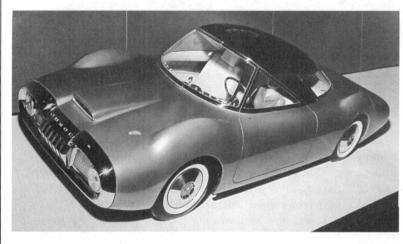

1953-Muroc

Designed as a sports coupe from Ford's Advanced Vehicle department, Muroc was one of the lucky dreams that got past the drawing-board stage.

Bump-up front fenders were features found later on Chevrolet Corvette and AMC Javelin models. Ford also used the arched hump on its full-size 1953 Ford XL-500 dream car.

It was named after the California dry lake where speed trails were held.

1955 La Tosca

Legendary Alex Tremulis is credited with the futuristic La Tosca. Designed to be remotely operable up to a distance of one and one half miles, the maneuverable toy had a top speed of five miles an hour.

Connected to the RC chassis was a removable fiberglass body for quick interchangeability during testing.

Design cues like the hooded headlights, large canted fins, and massive bumpers smoothly blended into the body, all became prominent features of the 1958-60 Lincolns and Continentals.

1957 X-1000

The X-1000 was a styling exercise highly influenced by supersonic aeronautical designs of the 1950s era. Note the bubble-type canopy, delta-shaped fins, and jet-pod fenders. The long torpedo-shaped taillights cantilevered off the inboard surfaces of the tail fins were designed to house electronic devices that would warn of approaching vehicles. Instrument panel and push-button controls were located in the center of the deep-dish safety steering wheel.

The shape of the hood and character line that flowed back to mid-body on the X-1000 looks close to those that eventually ended up on the 1958-60 Thunderbird.

3/8 Scale Dream Cars

1958 DePaolo

DePaolo represented exploration into vehicles with both sports car performance and features adaptable for use in mass-produced passenger cars. The action-looking side-molding treatment was to relay the feeling of motion that was conveyed by the wheels. Front fenders were bumped up like the Muroc concept.

1958 Nucleon

Looking deep into its crystal ball, Ford envisioned the possibility of atomic-powered transportation in the automobile's future.

Suspended between the two jet-style rear tailfins was the power capsule, which was planned to contain a radioactive core. Speed would depend on the size of the core, and power flow controlled by the driver.

The core could be recharged periodically at charging stations, which were going to replace gas stations.

Improving the aerodynamics of Nucleon were retractable front and rear bumpers. Long, slit beam horizontal headlights, which were a mere dream in 1958, are possible and available with halogen projector bulbs on 21st century vehicles.

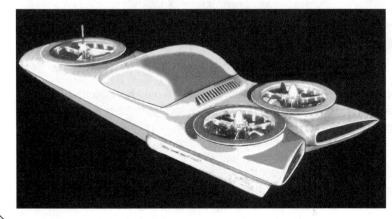

1958 Volante

Volante was envisioned as a future flying car, to be operated similar to a helicopter.

Shown in the photograph are three fan units arranged in a triangular pattern, which were designed to provide lift and thrust.

Located ahead of the driver/pilot was the unit composed of two counter-rotating blades and a motor. Each of the two rear units had a single set of blades that moved in opposite directions to offset torque.

When FoMoCo purchased Aston Martin, it finally had a Volante model, the DB7 Vantage Volante.

Ford

1958 La Galaxie

Many dream cars are not driveable, but purely styling studies, such as La Galaxic from 1958.

This was a six-passenger idea car, that had three adjustable front seats, and butterfly roof sections that raised-up when the doors opened. Handgrip steering replaced the conventional wheel, and radar was built-in for navigation. There was also a proximity warning screen on the dash, when objects came to close to the car.

Part of this dream car's nameplate, Galaxie, became a Ford luxury series in 1959. Similar rear-quarter design, along with the covered rear wheels, appeared on the 1964 full-size Ford Galaxie and Custom models.

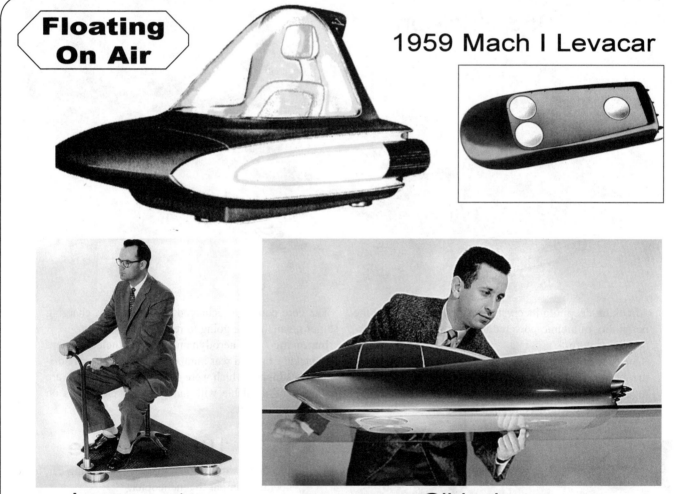

Floating On Air

1959 Mach I Levacar

Levascooter

Glideair

Shown above were ideas for Ford vehicles that levitated above the ground on a cushion of air. Each of the different designs operated by means of three levapads that supported the vehicle just a few thousandths of an inch from the road or water surface.

These levapads were mounted on a spherical bearing that permitted adjustments to the contour of the roadway. Tiny holes in each levapad released jets of low-pressure air, about

15 pounds per square inch, that would have been sufficient to raise it up. Engineers envisioned that either a gas turbine or turbojet engine would provide the propulsion.

These vehicles were described as, "…easily moved with the touch of a finger, and slide through air more easily that the blade of a skate over ice."

The first, full-scale levacar, the Mach I, was introduced at the Ford Rotunda in the spring of 1959.

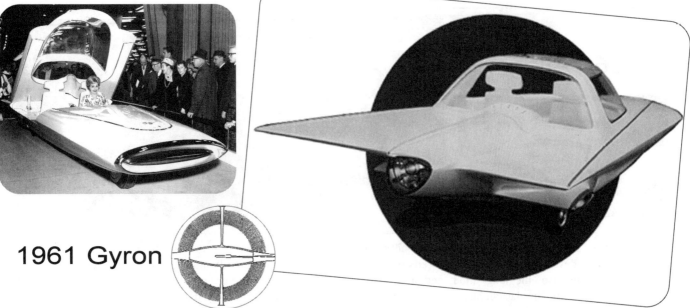

1961 Gyron

Luke Skywalker rode around in something that looked like Gyron, Ford's 1961 delta shaped dream car.

But, as Skywalker's vehicle hovered over the road, Gyron balanced and rode on two-wheels. Ford's inventive engineers envisioned that the car would be equipped with a gyroscope for stabilization.

Large one-piece canopy with fixed windows were raised or lowered automatically.

All controls in the Gyron were housed in a console between the specially contoured seats. These included controls to operate the gyroscope, air conditioning, the canopy control, adjustable foot rests, and a steering dial that made it possible for the car to be operated from either seat.

Though only theoretically in 1961, Gyron had a computer system that would make it possible to direct the car's planned travel route automatically.

1962 Seattle-ite XXI

Alex Tremulis was known for styling many outstanding vehicles, but a lesser known role was his leadership in Ford showing a bunch of 3/8 scale models of futuristic cars in the 1950s and 1960s.

One of the strangest was the Seattle-ite XX, which was made for display at the 1962 Seattle World's Fair. The six-wheel design with steering by the front four stands out visually, but that was only part of the plan.

Under its long hood was room for a variety of engines (if it was full-sized of course) that ranged from nuclear to fuel cells to electric to gasoline. As long as we're dealing with imagination, you could have a choice of a couple of engines at once.

Computers kept track of the engines and trip information for the driver and passenger. It was only a two seater.

Like many of the Ford designs of the future from the model series, they were advanced to the point that little has yet come to market. The four wheel steering was used on the Formula One racer a couple of decades later, however.

131

Ford

1962 Allegro

Described as "a car of the future that could be built today," the Allegro was developed by Ford's advanced stylists and engineers. Design-wise, the long hood, and a grille that extended forward of the headlights, were elements that became Mustang trademarks.

Inside the Allegro's compact passenger compartment were fixed seats, plus adjustable accelerator and brake pedals. Fixed-seat design contributed to overall rigidity and allowed for a reduction in the vehicle height.

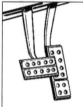

Adjustable pedals eventually appeared on Ford products.

Engineers tried something different with the development of a cantilevered-arm steering wheel with built-in memory unit.

The steering wheel was mounted on a horizontal arm that pivoted on the centrally mounted steering column.

Four years later, Ford released the Allegro II concept car, a two-seat roadster, shown during the 1967 season.

1963 Twister

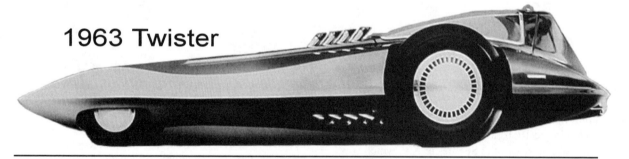

Research stylists at Ford tinkered with a dream dragster they called Twister.

Though it was only a 3/8-scale model, it cause a sensation when it was unveiled at the 1963 National Championship Drag Races in Indianapolis. Racing fans encouraged Ford to build the "Coke bottle"-shaped dragster, which also resembled a missile traveling at supersonic speeds.

Custom paint job blended from a nearly white hot nose through orange and red-orange to deep red at the rear of the model.

It was envisioned that two 427 cubic inch V-8 engines mounted radically would be used. According to the engineers, this arrangement would have yield as much as 950 horsepower.

Adding to the aerodynamics of the vehicle, was a fully enclosed streamlined cockpit that hinged at the front for entry/exit, and at the rear, a braking chute was contained in a simulated pod.

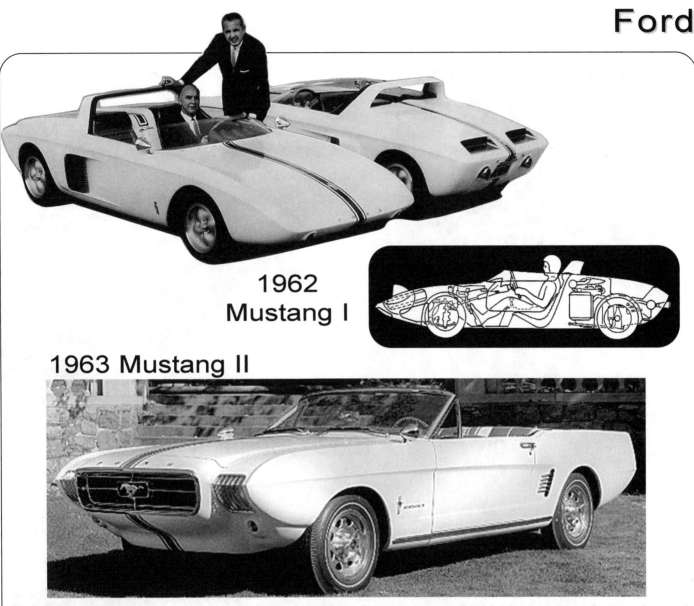

1962 Mustang I

1963 Mustang II

Who would have thought back in 1962, when the first Mustang concept car made its debut prior to the running of the U.S. Grand Prix, that it was the genesis of the pony car revolution. Shown above is Ford VP engineer H.L. Misch, shown above sitting in the driveable, aluminum-body Mustang. Standing along side was VP of styling Gene Bordinat. Both were responsible for the car's development. Directly behind them both was the second version of the two-seat Mustang, but this model was constructed of fiberglass and used primarily for auto shows.

In a press release from Oct. 7, 1962, Ford stated, "Mustang was the first car built by a major American manufacturer which fits into the European-dominated popular sports car class." The line illustration shows the layout of the 1,700-pound car, with the mid-mounted V-4 engine, which delivered 89 horsepower

for road version and 109 hp for the track. A four-speed manual transmission was mated to the engine.

Bucket seats were built as a fixed part of the body structure, while the steering wheel and foot pedals were adjustable for tall and short drivers.

The low, thin roll bar located behind the cockpit also served as an airfoil. Side vents were for real, pulling in cooling air to the two radiators. A full-length pan enclosed the underside to eliminate wind resistance. Unique feature was the horn pedal that was operated with the heel of the hand.

Deemed too radical for a high volume sports car, the 1962 two-seater led to the development of the 1963 Mustang II concept car.

Ford released the experimental Mustang II, and was encouraged by the extremely favorable public and press response.

This second version was developed as a two-plus-two, and was a disguised version of the coming production Mustangs.

So influential was the styling of Mustang II that 40 years later Ford still used variations of the triple-unit taillights, body character lines, side vent motif, and distinctive grille.

Ford

1962 Cougar 406

1963 Cougar II

1962 Cougar 406

For 1962, Ford used the Cougar name on a second concept car. The first was the 3/8-scale model from 1956.

Cougar 406 featured top-hinged, electrically operated gull-wing doors, used the new 406 cu. in. engine, and was built on a 102-inch wheelbase chassis.

Shown on the left is the third Cougar dream car, released by FoMoCo in 1963, but titled Cougar II. This very handsome two-passenger GT sports car would have made a timely contender to the popular Corvette String Ray. (Ford explained that GT, or gran turismo, is a term usually applied to two-seat coupes designed for super highways.)

Cougar II featured a fastback roof, concealed "pop-up" headlamps, and a serious, fully instrumented interior.

Powertrain was a high-performance 260 cu. in. V-8 engine that connected a four-speed transmission with a console-mounted gearshift lever.

It was claimed that Cougar II was engineered to reach speeds in the 170 miles-an-hour range.

When interior air pressure exceeded 15 pounds per square inch, a relief panel across the rear of the passenger compartment opened automatically.

This panel was required, since there was the possibility that at high speeds, the extreme pressure against the rear window might blow it out.

Cougar also had a unique spring-loaded window-lift mechanism that allowed adjustment to the curved side windows.

1965 XP (Bordinat) Cobra

A proposal to update the AC body used on Carroll Shelby's Cobra looked pretty much like a convertible version of the 1962 Cougar II dream car. It was under the guidance of Eugene Bordinat Jr., director for Ford Design, and became known as the Bordinat Cobra. It was powered by Ford's small block 289, but was said to have room for the 427-cid FE block. A single piece of Royalex plastic made up the dashboard.

Despite this and other efforts, the AC body continued to be used for Cobra production cars during the run and replicas have been produced for repro Cobras ever since.

Ford

1963 Thunderbird Italien

1963 Fairlane

Two Ford show cars that toured the 1963 show circuit were factory authorized custom versions of production models.

The Thunderbird Italien (Ford's spelling) was a styling study, with a top that departed from the traditional T-Bird squared-off design. A more aerodynamic roofline was used, giving the car a stunning new profile. Rear quarter windows swung out, and those side fender vents were a nice styling touch. The interior was finished in rich leather, including bucket seat front and back.

Though this streamline look never appeared on Thunderbirds, it predicted the coming trend of fastback roofs on other Ford models like Mustang 2+2, Torino Cobra, and 500XL models.

Traveling along with the Italien was an altered mid-size Fairlane. Its claim to fame was a landau roof and nearly rounded rear wheel opening, two elements not found on the stock model.

Body color was mother of pearl white, and a modern landau bar highlighted the roof, which was covered in a textured weatherproof material. Triple-line white-wall tires and genuine wire wheels with knock-off hubs added further elegance.

1964 Thunderbird Golden Palomino

Though the palomino name didn't exactly fit in with the elegant Thunderbird, the Golden Palomino made the auto show rounds in 1964. To call attention to the all-new 1964 T-Birds, Ford fixed up this example with pop-up roof panels that raised when the doors opened, Kelsey-Hayes wire wheels and special trim, inside and out.

It proved a hit on the show circuit, so much so that it was sent on a nationwide tour of Ford dealers during 1965.

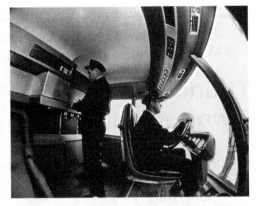

1964 Gas Turbine

Affectionately known as "Big Red," Ford's 600-horsepower experimental gas turbine transport was a sensation wherever it traveled. It's reported that at 70 mph, it rode smooth, that the turbine was completely noiseless, and produced non-smoky exhaust.

Envisioned as a long-distance, non-stop vehicle, Big Red would be the perfect truck for the coming 1970s, and the completion of the national superhighway network. It had a 600-mile cruising range, eliminating normal fuel stops, with only brief pauses to change drivers.

At full capacity, the turbine could move 170,000 pounds, which was a combined weight of tractor, trailers, and cargo.

The upper half of the 13-foot-high cab was where the driver and co-driver operated the vehicle. A motor controlled ladder allowed the drivers to climb up into the cab. The ladder then would stow away automatically beneath the floor. Placed in front of the driver were pedestal-mounted instruments and dials monitoring the turbine engine set above the windshield. Control pedals were mounted flush with the floor.

With a 6.6-foot-high cab ceiling, the co-pilot could walk around and make use of the built-in refrigerator, electric oven, wash stand, and disappearing toilet with electric incinerator.

1964 Aurora

Aurora, a styling experimental station wagon, was first shown at Ford Motor Company's exhibit of practical dream cars during the 1964 New York World's Fair.

Spear-shaped panels along the body sides were illuminated by means of electroluminescence that provided soft, blue-green running lights.

Front lighting was provided by experimental minibank headlamps, which were a series of 12 one-inch sealed beam units. A power-operated polarizing sunscreen that could change from opaque to transparent was located in the roof section above the front seats. The steering wheel was gone, replaced by small circular handgrips that turned together with the twist of the wrist.

A second version of a concept wagon, called Aurora II, was shown in 1969, after which the Aurora became known as the Aurora I.

Ford

1965 Thunderbird Town Landau

To dramatize the elegance of its experimental Thunderbird, Ford posed it in front of a painted outdoor cafe scene, showing formal-attired lovers seated at a table.

Previewed at the 1965 auto shows, this car was actually an early look at the special landau roof coming on the 1966 T-Bird. Featuring a broad rear roof pillar that extended to the door opening, it eliminated the rear quarter windows.

The idea was to offer increased privacy, but at the expense of the driver's rearward visibility.

Traditional landau bars were added to the roof's side, giving a distinctive appearance, as did the genuine wire wheels. The plush interior was fitted with experimental "wrist-twist" system, which replaced the steering wheel. Other styling features included a finely textured vertically fluted grille, rectangular headlights, and Silent-Flo Ventilation system.

1965 Galaxie 500 LTD

Appearing along with the Thunderbird Town Landau was the factory approved customized Galaxie 500 LTD.

A special horizontal chrome bar divided the production grille, and the vertical headlight bezels were extended further forward than normal.

All stock emblems and names were removed and leaded-in, and a custom medallion was added to the lower front fender behind the front wheel.

Like the above Thunderbird model, the 500 LTD also rode on classy chrome wire wheels.

The four-door hardtop roof used a stainless steel roof panel from the front window to mid-roof and padded material from that point to the rear window.

Those arrows near the front and rear windows were demonstrating Ford's Silent-Flo Ventilation system.

1965 LTD Executive Limousine

According to Ford V.P and general manager Donald N. Frey, this stretched LTD four-door hardtop was developed to test the public reaction to an eight-passenger limousine that would have sold for several thousand dollars less than similar units on the market.

It was also clever marketing. Ford could promote that the inherent quietness, smooth ride, and quality of a production LTD was suitable to serve as a limo in the world of furs and executive secretaries.

Even the interior appointments in the prototype limo used the same material found in the 1965 LTD.

This included the limousine's dual pedestal-mount seats that provide room for five in the rear compartment.

Known for its special vehicles, the Dearborn Steel Tubing Company developed the limousine concept for Ford Division. It extended the body and chassis two feet. To handle the added passenger load, chassis and suspension were beefed-up.

1966 Black Pearl

Looking like a mild California custom, this factory modified LTD two-door hardtop, was painted in a specially formulated Firefrost black metallic. Hence, its name, "Black Pearl."

Exterior door handles, along with the deck lid keyhole assembly and block letters on the hood, were removed, achieving a clean uncluttered design.

At the rear, the taillights were deeply tunneled into the fenders. To top it off, the roof on the Black Pearl was clad in a padded, black vinyl material, and the car sat on elegant wire wheels with triple stripe white-wall tires.

Interior included pearl-white seats with satin and leather bolsters for the cushions and seatbacks. Covering the floor was deep, pearl-white mouton carpeting.

Ford

1966 Fairlane GT A Go Go

Dancing in tune with the hip, youthful trends of the mid-1960s, came this cool Fairlane show car.

Perfectly titled as "GT A Go Go," it was a tastefully modified two-door hardtop.

Most notable features were the canted air intake ports on both sides of the hood, and the intake screens that replaced the lower headlights. The rushing air through those vents was to cool the front brakes. The unique exhaust system on the 390 V-8 engine allowed for street or track driving. Under normal use, the exhaust streamed out of the dual pipes built into the rear bumper.

During competition, the driver switched a cutout sending the exhaust through tuned straight pipes with outlets in the rocker panel molding, ahead of the rear wheels.

Finished in a white metallic paint, the body was accented by blue racing stripes that ran the full length of the hood, roof and trunk lid. Front and rear bucket seats were upholstered in blue metallic vinyl, as were interior panels. Special front fender decals were of four tiger heads and a Playboy bunny logo. These suggested that the GT A Go Go raced and beaten four Pontiac GTO tigers, plus gave a spin to a pretty Playmate.

Legendary customizer Gene Winfield constructed the car from designs out of Ford's Corporate Projects Studio.

1966 Magic Cruiser

An imaginative hybrid concept of the 1960s was Ford's Magic Cruiser. Designed to appear as a sporty fastback hardtop, it could change into a station wagon with the push of a dash-mounted button. The specially constructed top, along with two window side panels, would rise to provide additional seating area. Closing the tailgate and raising the rear window complet-

ed the transformation. Lowering of the tailgate permitted easy entry to a rear-facing third seat, and for more cargo area, the second and third seats could be folded down.

Created during a period when Ford's station wagons had immense popularity, and the merging sport car market, the Magic Cruiser seemed like a logical solution, but probably was cost prohibitive.

Custom-constructed by George Barris' Kustom City, the car was finished in a luxurious gold pearl paint, and special one-piece tempered glass headlights were installed. The powerful 7-liter, (428 cu. in.) V-8 was under the hood.

Ford updated the Magic Cruiser with 1967 bodywork and used it on the show circuit for a second season.

1967 Magic Cruiser

Ford

1966 & 1968
Bronco Dune Duster

This is one of those concept vehicles that lived more than once. First released Feb. 4, 1966, it appeared at auto shows, then was reintroduced Feb. 20, 1968, for another round of shows.

Ford had Barris Kustom of North Hollywood, California, construct the Dune Duster, as a special show version of its new four-wheel-drive vehicle.

Barris started with a stock six-cylinder Bronco roadster, which was painted a specially formulated golden saddle pearl. They then added an NHRA-approved roll bar, with integral headrest, as well as walnut appliques and exposed chrome exhaust pipes. Behind those side pipes was heat shielding rocker panels, stylishly formed of black and white anodized aluminum.

The stepover door panel with padded sill had a built-in step and assist handle. Triple rubber snubbers protected the bumpers from scratches, and chrome wheel lip moldings accented the steel alloy hubs, with knockoff caps.

Protecting the rear compartment was a tonneau cover, which utilized quick-fastening snaps. Stainless-steel rail topped the sides of the load bed, and a performance-type gas filler added to the sporty look.

The interior included a walnut steering wheel and suede upholstery. Not apparent from this photo was the hood air scoop.

Quite likely, the Bronco Dune Duster also reappeared in 1971 with different paint as the Bronco Wildflower.

1966 Falcon
Apartment

Ford stylists chopped the roof on a Falcon Club Wagon, reduced the overall height by seven inches, removed the second and third seats, and then reworked the interior to resemble a comfortable living room.

Appropriately called the Apartment, it was furnished with wall-contour sofa, tables, lamps, television, and thick-pile nylon carpeting. Elegant overhead ceiling beams, and door panels of wood blended well with the soft palomino interior color scheme.

Exterior was painted in an unusual copper colored metallic-flake finish. Other features included a Stereosonic tape music system, and contoured bucket seats.

Conforming to the Apartment's low-slung contour, the two side doors on the passenger side were replaced by a single door.

Powering this home-on-wheels was a 289 cu. in. high-performance V-8 engine, connected to a Cruise-O-Matic transmission.

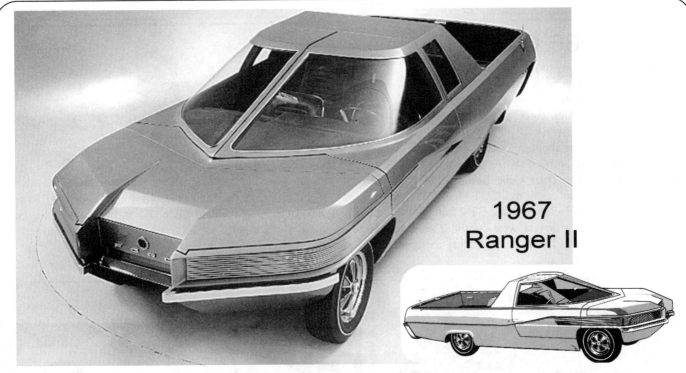

1967
Ranger II

Promoted as a futuristic pickup, this ultra-modern two-passenger truck could converted into a four-passenger pickup/sedan combination. The rear panel of 1967-68 Ranger cabs could move 18 inches into the bed of the truck, then a roof section filled the gap and two additional bucket seats could be dropped in place. Aircraft-type canopy doors operated hydraulically.

Ranger III was a refined version of the pervious year's concept. Other "better ideas" included a power-operated hood that was opened from inside the vehicle.

Both Ranger II and III were 18 feet long on a 120-inch wheelbase, and had rosewood flooring.

These weird looking vehicles were crafted out of an F-250 pickup, and equipped with a high performance, tri-powered, 390-cubic-inch V-8.

Ford began to use the Ranger name on production trucks beginning with the 1950 Marmon-Harrington panel conversions.

1968
Ranger III

Ford

1966 GT-P

Though it looks ready to race, the GT-type vehicle car shown here was actually a full-size clay model. Ford's Advanced Concepts department created the design to carry the U.S. colors in the International racing circuit.

What was important about this racing car was the major role that Ford allowed stylists to have on the vehicle, under styling chief Gene Bordinat. Their goal was to create a successor to the GT Mark II.

Standing a mere 38 inches high, the GT-P featured the latest in aerodynamics. Racing drivers were consulted on details, like Bruce McLaren who had ideas on the seating configuration.

It was estimated that the car would weigh between 1,750 and 1,900 pounds, and would be powered by a 427-cubic-inch engine. Those figures would have put the car at a power-to-weight ratio of about 4.1 pounds per horsepower.

1967 Mach 2

Shown directly above was the public debut of the experimental Mach 2 high-performance two-passenger sports car. Designed for both street and competition use, the car had a mid-mounted engine with carburetor intake ports on the rear deck.

The coved-back, fiberglass body, with semi-monocoque construction, stood a mere 47 inches high. Front-hinged doors were cut into the roof, making it easier to entry/exit the vehicle.

Ford let it be known that it cost $150,000 to build the one-off vehicle.

Two model years later, Ford added the Mach name to its model line-up, but called the Mustang the Mach I.

1967 Allegro II

Ford released the Allegro II as a fresh idea in a two-seat sports car. Basically, it was an update to its 1955-57 Thunderbird philosophy.

Wearing gold stripe sidewall 13" tires, Allegro featured an integrated roll bar, hood lock pins, and a tachometer mounted in the steering wheel hub. A digital speedometer was flush mounted into dash. The fixed seats and adjustable foot pedals were similar to those shown in the 1962 Mustang I.

The fully wraparound windshield blended smoothly into the roll-bar pillars. A steering wheel was on a cantilevered arm that with the touch of a button could pivot up or down, plus, slide in and out.

For easy entry or exit from the interior, the steering wheel also swung out of the way. Built on a 99-inch wheelbase, Allegro stood only 41.25 inches to the top of the roll bar, with a body 10 inches lower than the production Mustang.

1967 Mach I

Ford did some extensive modifications to its production Mustang, and created an even sleeker Mach I idea car. Rectangular headlights, still not legal in all 50 U.S. states, were set horizontally in the fenders and twin-louvered hood distinguished and the front end

Unlike the production Mustang, the air intake scoops just behind the doors actually worked at cooling the rear brakes. Quick-release fuel-filler caps were located on roof pillars behind the fixed side glass, and the rear window/deck lid opened with hydraulics from the Mach I interior.

Large wheel openings were flared to accentuate the special wide-oval, low profile racing tires and cast aluminum alloy wheels. Rear fenders flowed into the ducktail air spoiler, and the triple taillights blended with the full-width ribbed rear panel. Center mounted exhaust outlets were notched into the rear bumper.

1968 Techna

Ford's Techna concept car lived up to its name, featuring over 50 technological innovations.

A cantilever roof, similar to the 1956 Chrysler Norseman, eliminated the front corner posts, and featured a specially constructed windshield of soft polyvinyl, laminated between strength-tempered glass. The six-foot-long powered-operate, parallel-hinged doors, allowed the Techna to park within 18 inches of another vehicle.

The complete front clip tilted forward, like the XK-E Jaguar, allowing easy access to service the entire engine. For routine inspection of engine fluid levels, carburetor, and distributor, there was a convenient 14x24 inch hatch that opened in the middle of the hood.

A small driveline tunnel was located between the left and center occupants, rather than in the center of the car, providing a more spacious interior.

The frame on the Techna was just three-quarter length, which provided a crush zone up front and, with the absence of a rear frame, gave more trunk space. The spacious truck also housed the battery and electronics for the AM/FM radio.

The stylish body was constructed of sandwiched composite material, with plastisol-urethane foam-molded trim pieces.

Ford

1968
Torino
Machete
Style I

1968
Torino
Machete
Style II

Ford tried something different in auto show special vehicles for 1968. It modified two 1968 Fairlane Torino GT fastbacks, with the same custom touches, but painted each in a different two-tone paint combination. Notice the highback front seats.

Like many show and production cars, Machete featured concealed headlights behind electrically operated doors in the grille. Ford described the restyled grille as black, twin horizontal air scoops. Quad exhaust tips were tastefully notched into the lower rear fenders of both Machete Style I and Style II.

Style I was finished in a special two-tone pearlescent white and silver finish. White-coated taillight lenses were nearly flush with the lower rear deck panel. When the lights were off, the taillights were hidden, making the entire rear solid white.

Style II also had concealed taillight lenses, but they were coated black. The side featured black graphics that were contrary to convention, as it began at the rear of the car, and ran to the front. The lower stripe was dissected by the wheel arch and stopped just before the door.

Ford revived the Machete name on a Lincoln concept car for 1988.

Thunderbird Saturn Concepts

For two consecutive years, 1968 and 1969, Ford displayed a concept car it called "Saturn." This was 16 years before GM had a concept it titled "Project Saturn," and 22 years before the first production GM Saturn automobile.

Ford's Saturn I and II were highly modified production Thunderbird two-door hardtops, and it is likely they were even versions of the same car.

They each featured a roof that was lowered two inches, and the front end extended four more inches than the stock Thunderbird.

Both versions had built-in computerized travel information monitors located in the dash. The monitors advised the direction the car was traveling, when to turn and the road/traffic conditions ahead. This sounds like today's satellite navigation systems, but in 1968-69, a punched "trip control" computer card was needed to program for a pre-select destination.

Located in the upper right portion of the control panel was a small screen that pictured a map layout of the route ahead. On the left portion of the control panel was another screen that showed the driver the distance and direction of the next turn, etc. A radar screen in the center of the dash provided a clear view of traffic ahead, regardless of the visibility outside the car. Included were a two-way citizen's band radio and portable tape recorder. With the microphone built-in to the headlining above the dash, the driver could use the tape recorder or transmit over the radio, while keeping both hands on the steering wheel.

An interesting feature on Saturn I and II, was the horizontal sidelights in the rear fenders that would pop out to function as backup lights when the transmission was is in reverse. Another better idea was the hidden light in the rocker panel beneath the door for safe entry and exit at night.

Design-wise, they appeared similar, though each had unique elements, as listed below.

1968 Saturn I

*Full-width grille and exposed rectangular headlights. Park, turn, and side maker lights located along centerline of grille and wrap around side of grille opening.
*Vents in fender behind front wheels are for oil coolers.

*Painted iridescent candy-apple red, shaded from dark bottom to light at the top.
*Interior seats trimmed with shaded red knitted vinyl in a wide waffle pattern.

1969 Saturn II

*Split full-width grille with center-mounted dual roadlamps, and built-in twin lights flush-mounted in both front fenders.
*Gold metallic exterior.
*Interior seats tailored in gold metallic fabric.
*Wide wheels had reflective paint on hub centers.

Ford

1969 Super Cobra

Ford designers had a ball when they created the sexy Super Cobra from a stock 1969 Fairlane. This sleek SportsRoof show car was lowered about two inches and the front-end was extended nearly eight inches. The windshield was slanted back, adding to the Super Cobra's racy profile.

Thin horizontal chrome bars filled the grille cavity, divided by a vertical section that housed an imbedded Cobra medallion. Poking proudly through the hood was a wide, tall shaker airscoop, connected directly into the 428 engine's air cleaner.

Built-in to the backside of the scoop was a tachometer, facing the driver. The radically styled rear end housed a one-piece sunken taillight that contained eight spaced brake lights that would flash an easy-to-read warning message at the touch of the brake pedal. Lower down, at the center of the rear panel, sat acoustically tuned twin exhaust pipes, placed side by side. Black metal louvers covered the rear window, and special 15-inch trident cast aluminum wheels with chrome rims added the finishing exterior details. The interior was a candy-murano, hot-red finish and went well with the Super Cobra's bright red exterior.

1969 Ranchero Scrambler

A companion car to the above Super Cobra was this handsome modified Ranchero, titled "Scrambler"'

It had similar front and rear styling details, with slight differences in the grille texture, and dual exhaust locations.

Like the Super Cobra, Scrambler had a 428 Cobra-Jet engine connected to the through-the-hood "shaker" air scoop. Extended sail panels running the full length of the pickup's box created a tunnel effect. The leading edge of the tailgate formed into a rear spoiler, with a full width taillight recessed into the middle of that tailgate.

Color-wise, the exterior was a special ivy gold pearl and color-keyed vinyl roof. Inside, the two-seat high-back buckets were done in a dark ivy vinyl with ivy gold accent stripe across the upper part of the seat back. Dark ivy nylon carpeting matched the upholstery.

His and her mini-scrambler motor bikes sitting in back were novel items for a concept vehicle of the late 1960s.

Ford

1968 Fiera

Basically a customized 1968 Ford XL fastback, the Fiera offered interesting styling modifications, aimed at the GT crowd. Giving the car a more streamlined appearance, research designers lowered the roofline, angled the windshield back, and slanted the rear window a rakish 15 degrees.

The full-width grille was deeply recessed and on each side of the center divider sat bright rectangular frames housing auxiliary driving lights. Headlights were behind retractable doors, and the parking lamps, also hidden, would shine through the grille when in use.

At the front section of the hood were twin louvers that provided extra cooling for the monstrous 428 cu.in V-8.

Rear wheel openings were made larger for the wide-oval tires, and to emphasize Fiera's racy appearance. A band of bright accent lines ran across the rear panel and over the recessed taillight lenses.

Iridescent autumn copper paint was applied to the body shaded from light at the top to dark at the bottom. The interior was done in gold-tone cloth/vinyl.

1969 Aurora II

Following up on the original Aurora research vehicle from 1964 (though looking nothing like it), the Aurora II was also a one-of-a-kind station wagon. Modified from a production LTD Country Squire, the pearlescent white gold Aurora II offered some unusual features.

The Aurora II had only three side doors. The rear passenger door on the driver's side had been eliminated, because of the curved lounge seat, shown in the photo to the left. Notice that the center pillar on the passenger side also has been eliminated. When both right doors swung out from the center, there was nearly six feet of opening to the entire lounge area. The front passenger seat was a "swivel chair" that could turn to face the center, three-passenger "sofa" seat.

A rear lounge area was accessible through the doorgate. This rear seating was also done in a curved lounge design; plus, an eight-inch Philco television set came built into the interior panel.

Other high-tech electronics of the era included AM/FM stereo radio and 8-track stereo tape recorder/player.

150

1970 Mustang Milano

Named for Milano (Milan), Italy, this highly modified 1970 Mustang SportsRoof was a sensation at the auto shows. (It was one of five special Ford Division show cars on displayed that year.)

It served as a preview of the all-new 1971 Mustang SportsRoof.

Painted ultra violet, the Milano was a full seven inches lower than a production Mustang, and reconfigured into a two-passenger grand touring machine.

Featured up front were headlights and high-powered driving lamps that were concealed when not in use, and a special hood with NACA-type air scoops for ram-air induction. At the rear of Milano were unique taillights that indicated three phases of travel, by changing color depending on the rate of speed. While accelerating, they glowed green; coasting, they were amber,

and during braking, they turned red.

This concept car's interior was color-keyed to the ultra violet exterior, with purple mohair carpets, high-back bucket seats that were upholstered with blue-violet fabric inserts, and light-purple leather trim.

The two female models directly above are demonstrating the electrically operated hatch, which raised for access to the luggage compartment.

1970 Econoline Kilimanjaro

Shown above are two versions of the Kilimanjaro concept vehicle. Decorating the front, rear, and sides of each van was a band of simulated leopard skin, and the body was finished in Bush Jacket Beige. The articulated side window could open and fold back for open-air viewing while on a safari.

Kilimanjaro was a rugged and spacious four-wheel-drive show vehicle, designed to maneuver through swampy jungles or desert sands carrying hunters, rifles, ammunition, and a two-way communication system. On the driver's side, there were foot holes running up the vehicle's body, making it easy and faster to get on top of the roof. Power winches were mounted up front, and a spare tire was housed on the roof top.

Modified Mavericks

Ford tried a retro-look on its popular Maverick model, which resulted in the curious-looking Runabout and Estate Coupe.

Though retaining some Maverick identity, the designers created one as an open four-seater, and the other with a landaulet roof covering. Both cars added features found on 1920s automobiles, like a bustle-back design, restraining straps over the external trunk, and free-standing taillights.

This was all blended into modern elements as a front air dam, thin wraparound chrome bumpers, dual racing mirrors, and a hood-mounted tachometer.

1970 Maverick Runabout

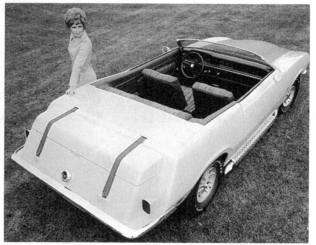

The Runabout had chrome exhaust pipes, covered with a perforated heat shield, that ran along the passenger-side rocker panel. It was painted brilliant Grabber Yellow, with contrasting avocado green hood that complimented the avocado leather interior trim.

1971 Maverick Estate Coupe

The Estate Coupe had a dark green padded "Landaulet" roof over the rear seating. The body was finished in limefire green, a special metallic show color that used a subtle gold-flake base, and the avocado interior complimented the exterior.

Rectangular quartz-iodine driving lights are separated by a chrome horizontal bar grille. Parking-turn signal lights were placed above the headlights and encased in the same chrome frame for an integrated look.

Both versions wore cast-magnesium wheels with a spoke design reminiscent of the classic wire wheels.

1971
LTD Berline
1972
LTD Berline II

The Berline, designed as a one-of-a-kind LTD for the 1971 auto shows, was also renamed Berline II and featured again during 1972. Basically the same car was used, with different wheels and tire designs.

Both had the unique grille and body-colored bumpers in front. The landau-style roof carried vinyl material on the forward half with the vinyl continuing down the belt line just behind the door.

The body was finished in a special two-tone treatment of deep Tangier blue and a silver-flecked white paint.

Broader roof pillars with the absence of a rear quarter window gave the SportsRoof an even sleeker appearance. It also gave more privacy to the rear seating, but did nothing for the driver's rear visibility.

Adding to the car's long, low look were black-ribbed rocker panels, with black extensions ahead of the front wheels and behind the rear wheels.

Taillight configuration incorporated a new optical principal, whereby abundant light was funneled through tiny slits in the lenses.

1971 Bronco
Wildflower

Bronco Wildflower was no shrinking violet. It incorporated a roll bar with integral headrests, stepover door panels with padded sill, exposed chrome exhaust pipes, and a walnut steering wheel.

Bright pastel paint and trim added further highlights to the vehicle.

Though the exterior is decorated differently, the Wildflower looks like an updated version of the 1966/68 Bronco Dune Duster.

Ford

1971 Thunderbird Tridon

Ford's T-Bird Tridon show car had the look that Batman or Green Hornet would have loved. Its bold, protruding front grille divider, long hood, and forward-thrusting fenders formed a pronounced tri-element design, which gave the car its name. The rare overhead view of the Tridon shows off the tinted skylight strip that extended across the roof and down the sides of the pillars to the beltline.

A custom paint job included 20 coats of a murano lacquer called Moongold Mist. To harmonize with the paint, all exterior glass, including the skylight strip, was tinted amber. When the car appeared at shows, auto reporters speculated that all future production cars would offer an array of tinted glass, in hues that matched exterior colors.

Tridon's seats were finished in synthetic lamb's wool, and the floor was draped in mink mouton carpeting.

Special turned aluminum wheels with a circular brushed finish were held to the wheel by bolts around the entire perimeter of the outer wheel surface. Firestone Tire & Rubber Company created special tires exclusively for the Tridon.

1972 Maverick LTD

Some prototype cars created for the annual auto shows displays are nothing more than slightly altered production models. A perfect example is the Maverick LTD. Major modification were the addition of quarter windows in the "C" pillar at the rear of the car, and a power sunroof.

Painted white pearl, it had tan vinyl on the roof, as well as inserts in the bumper guards and body side moldings.

The interior was done in leather trim on the seats, doors and headliner. Under the hood was a 302 cu. in. engine with a two-barrel carburetor.

Though it was a nice edition for the Maverick model line, this luxury Maverick never made the dealers' showrooms.

1973 Experimental Safety Vehicle

Ford, as well as other manufactures of the early 1970s, were tackling the development of safer vehicles. One concept idea was the Experimental Safety Vehicle (ESV), revealed by Ford during the Department of Transportation (DOT) Transpo '72, and then featured at auto shows the following year.

Resembling a conventional Galaxie 500 sedan, the added safety items altered the overall appearance. A long hood, with energy-absorbing frame, pushed the ESV past DOT's overall length objective of 220 inches, so the car's rear deck was shortened to meet the requirements.

Ford claimed that 65 percent of crash energy would be absorbed by the car's heavier frame and 35 percent by the front end. Front and rear aluminum bumpers extended further than production Fords, allowing room for hydraulic struts, which anchored the bumpers to the frame. The bumpers yielded on impact at 10 mph and sprung back into position. Answering rollover collision concerns, ESV had a "roll cage," similar to

those used in race cars of that era.

DOT specified a "passive" occupant-restraint system that required no action by the five occupants. The answer was air bags, which were still experimental. Four bags were built-in, including the steering wheel hub, a second one in the dash panel, also intended for the driver, one in front of the right front-passenger, and a larger air bag mounted behind the front seat for rear-seat occupants.

1973 Pinto Sportiva

Pinto was still a popular model in 1973, with sales over 500,000 units, when Ford teased its fans with a sharp looking Runabout.

Called, "Sportiva," this concept was a two-seat roadster, with removabe roof panel, and a stylish integrated roll bar. Further modifications included chrome-plated brass moldings, horizontal eggcrate chrome grille above and below the bumper, plus driving lights set into the grille.

The body was coated in 23 applications of silver pearlescent paint. Shades of silver were also used on the leather bucket seats, along with black-and-white plaid cloth inserts, and red piping. Door panels, dashboard, and console top were trimmed in silver leather, with pewter shag carpeting covering the floor and rear package shelf.

Ford

1973 Explorer SUV

What a wide vision Ford had when it designed the futuristic Explorer SUV.

Extremely low height gave the recreational pickup a racy appearance, and with the front axle setback, a larger interior.

Powering this Southern California surfers' dream vehicle was the monstrous 429-CID V8, mounted midship. The louvers placed behind the doors vented the engine compartment.

Adding to the functionality of Explorer was a foldable tent that could be used inconjuction with the long truck bed.

1974 Mustang II Sportiva

To add excitement to the debut of the new, but not so exciting downsized Mustang II, Ford created the special Targa-styled Sportiva II for the auto shows. With roof panel and rear window removed, this coupe turned into a convertible.

Body was painted white, with black accent, and the chrome wheels had bright yellow centers.

Ford

1975 Flashback

Ford's Flashback concept car shows what happens when the retro-look goes wrong. The oddly shaped two-seat prototype tried to combine ideas and lines from classic cars of the past with features of a modern lightweight vehicle.

The styling cues from the past included the long sculptured hood, protruding headlights, hood, bustle-back with leather straps, and side louvers and large-diameter wire spoke wheels.

Flashback could be classified as an interesting experiment during the madding quest for fuel-efficient sporty cars in mid-1970s America.

1976 Prima

Prima was four concept vehicles in one: a pickup, a station wagon, two-seat coupe, and a 2+2 fastback. Three steel interchangeable tops for the rear section permitted various conversions. These roof panels were clamped into place with latches similar to those used to close down a convertible top. The fastback top included a hatchback or third door in the rear. When Prima is a station wagon, the rear door lifted up and the bottom section lowered for easier access to the cargo area.

The body design was done by Ford's Design Center in Dearborn, and the red all-steel body was formed and assembled by Ford-owned Ghia in Italy.

Accenting the red color, the lower body was painted black, and white forged-aluminum wheels set off the combination. Power came from Ford of Britain's 1,100-cc four-cylinder Kent engine mated to a four-speed manual transmission.

A tan interior featured contoured leather front bucket seats and a rear seat that folded down to form part of the cargo floor on the pickup version and added carrying capacity for the fastback and station wagon models.

This multi-roof concept was featured again by Ford as the 1978 Fiesta Fantasy and by Nissan in the 1987-90 Pulsar production vehicles.

157

Ford

1978 Corrida
by Ghia

Hard to imagine, but this futuristic vehicle was based on the plain-jane European-built Ford Fiesta. Top-hinged gull-wing doors folded in the middle, permitting them to be open/closed in confined parking areas.

The third door at that the rear of Corrida was actually two in one. While the glass hatchback top section raised up, the lower section hinged at the bottom and could be locked in an open position. This increased the cargo capacity.

Up front were retractable headlights. The body and wheels were of aluminum construction.

1978 F-250
Little Louie

Imagine cruising around in a smaller version of Ford's heavy-duty Louisville trucks. That was the idea behind the creation of the "Little Louie" concept vehicle.

Obviously based on an F-250 extended cab pickup truck, it was dressed up with dual chrome-plated air horns, vertical exhaust stacks, eight-spoke deep-dish chrome wheels, and a mini-sleeper bunk.

1978 Fiesta Fantasy

Ford followed up its multi-purpose 1976 Prima idea (or rather ideas) car with the Fiesta Fantasy. Like the Prima, several different body caps changed the type of vehicle. The Fantasy was based on the European Ford Fiesta, which was imported to the U.S. from Germany

The different toppings affected the back half of the roof. There was a soft top (above), pickup truck (above left), wagon (above right), and (not shown) a coupe and two passenger sportster. The Fiesta was popular here from 1978 through 1980, but disappeared when the 1981 Escort came to market.

1978 Tuareg

Ford built this rugged off-road creation from the modest European Fiesta. It used large sand/mud tires and beefed-up suspension for increased ground clearance.

Flared wheel arches blended into the running boards, the hood featured five large functional louvers, and tubular steel bumper bars were placed front and back.

Built on a 90-inch wheelbase chassis, Tuareg used a tiny 1.1-liter engine and a four-speed manual transmission.

On the roof were a heavy-duty roof rack and halogen searchlights.

The car was first shown at the 1978 Geneva Auto Show, and appeared in America during the following year.

Copies were made and sold in Europe.

Ford

1978 Megastar

1979 Megastar II

Both Megastar I and II gave good indication of how Ford designers of the late 1970s envisioned future, five-passenger, family vehicles. With wedge-shape aluminum bodies, they had a 101-inch wheelbase, which was four inches less than the new Ford Fairmont.

Actually, the Megastars were based on the European Granada, with the front section of the car extended three feet ahead of the front axle.

"By extending the front section, we achieved a small frontal area which added to aerodynamics, performance and fuel economy," stated builder Ghia's managing director Filippo Sapino during the debut of Megastar I.

Their short, square tail section was designed for high-speed directional stability and again, for added fuel economy benefits. Copper-tinted windshields and door glass compli-

mented the honey-colored velvet-like upholstered material.

Megastar I offered incredible occupant driving visibility, as 80 percent of the car's four doors and 60 percent of the rear doors were glass, and up front was a deep, wide-curved panoramic windshield. Both I and II had front and rear bumpers that were foam-filled to absorb impact.

Megastar II moved the spare tire into the engine compartment, extended the front further than the original and added a tailgate. It was a two-door model.

Power for Megastar I came from a 3-liter V-6 engine, but it was an even smaller 2-liter four-cylinder that was installed in Megastar II.

For the record, the 1978 version was known as Megastar, but when the second version followed in 1979, the original was unofficially referred to as Megastar I.

1980
Fiesta GTK

Ghia continued its design theme begun on the 1978/79 Megastar I and II, and created the Fiesta GTK family station wagon.

The long wedge-shaped hood and sharp kick-up over the rear wheels was also evident on the 1984 Ghia Barchetta and 1988 Ford LIV concept vehicles.

Exterior was finished in metallic gold, and though the wheelbase of the three-door Fiesta GTK was only 94 inches, its interior provided maximum room for a driver, passengers, and their luggage.

A tubular instrument panel that was an extension of the circular center console, an on-board computer and digital display instruments highlighted the interior.

What was odd for this '80s futuristic car were the five-spoke wheels that looked like those used on 1972-74 Mustangs.

1980 Ghia Navarre

Ford Design Center worked with Ghia to create the Navarre five-seat coupe. Their purpose was to blend European styling themes into a downsized vehicle for the American market.

Surprisingly, instead of the typical 4-cylinder engine used on concept Fords during the early '80s, Navarre was equipped with a muscular, 5.0-litre V8.

The sleek, unit construction steel body featured an aerodynamic front hood that flowed downward into the six-unit lighting system. Actually, the inboard units next to the grille were the road lights.

Ford

Probe Series 1979-1985

Ford's Probe series of experimental concept cars was an ongoing effort to push beyond aerodynamics into the era of airflow management. Airflow management uses a car's outer surface to redirect airflow in a controlled way.

All the Probe concepts knifed through the air, each year topping the previous coefficient numbers. Innovations like flush side glass, full underbody shields, a double-wing rear spoiler, and a deployable valance helped to achieve remarkable successes.

1979 Probe I

1980 Probe II

1982 Probe III

Probe I was the size of a Mustang. The original Probe was a three-door hatchback that weighed in at a fuel-saving 2,750 pounds. Its sleek-surfaced composite body, designed by Euro-stylist Uwe Bahnsen, underwent extensive wind-tunnel testing and achieved an airdrag rating of .22, lower than any American car at the time. Power would be a four-cylinder engine with turbocharging and projected fuel economy of 39-mpg in city driving.

Probe II had body characteristics more like a 1985 Chrysler LeBaron GTS. The second version did not seem to fit with the other four Probe concepts. In fact, Ford speculated at the time that the more conventional-looking Probe II could be on the market within a few years. While no engine was stipulated, talk was centered on a possible new fuel-efficient diesel powerplant.

Probe III was done before the introduction of the European Sierra five-door hatchback, Ford fabricated the Probe III concept from an early fiberglass model of the Sierra.

It was designed as a five-seat family car for the year 2000. The lower panels wrapped under the body for improved air-flow, with a section that would move down when Probe exceeded 25 mph. The 1983 Sierra XR4i sports coupe offered the biplane rear wing that appeared on Probe III.

Probe Series 1979-1985

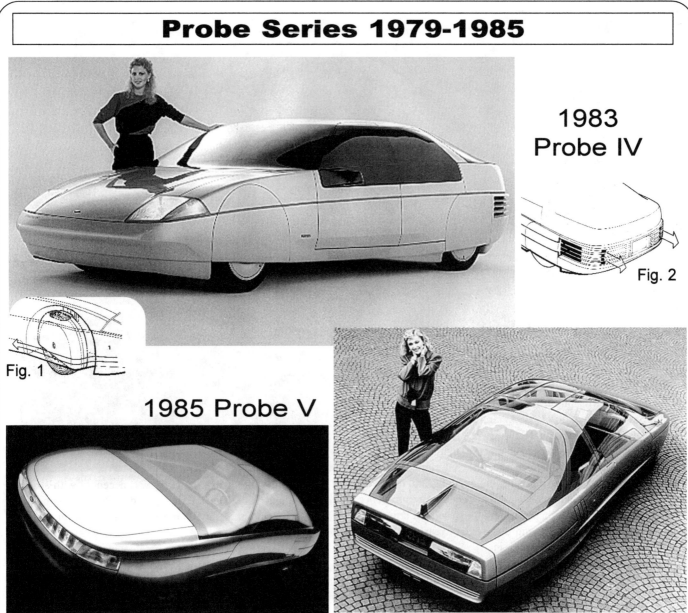

1983
Probe IV

Fig. 2

Fig. 1

1985 Probe V

With *Probe IV*, Ford's engineers and designers created the lowest coefficient of drag (Cd) of any conventional five-door vehicle in the world for 1983. It took only 2.5 horsepower to move the Probe IV, compared to 6.2 horsepower for the 1983 Thunderbird.

Fully shrouded wheels, flush glass, and the covered headlights, were the most striking exterior features. It also had a full belly pan, moveable front air dam and unique flexible front-fender skirts. These skirts, made of material similar to tires, screened out the wind but still allowed the wheels to turn for steering (Fig. 1). A stationary cap mounted over the wheel kept the rotating wheel from contact with the flexible skirt.

Since there is no grille opening for the front, the radiator and air-conditioning condenser were housed behind the rear wheel wells. Air-intake openings were located behind the rear wheels, and the exhausted air actually helped to improve the Cd by .005 (Fig. 2). The turbocharged 1.6-liter, four-cylinder engine was tilted at a 70-degree angle to fit under the low sloping hood.

Probe V was the last in that concept series, and was the most advanced aerodynamic of the five models. With a coefficient of drag (Cd) of .137, it surpassed Probe IV's .15 record, to be claimed the lowest Cd of any driveable car in the world. It also topped the Cd of the F-16 jet fighter aircraft.

Added to Probe V was a dorsal fin on the rear deck, which gave it remarkable sideward stability. The full-width front headlights were reinterpreted on the first generation Mercury Sable. The rear engine cover and large rear window lid slid back when opened, and the side doors opened parallel to the body. Similar to early 1990s Pontiac Bonneville SSEi models, Probe V used a head-up instrument display that projected a digital speedometer on the windshield directly in front of the driver.

1980
Mustang IMSA

Designed and constructed as a high-performance concept, the rugged looking Mustang IMSA was named for the International Motor Sports Association (IMSA) circuit.

Normal Mustang exterior features were replaced by aerodynamic pieces. Turn signals and driving lights covered with smoked plastic covers blended into the redesigned air dam. Clear plastic covered the four halogen headlights and even covered the Gotti modular wheels, all to reduce air turbulence. Wide fender flares were shaped to smoothly route air around the super-wide Pirelli P7 tires, and a full-width rear deck spoiler added stability for high-speed driving.

The unique hood featured louvers, a warning light module (for turbo boost, engine temperature, and high-beam headlights), and an engine-mounted "shaker."

Unfortunately, this Mustang had only a turbocharged 2.3-liter four-cylinder under the hood.

Finished in white pearl, the body was accented with striping in orange and gold. The interior included Recaro competition buckets, four-point safety harnesses, and a custom steering wheel pad.

In the hub were six switches to operate wipers, washers, headlights, driving lamps, horn, and turn signals. This allowed the driver to activate any switch without removing hands from the steering wheel.

Even with the special components and attention given this car, it never did compete in any IMSA races.

1981 Mustang RSX

Ghia created an entirely new concept off the four-seat Mustang, and named it Rally Sport Experimental, or RSX. It shortened the wheelbase by 14.2 cm, made the car lighter, slightly narrower, and lower than stock. As with many concepts of the era, a small four-cylinder was seen as the engine of choice.

This one was a 2.3 liter, connected to a four-speed manual, and the car also featured power steering.

Finished in orange metallic, it featured simulated all-glass doors, which used black tinted Plexiglas panels bonded over the lower door panels. A rear airfoil was added for directional stability.

1981 Super Gnat

If the Super Gnat looks tiny, realize that it was nearly 16 inches less than the subcompact Ford Escort. A three-cylinder engine was proposed, which would have provided adequate power to move the 1,500-pound vehicle. Fuel efficiency was the goal for this two-seater commuter car, and it was seen as a possible solution for the energy-conscious environment of the early '80s.

Ford

1981 Bronco Montana Lobo

Ford took the development of four-by-four vehicles beyond what was offered in normal off-road cars and trucks in the early 1980s with the debut of the Bronco Montana Lobo. Its design appeared futuristic, but was inherently practical for almost any chore.

A special feature was the removable bubble-tinted doors. When the bubble doors were in place, entry/exit of Lobo was a slide-open glass door between cab and cargo bed. When the rear tailgate with the attached ramp was lowered, the hauling of motorcycles and snowmobiles would be much easier.

Its custom body was painted mustard gold, with black used on the grille, bumpers, and flared wheel openings. Large side rails with louvered panels ran parallel the entire length of the rear fenders, and the overhead airfoil with suspended road lamps, blended beautifully into the side panels.

The chrome dual side-mounted exhaust pipes were a nice touch. Notice that the bubble doors were not in place on the Bronco Montana Lobo while on display during the 1981 Chicago Auto Show, but they appear in the Lobo photo, in the Ford color section of this book.

Pontiac would corral the Montana tag in the 1990s on a concept vehicle and later for use on its minivans.

1981 POCKAR

Since the mid-1970s, Ford and Ghia experimented with agile little urban cars that would have super miles-per-gallon ratings.

Pockar was 33 inches shorter than the subcompact Fiesta, but three inches taller.

Amazingly, as tiny as it appears, there was room for five passengers. Space was obtained with ideas like placing the spare tire and jack vertically behind the front body panel, and storage bins in the door panels.

Notice that the lower half of the door panels could open from the outside, which allowed access to the storage bags from either inside or outside the vehicle.

The grilleless front and rectangular headlight design appeared on Ford vehicles starting in 1985. The first generation 1989-92 Probe had the same type of wind-cheating integrated sideview mirrors.

Ford

1982 Ghia Cockpit

The search for miles per gallon in the "energy-crisis" era brought Ford to develop a design very similar to the 1950s Messerschmitt KR-175 three-wheel design of a tandem seat minicar. The Cockpit featured a rear-mounted 12-hp, 200 cc single motorcycle-type engine that was said to be good for 75 mpg. Like its predecessor, occupants sat under an airplane type canopy.

The three-wheeler had a roll bar over the driver and was operated by a conventional steering wheel, as opposed to tillers on other similar vehicles.

Shown in the photo above right is the Ghia Cockpit as it appeared during the 1982 Chicago Auto Show.

1982 AFV

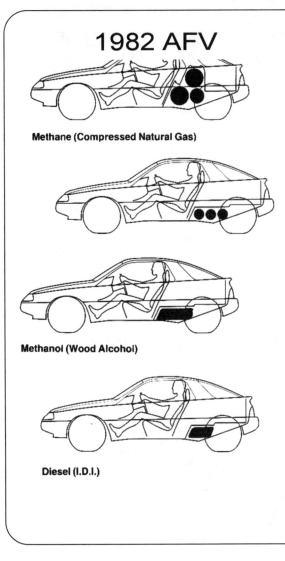

Methane (Compressed Natural Gas)

Methanol (Wood Alcohol)

Diesel (I.D.I.)

Designed as a two-passenger commuter vehicle for the near future, Ford's Alternative Fuel Vehicle (AFV) was an answer to GM's battery-powered electric concept cars.

The 1.6-liter engine was capable of running on methane (compressed natural gas) and was adaptable for methanol, ethanol or liquid propane. Fuel economy was evident, with 32 mpg when it ran on methane, and 35 mpg with propane, methanol or diesel.

The illustrations on the left indicate the location of four different fuel containers. Plans included that home compressors would be available for refueling the AFV.

This might have been just a concept, but beginning in 1983, Ford began selling propane-powered Granadas to fleet buyers. AFV design elements such as wraparound headlights and sloping front end began appearing on 1983 Ford production automobiles.

167

Ford

Compact Van Concepts

1982 Ghia Aerovan

"In the near future," Ford Motor Co. stated in 1984, "we will introduce a vehicle similar to the Aerostar concept." It kept that promise with the 1986 Aerostar compact van.

One of the earliest attempts shown to the public was the two-door *Ghia Aerovan* from 1982. It's amazingly close in design to the production 1986-97 Aerostar, especially the slanted nose.

Appearing at mid-1980s auto shows, the *Ghia APV* (All Purpose Vehicle) was a prototype of the family car for the 1990s. Looking similar to a mini-Aerostar, APV dimensions were about the same as an Escort station wagon. Though small in stature, there was room for seven passengers, with the addition of a third bench seat. All side glass was flush-mounted, the windshield was slanted at a 60-degree slope, and the rear wheels were partially covered. AP, was designed to be front-drive, with a 1.6-liter transverse four-cylinder engine.

The *1984 Aerostar* concept featured a fresh, aerodynamic profile, and state-of-the art electronics.

Ford's objective was to build something more than a car, but better than traditional vans. Aerostar's compact design had seating for seven adults, but could fit in home garages. Proposed power ranged from a 4-cylinder to V-6 or turbocharged diesel engine. First-year production Aerostars did offer a 2.3-liter 4-cylinder, and an optional 2.8 V-6.

1984 Ghia APV

Compact Van Concepts

1984 Aerostar

1987 HFX
Ghia Aerostar

Called the family vehicle of tomorrow here today, the Ford Ghia Aerostar was a rolling laboratory of advanced technology.

Many of the improvements were not available at the time on most vehicles. Innovations included clear windows that could change to a dark privacy mode at the flip of a switch, and liquid crystal diode (LCD) message display on the exterior liftgate.

Those messages said such things as "send help," or "do not pass." Additional safety items included run flat tires and wheels, and a sonar system to warn when to close to another vehicle, and assisted during parking.

The HFX Aerostar included Ford's sophisticated electronically controlled all-wheel-drive E-4WD system.

Ford

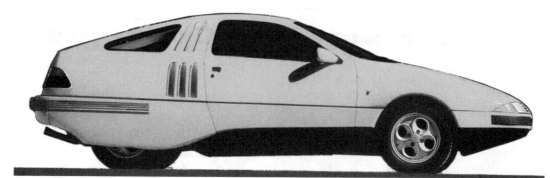

1982 Ghia Brezza

Designed for outstanding aerodynamic efficiency, the Ghia Brezza concept was a real eye-catcher. From the partial belly-pan up front to the enclosed rear wheels, this car was designed to slice through the wind. The louvers placed behind the doors were for the mid-mounted Escort powertrain. Areas of the rear quarter panels, especially the wrap-around taillights, bumper mouldings, and the shape of the fixed side window, directly influenced the styling on the 1984 Ford Tempo.

Shown on the right is a rare photo of the Brezza's dashboard and steering wheel.

1983 Ghia Barchetta

1988 LIV

Shown above is a pair of roadsters that closely resemble each other, for a good reason. The top two images show the original version from Ghia Studios, which was titled Barchetta. It made its American debut at the 1984 auto shows.

This was a front-wheel-drive two-seater, built on a 90-inch wheelbase. Several years later, Ford took the same layout and styling to construct the car in the photos directly above. This version was titled LIV, which stood for Low Investment Vehicle.

Both versions developed by Ford Advance Vehicles were created to determine if the use of plastics would reduce investment costs sufficiently to make low-volume popular-priced specialty cars economically feasible. A 4-cylinder high output 1.6-liter engine powered Barchetta and LIV, but the Barchetta was mated to a four-speed manual transaxle, while LIV had a five-speed transmission.

For those interested, Barchetta was designed around the European Fiesta platform, and was the impetus for the Australian-assembled 1990 Mercury Capri XR2.

1984 Mustang PPG

1984 Thunderbird PPG

PPG pace cars were beginning to appear at the mid-1980s national auto shows, with exciting automotive designs.

Above, the modified Mustang SVO was powered by a 3.8-litre V-6 equipped with twin Garrett turbochargers and Bosch L-Jetronic injection. Horsepower totaled 380 at 5500 rpm. Designed by Ford, and engineered by its Special Vehicle Operations (SVO), this wedge-shape pace car was one of three FoMoCo vehicles pacing Championship Auto Racing Teams (CART) during the 1984 season.

The other is the Thunderbird shown at the right, and the third was a Lincoln MK VII. PPG stands for Pittsburgh Plate Glass Co., which sponsored CART.

1984 Ghia Vignale Mustang

Based on a Mustang SVO platform, this Ghia creation had a permanently engaged four-wheel drive system, and was powered by a turbocharged 2.3-litre engine. Horsepower rating was 176.

Added to the aerodynamic shape of this Italian Mustang were flush glass, contoured windshield with single wiper, lower-profile headlights, and a partial belly pan. The side windows were fixed, but there were small rectangular sections that opened for fresh air and tollbooths.

Two small electronic devices were built into the contoured front end, one to monitor the outside temperature and the other that was a parking sensor.

Ford

1985 Ghia TSX-4

TSX-4 stood for Touring Sport Extra-4 Wheel Drive. This was a luxury five-door sports sedan that looked like a station wagon. Though it was not termed a wagon, it was promoted as having the carrying capacity of one.

An innovative rear tailgate window continued up and over the roof, allowing the rear passengers to have a heavenly view. Ghia used the floor pan of a Ford Tempo sedan, and powered the TSX-4 with a 2.3-liter engine that supplied 120 horsepower and was transverse mounted.

1986 Cobra 230 ME

Back in the mid-1980s, there was talk that the wedge-shaped Cobra 230 ME was going to be Ford's new two-seat mid-engine sports car of the 1990s.

It would have been nice, since a traversely mid-mounted 230 horsepower engine powered it. This dual overhead cam inline four-cylinder was equipped with electronic fuel injection, and intercooled tubocharger.

Ford estimated that the 230 ME would have had a top speed of 130 mph and run 0-60 mph in less than 6.0 seconds.

Design details included dual spoiler wings that spread across the rear window and a roof scoop that drew cool air down to the horizontally placed radiator.

Out front, there was a low air dam, and just ahead of the rear wheels were large air intakes scoops.

1988
Bronco DM-1

In the late 1980s, Ford sponsored a design program for industrial art students.

The winning design, shown above in a public relations photo and on public display, was a five-seat sport-utility vehicle, created by Derek Millsap.

Ford honored the young stylist by adding his initials to the name of this concept, Bronco DM-1.

This small four-wheel drive vehicle had a steel-reinforced fiberglass body, a large hatch that extended into the roof and built-in rollbar. It appeared at American auto shows in 1988.

1988 Saguaro

In a quest to prove that not all utility vehicles have to look alike, Ford conceived the sleek Saguaro. Seen as a multipurpose, concept utility, it had the versatility of an intermediate-size four-door station wagon. Aerodynamic design details include flush door glass, flush door handles and a steeply raked windshield angle. A cleverly designed rear liftgate could wrap over into the roof, allowing large objects to be loaded into the cargo area, including the seventh passenger.

The seven-passenger Saguaro was a step forward in Ford's quest for truly aerodynamic vehicles.

It appeared first in Italy, where it was built by Ghia, and traveled the American auto-show circuit, beginning in 1989.

Ford

1988 Splash

Four transportation students from the Center for Creative Studies in Detroit created the Splash concept vehicle, with Ford's assistance.

Jack Telnack, Ford VP of Design at the time, gave the students an objective to create a vehicle that would appeal to young drivers for year-round fun. The winning design was this radical, sexy-looking concept shown here. In its various forms, Splash could be a sea, ski, or surfing vehicle, even a sports car.

Versatility came from the all-wheel drive and a special variable ride height and altitude system.

A removable roof panel, side, and hatch windows turned it into a convertible.

Interior fabrics, fluorescent blue with magenta accents, were made of the same durable, rubberized material used in scuba wet suits.

An integral roll bar and special four-point safety belt system added to the overall safety. Other features were retractable high-mount driving lamps, and deployable mud flaps that could be lowered when off-roading.

The young design winners were, from left, Brad Baldonado, Ricky Hsu, Chris Gamble, and Warren Manser.

1989 Ghia Via

Ghia Via was promoted as a 10-year advanced look at a Ford from the year 2000. Some of 1989 Ghia Via's aerodynamic features did influenced styling of future Probe and Taurus autos.

Fiber optic technology allowed Ghia Via's headlights to perform as either foglamps, or spotlights, and a Targa-type glass roof panel was photosensitive and darkened in sunlight.

The Ghia Via started touring American auto shows in 1990.

1990 Surf - See color section

1990 Shoccc Wave

Featuring cab-forward styling, the 1990 Shoccc Wave had the overall feel of the 1993 Probe sports coupe.

A big difference was in the powerplant. Shoccc Wave borrowed the 220 horsepower Yamaha 3-liter V-6 engine from the Taurus SHO. The interior featured an instrument binnacle mounted to the steering column.

1990 Zig & Zag

Ford Motor Co's Ghia Studio created Zig and Zag as logical alternatives to conventional types of transport by reducing size to a minimum.

Power sources discussed included electric motors or experimental minimally sized two-stroke engine that would gain extra inches for interior room.

Zig was the two-seat mini convertible, with amenities that included a removable compact disc player. For added cargo space, there were large door bins, and a back-seat access to the luggage space via a roller-type door.

Zag was seen as a multipurpose leisure minivan with a retractable roof-mounting system. This set-up allowed transportation of large items, such as mountain bikes.

Ford

1991 Contour

The all black four-door Contour was a taut, sleek, concept car that was designed around an extruded aluminum space frame and featured the unique T-Drive powertrain. This innovative layout utilized a transversely mounted engine and longitudinal transmission. This allowed the designers to reduce the size of the engine compartment.

Ford's engineers took two four-cylinder engines and created a straight eight for the Contour.

The 1991 Lincoln-Mercury Mystique concept used the same setup.

Trying something different, the Contour's taillights were integrated within movable aerodynamic spoilers.

1991 Ranger Force 5

Ford took a production Ranger and created a low-slung, futuristic pickup for the auto-show tours.

Designed to perform as fast as it appeared, Ranger Force 5 was equipped with a high-output 5-liter engine and Mustang's fuel management system. Matched to a five-speed manual transmission, the engine featured a customized dual exhaust system that was routed though ports in the rear ground effects package.

Special aerodynamic pieces included a tilted-forward hood that was two-inches lower than normal, and a roof spoiler that housed an integral moon roof.

A center-mounted rear wing was articulated for added rear-wheel traction. The spoiler disappeared into the contour of the tonneau-covered box for normal driving. The custom color scheme ran from a deep purple at the top of the cab that was lightened through shades of reds and whites as it reached the truck's bottom.

1991 Desk Drive

Billed as an office on wheels, Desk Drive was equipped with all the latest technology. Ford's objective was to demonstrate the versatility of its popular Explorer compact sports-utility vehicle.

A fast-paced executive or motor journalist could travel off-road with the 4x4 Desk Drive, while keeping in touch via computer, fax, and copy machines.

Most of the electronic componetry was controlled by voice command. For an office break, there was a refrigerator, TV, microwave oven, and, of course, a coffee maker. To facilitate the required office space, the roof was raised about four inches. A satellite dish on the roof kept the vehicle in constant communication. Power came form 4-liter electronically fuel injected V-6 engine.

1992 Connecta

Ford's Ghia Studio in Turin, Italy, designed and built this bubble-back concept car, which was powered by electricity. It had the same drive train and battery technology as Ecostar, Ford's urban electric delivery van.

Both vehicles used the sodium sulfur battery invented by Ford back in 1965, which provided over twice the energy storage of lead-acid batteries. This technology allowed frequent recharges, and enough power and range to serve as the family taxi.

A current inverter took direct current (DC) from the battery and converted it to alternating current (AC) to run the motor.

Connecta's oddly shaped aerodynamic body was made of a combination of carbon fiber and Kevlar, and painted in a three-coat metallic pearlescent aquamarine finish.

A double-skinned glass roof provides insulation from the elements, plus a wonderful view of the sky. A solar panel in the car's top surface would automatically power the rear roof vent.

The Connecta was designed with a single door on the driver's side, and two doors on the passenger side. Opening from the center, as shown above in the cutaway illustration, the double doors made for ease of access to front and rear seats. Notice that there is no center post.

Suede-like paint was used on the interior, and the Goodyear ultra low profile, rolling-resistant tires were unique. To drain less energy from the battery, high efficiency projector beam head and taillight bulbs were used.

1992 Ecostar

Ford

1992 Explorer Drifter

For roaming the city streets or back roads, Ford came up with a hot looking 1992 concept, applied titled, "Explorer Drifter."

This open-air two-door, 4x4 ran on natural gas.

A deep fresh front fascia gave better aerodynamics and housed twin road lamps. Large side rails blended smoothly into the rollbar that also housed built-in road lamps.

For cruising or tailgate party enjoyment, there was a super-premium stereo system, and a cellular phone.

1992 F-150 Superflare

Painted an intense cobalt blue, the F-150 Superflare was a custom truck developed as a concept for auto show display only. Dual power bulges in the hood and unique body cladding gave the two-seater an aggressive look.

Ford stylists gave a fresh look to the F-150 by cleverly continuing the roof road lamp/rollbar down the sides of the crewcab body, and grafted it into the rocker panel moldings.

The 7-foot pickup bed, cellular phone, and super-plush carpeting were special touches, as was the handsome saddle leather seating material. Note the large three-blade chrome wheel design, a minor design trend among customizers in the early 1990s.

Another truck on display with Superflare was the 5.0-liter V-8 powered, bright yellow Boss Bronco concept.

1993 Ranger Jukebox

Ford created the Ranger Jukebox for music lovers. Installed in this California-style cruiser was a 2,500-watt eight-speaker stereo system.

This low-rider concept had neon lights concealed under the bodyside cladding that pulsated in beat with the music.

A wraparound windshield blended smoothly into the side windows, and hidden away was a convertible top. Jukebox rode on 17-inch deep-dish chrome wheels.

1992 Ghia Focus

If the Ghia Focus looks a little organic for a car, it stems from the designer's use of shapes derived from natural human and animal forms. For environmentalists, earth-friendly materials, like a wood veneer floor and leather, were used.

Exterior nostril hood vents up front, freestanding tubular side moldings, and tiny buckshot taillights were bold attempts at breaking conventional thinking.

Ford gave credit for Focus' appearance to its young American designer Taru Lahti, directed by VP of styling, Jack Telnack.

Battleship-gray body panels were made of weight-saving carbon fiber composite materials.

Focus was based on the European Escort RS2000 four-wheel-drive vehicle, with a chassis shortened by 3.9 inches.

Though the design was controversial, there were no complaints about the Ghia Focus' 216 horsepower Cosworth 2-liter, 16-valve, turbocharged four-cylinder engine.

1993 Eddie Bauer Expedition

This Eddie Bauer Expedition was a dream vehicle for people who love the outdoors, and rely on their trucks. Special features and equipment included storage compartments, a built-in stove, a refrigerator, and a pullout protective awning that was integrated into the unique bed cover. In the rear of the custom Expedition were two passenger seats and the refrigerator.

The pullout awning, which ran the length of the eight-foot pickup bed, was adjustable and self-supporting.

Though hard to tell from the photo, the Eddie Bauer Expedition's exterior was finished in a camouflage paint treatment. Also featured were a new grille, heavy-duty Warn winch, and Pia running lights that were recessed in the bumper.

A 5.8-liter electronically fuel injected V-8 engine was the power plant.

Ford

1993 Mustang Mach III

To celebrate the 30th anniversary of starting the pony car revolution, Ford released a sleek concept car called Mustang Mach III. This open-air roadster with carbon-fiber body panels nicely blended many of the 1965 Mustang styling cues with 1990s state of the art design and technology.

It also gave clues to the coming of the then all-new 1995 production Mustang.

Cut-down and shortened windshield, cat's eye headlights, and 19-inch chrome five-spoke wheels are handsome custom details. At the rear were the trademark three-bar taillights, though this time laid-out horizontally. This 1990s concept featured adjustable pedals, similar to the idea on the 1962 Allegro dream car.

To match the powerful body proportions, Mach III pumped out 450 horsepower from a supercharged 4.6-liter V-8, equipped with a "cold pack" manifold intercooler. Connected to a six-speed transmission, this dream stallion had an estimated 0-to-60 mph time of less than four and a half seconds, with the engine running on either regular gasoline or methanol.

1994 Power Stroke

Painted bright yellow, the low-slung Power Stroke gave a glimpse of Ford's idea for a possible future truck.

Based on the F-350, this no-nonsense extended bed pickup was powered by a direct-injection turbo-diesel engine. This was a new powerplant for Ford, rated as a 7.3 liter V-8, producing a strong 210 horsepower.

The fish-mouth chrome grille opening and the sleek projector-bulb cat-eye headlights gave Power Stroke a fresh look in truck front designs.

Custom touches included a 10-inch lengthened wheelbase, A-pillars hidden by wrap-around windshield, curvaceous flared running boards, and roof auxiliary lights.

As handsome as the Power Stroke was, the two-by-two 17-inch eight lug chrome dualie rear wheels gave it a serious working truck appearance.

1995 GT 90

With a salute to the legendary GT40, Ford debuted the GT90 to showcase new automotive technology. Featuring angular "edge design" features, GT90 used an aluminum honeycomb monocoque chassis with tubular steel reinforcements. GT90 was the first concept to use Ford's "new edge" approach to design.

Mounted mid-ship, the 720 horsepower quad-turbo

6.0-liter engine was a special built V-12 design.

The engine was mated to a Ferguson five-speed racing transaxle, delivering power to the rear wheels.

Built into the side mirrors was an infrared blind spot warning system. There were also special rear spoiler, high-intensity discharge headlights and ionized discharge taillights.

Leather racing bucket seats, floating gauge cluster, and 10-speaker sound system highlighted the GT90 interior.

1995 Synergy 2010

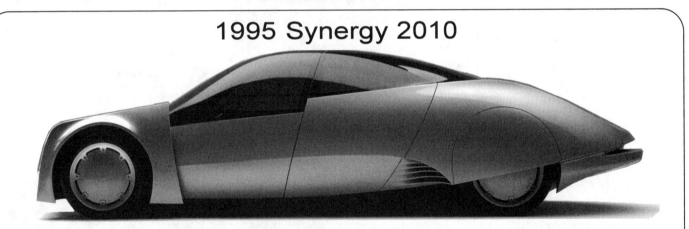

Ford took its Edge Design thinking to the extreme with their Synergy 2010 concept vehicle. Tall, thin, front fenders served to directed airflow for better areodynamics.

In cooperation with Chrysler, General Motors, the U.S. government, and domestic suppliers, Ford was in the Partnership for a New Generation of Vehicles (PNGV) program. Their efforts were to accelerate the development of energy conversion, energy storage, power conditioning, and mass reduction.

Three separate powertains were discussed to propel the

Synergy 2010, which included an internal combustion engine hybrid electric, gas turbine hybrid electric, and fuel cell hybrid electric.

Weight reduction through advanced materials improved fuel economy, and at a projected 2,200 pounds, the Synergy 2010 weighed about 1,100 pounds less than a contemporary mid-size sedan. The interior included video-screen gauges and voice-command controls.

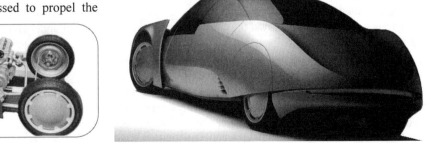

Ford

1996 Indigo

Ford's involvement in Indy Car racing is a long one, going back to a factory effort led by Preston Ticker in the 1930s. However, it was the modern-day picture FoMoCo was concerned with when it released the Indigo concept car for the 1996 show season.

Turbocharged Ford Cosworth V-8 powered cars were a staple of the CART PPG Indy Car World Series. However, that engine was not in the Indigo but rather a V-12, based on a pair of the 3.0-liter Duratec V-6s used in the Ford Taurus and Mercury Sable. The output was 425 horsepower, about half of a Cosworth, less than half the size.

When viewing the Indigo at shows, the engine was well down on the list of features the motoring public noticed, however. The open wheels and front wing/bumper had a bit of a Plymouth Prowler look for the open two-seater. Access to the interior was via swing-up doors. The instrument panel was said to have been influenced by a Formula One racer, another area where Ford Cosworths were a factor. Gears were selected by pressing a but-

ton on the Nardi steering wheel, also similar to Formula One. There were four-point seat belts like race cars, but airbags were also installed, like an ordinary car for the street.

The whole thing weighed in around 2,300 pounds and 0-60 was an under-five-second experience.

The carbon fiber/aluminum honeycomb body was built by G-Force Technologies Ltd. in West Sussex, England. Somewhat strangely, G-Force was chosen to build race cars for the Indy Racing League (IRL), which was a rival to CART. Ford has chosen to stick with CART and avoid IRL, right up to the time this was written.

1996 P2000 Prodigy HEV

Ford's P2000 Prodigy HEV was a stylish four-door sedan powered by a stored hydrogen fuel cell. The goal set for this concept family sedan was to achieve the same performance as a V-6 powered Ford Taurus, with a fuel cell engine that delivered the equivalent of 90 hp.

Using a Low Storage Requirement (LSR) hybrid electric powertrain, Prodigy HEV achieved 80 mpg and 660-mile driving range on diesel fuel, which translates to a 72 mpg gasoline equivalent. Primary propulsion was provided by a 1.2L direct-injection, aluminum (DIATA) 74 hp engine.

An integrated starter-alternator system provided instant restart, allowing fuel shut off when coasting or stopped.

Along with the hybrid set-up, this idea car achieved sensational fuel economy by an overall 30 percent weight reduction, achieved through computer optimization and lightweight materials. Aerodynamic drag was also improved through cameras/monitors (replacing side view mirrors), grille shutters, and bellypans. An automatically shifted manual transmission provided the convenience of an automatic with a 20 percent efficiency gain.

1998 Libre

Libre was a fun-to-drive, four-passenger sporty convertible with unique twist quad-doors. Like production Ford extended-cab pickup trucks, the quad-door concept would provide a more open rear seating area and allow for easy entry and exit.

Built off the versatile European B-platform, used for Fiesta, Ka, and Puma, as well as the Brazilian-built Courier pickup, Libre showed that the use of a single platform for a variety of vehicles could lead to reasonable cost niche vehicles.

Simple and straightforward body shape and contours gave the Libre a strong, clean appearance. Shapely angled windshield (set at 66-degrees) added to the vehicle's aerodynamics, yet did not compromise front seat occupants' headroom.

The body, finished in bright red metallic paint, featured innovative lighting technology. The headlights were three individual tubes, with the two larger tubes housing reflector beam lamps, and the third, smaller tube was the amber turn signal. Two round fog lamps were built into the front fascia, and geometric taillights sat high on the decklid, with an auxiliary stoplight.

Though it was a convertible, this concept did not feature a functioning soft top. It was explained that a variety of different types of soft and hard tops could be available.

A fuel-efficient powertrain consisting of a 1.25-liter Sigma engine and five-speed manual transmission allowed Libre to achieve an estimated 40-miles per gallon highway economy.

The handsome interior of exposed red sheet metal blended with the four tan leather bucket seats. To start the car, a twist of a knob and the push of an ignition button on the center console eliminated the need for a conventional key.

Ford

1998 Thunderbird

2000 Sports Roadster

Since the introduction of the 1958 "Squarebird," the motoring public and the press have been telling Ford to bring back the two-passenger Thunderbird. Ford produced the original Thunderbird with the bench front seat in the 1955, 1956, and 1957 model years. Only problem was, it could sell many more four (and more) passenger T-birds than the early models.

Thunderbird went through many changes, not all for the better, over the years, but the market for two doors was shrinking and production of the Thunderbird ended with the 1997 models. However, a future T-bird was promised. That prophecy was fulfilled at the 1998 North American International Auto Show when the Thunderbird concept was shown for the first time.

With styling led by J. Mays, a recent recruit from Volkswagen, the Thunderbird concept paid attention to what made the 1955-57 Thunderbirds modern classics. A bumperless 1955 influenced grille, obligatory hood scoop, sensible side styling, round taillights, wraparound windshield, and 1950s dash all hit the right buttons. The removable hardtop, of course, had a porthole on each side. Classic "Birders" know what that means.

Power was V-8, rear-wheel drive as it had to be, but instead of a Y-block V-8, the Lincoln LS drive train, with its 3.9 liter engine, was the source.

Production was announced and, limited to around 25,000 examples a year, the Thunderbird made its showroom appearance as a 2002 model. Future pre-production examples were shown and the production cars themselves were little changed from the concept car, a tribute to getting it right the first time.

Making the show-car rounds in 2002 is a Sports Roadster concept, which combines the rear-deck styling of the 1962-64 production Sports Roadsters with the 1950s two-passenger models.

The original Sports Roadsters had a fiberglass cover for the two rear seats to make the cars look more like a two-passenger car.

The new concept visually works well and likely will become a future version of the production Thunderbird.

2000 Windstar Solutions

Windstar Solutions debuted at the 2000 National Kitchen and Bath Industry Show. Integrated into a 2000 Windstar production minivan were custom-designed Maytag appliances.

Maytag's exclusive ClimateZone technology food drawer was featured in the cargo area and a refrigerated compartment in the rear passenger area. It was perfect to heat up a baby bottle, hot chocolate, tea, soup, and even popcorn.

A mechanical trash compactor was located between the front seats, and a trash bin in the vehicle cargo area.

The Hoover wet/dry utility vacuum was placed in the side panel adjacent to the second-row passenger seating.

A miniature Maytag combination washer/dryer is built into the rear cargo area.

Ford

2001 F-150 Lighting Bolt

The F-150 Lighting Bolt concept truck was inspired by rock-and-roll and the current fascination with body art.

Painted a cherry red metallic color, the F-150 pickup truck was detailed with hard-core, Maori tattoo designs, including one on the bed cover. Lightning Rod's sleek body was lowered and stretched, the roof was chopped one-inch, and the overhangs were shortened.

Muscles behind the good looks came from a supercharged 5.4L SOHC Triton V-8 that produced 380 hp.

The bright red exterior color was carried through to the interior, with a leather-wrapped dashboard and exposed, natural aluminum color instrument panel. A milled aluminum three-spoke steering wheel was partially wrapped in red leather, and the tattoo theme appeared on the leather-wrapped bucket seats and headliner.

2001 Explorer Sportsman

Bowing at the North American International auto Show in Detroit, but aimed at jungle safaris and the like, was the Explorer Sportsman. While Explorer versions have been going up market and increasingly highly styled, the Explorer gets back to basics and looks to be aimed at the market for the Land Rover, which is now owned by Ford.

Two sunroofs, a rugged roof rack, and squared off styling disguise the Explorer underpinnings.

Ford also showed off the EX at the show, which was more like a dune buggy than an SUV, as it had minimal body work.

Ford

2001-02 Forty-Nine

2001 Coupe

2002 Convertible

If the retro look could put the Thunderbird back into production and into the minds and hearts of America, what could it do for the conventional four-passenger car?

With J. Mays, Ford vice president of design on board, it would be sure worth finding out. Mays, who came to Ford after doing the Volkswagen New Beetle, shepherded the two-passenger Thunderbird concept into reality. His effort with the Forty-Nine, as the new concept was called, was no less spectacular.

Publicity claimed the all-new 1949 Ford was a basis for the design, but the Forty-Nine was an amalgamation of several Ford designs, ranging up to the 1960-61 Starliner. It was also a tribute to the custom cars of the 1950s which chopped, channeled, and did just about everything to the postwar Fords.

The roof featured an all-glass upper structure, a vintage non-specific grille, simply contoured sides, and a rear deck/trunk that did have 1949-51 influence.

Interior-wide, the Forty-Nine looked more like a 1960s show car with bucket seats front and rear and a raised con-

sole down the middle. The single-dial gauge cluster had 1949-51 heritage, while controls were placed in the steering wheel. Of course the tunes situation was 21st century with a 200-watt CD/stereo system with lots of speakers.

No 1950s incarnation would be complete without the horses, but there was no flathead V-8 here. A Thunderbird 3.9 liter V-8 could legitimize its "Powered by Thunderbird" badge under the hood, where chrome abounded, as it should be.

After the Forty-Nine's spectacular reception at the North American International Auto Show in Detroit and equally positive reactions at other shows, rumors of production status abounded. However, Ford's financial and legal problems that took the stage for much of 2001 resulted in budget cuts and the Forty-Nine program was among the first.

Despite the lack of a future, a convertible version of the Forty-Nine appeared at the 2002 Detroit show. It updated and themes on the original. It is interesting to ponder what a pair they would have made. The Forty-Nine convertible was not as extensively shown as the hardtop.

> "The inspiration for the Forty-Nine concept comes from the passion and excitement of the original, combined with the imagination of people across America who customized the car and turned it into what they thought a really great car should be."
>
> J. Mays, vice president of design.

2002 Mighty F-350 Tonka

By being painted a striking yellow, the Mighty F-350 Tonka concept was paying tribute to the traditional Tonka palette.

Chiseled-body features included a drop-down belt-line, pronounced power dome hood, and massive chrome grille with side nostrils. Some of these are design details coming on the next generation of Ford F-Series pickups.

Chrome was applied generously throughout the truck, and the extruded head and taillights underscored the architectural feel of the steel beneath the body.

Light Emitting Diodes provided a crisp and efficient headlight and taillight source. Lighting also ran along the fenders, was used within the embossed tailgate badging, and throughout the midnight blue leather and stainless steel interior.

The absence of a B-pillar allowed the full-size rear-hinged, rear doors, to extend easy access into the large cabin.

Muscles moving the Mighty F-350 Tonka was a 6.0-liter Power Stroke 32-valve, direct injection diesel V-8 concept engine. It was connected to the PowerTorq five-speed auto trans. Assisting the powertrain was a Hydraulic Launch Assist (HLA) system, which recovered energy from the vehicle deceleration, stored it in the form of hydraulic pressure, and then reused it during acceleration.

2002 GT40

In April, 1964, the first "Ford GT" wowed the motor press in New York. This low-slung, mid-engine GT40 was introduced to do battle with the world's best in endurance racing. Just over 100 of these historic cars were built, with major wins at the Le Mans (France) 24-hour race in 1966, 1967, 1968, and 1969.

These 1960s versions were fitted with the all-aluminum 4.2-liter Indianapolis V-8 and a 4-speed Colotti transaxle. The number 40, which signified nothing more than the car's height in inches, was added retrospectively with the introduction of the Mark II. An example of a 1960s' version of the GT40 shown in the photo on the right is posed behind the 2002 concept. This allows comparison to the cars similarities and differences.

The new GT40, created by Ford's "Living Legends" studio, is more than 18 inches longer and stands nearly four inches taller than the original. Yet, despite being physically larger, it is unmistakably a GT40.

An all-aluminum MOD 5.4-liter V-8 engine, an aluminum spaceframe, and a competition-tuned suspension provide the performance credentials of Ford's GT40 concept.

Intended to be a world-class road-going car, Ford used its largest modular supercharged and intercooled DOHC 32-valve V-8 engine, which produces 500 horsepower and 500 foot-pounds of torque. Both figures are comparable to those of the 7-liter engine that won the 24 Hours of Le Mans in 1966 and 1967. At the wheels, engineers chose Alcon 6-piston monoblock calipers and dinner-plate-sized cross-drilled discs for excellent stopping power from high speeds.

The wheels themselves - 18 inches at the front and 19 inches at the rear - were custom-fabricated for the concept car and are wrapped by substantial Goodyear raised-white-letter tires.

Ford's SVT chassis engineers created an all-new aluminum spaceframe.

Look for the new GT40 to appear at racecourses, as the manufacturer has approved production on these exotic vehicles.

1952 Continental Nineteen Fifty X

First revealed to the public in January of 1952, Ford Motor Company offered this stunning prototype as a possible future Lincoln Continental. It was billed as a "Car of Tomorrow," and it was a trendsetter from the start. After its introduction, its name was changed to the Ford X-100.

Unlike many dream cars, most of the design elements from the four-seater Continental Nineteen Fifty X eventually appeared on production models.

The 1956-57 Lincoln hooded headlights, front fender crease lines and semi-covered front wheel well openings are perfect examples.

In 1958, Ford used nearly an identical chrome hood scoop that flowed into a raised power bulge, and the 1958-60 T-birds feature a similar wide, formal-looking rear roof panel. But the car most influenced by the Continental Nineteen Fifty X was the 1961-63 Thunderbirds, with their mini tail fins and rounded fenders blending into the protruding rocket-shaped taillights.

Shown in the photograph above, the non-glare glass top over the front seat was retracted mechanically into the leather-covered canopy.

Ford hinted at a radical new engine design, which featured Turbo-dyne high compression combustion chambers and multiple throat carburetion system for use of high-octane fuels. The company kept the engine size, horsepower' and performance numbers a secret. It would have had to be a powerful one, as the car weighed 5,900 pounds.

Low and sleek, at over 18 feet long, the Continental X100 carried 24 electric motors, two batteries, and an extra charger.

1953 Anniversary and Maharajah

Maharajah was a Lincoln Capri four-door sedan finished in an ultra-luxurious gold pearl paint and a white roof. Interior metal trim was also done in gold. Traveling along with the Maharajah were the Midshipman, the Cadet, and the Anniversary show cars.

The Anniversary Capri convertible was Lincoln's tribute to FoMoCo's golden anniversary. It was trimmed in 14-carat gold, with $4,000 worth on the bumpers, grille, and trim.

Painted aquamarine with a white roof, the Midshipman. was styled in yachting tradition. Inside the car, the major heavenly star constellations were etched in the plexiglass material that lined the ceiling.

A Capri four-door sedan, named the Cadet, was decorated in the colors and decor of West Point. Handsomely painted in a pearl essence that matched the blue-gray of the military, Cadet's interior metallic surfaces and hardware were all finished in polished brass.

1953 XL-500

No matter what Ford Motor Company make the 1953 XL-500 dream is listed under, it is likely to cause controversy. It had a Lincoln chassis, it was most often displayed in the Lincoln-Mercury displays at auto shows, it was listed in some media reports of the time as a Ford, and its name and basket roof styling feature wound up on future Fords.

Since it had to go somewhere, the chassis and the styling cues of the 1956 Lincoln swayed the vote and it is classed as a Lincoln.

The roof B-pillar was the trademark of the 1955 and 1956 Ford Crown Victoria. The glass roof was half duplicated in the Skyliner models. However, the XL-500's top was transparent, front and back. As for future production features, throw Edsel into the mix, as it and the 1958 models and the XL-500 had push-button automatic-transmission controls in the middle of the steering wheel. Edsel's were in a circle, the XL had a vertical row. The horn moved to a treadle control on the floor in the dream car.

The XL's other controls were on a pedestal at the center of the dash. One of them operated the automatic jacks.

The fiberglass body was painted scarlet red. From the side, the partially enclosed front wheels and front fender line previewed the all-new 1956 Lincolns. A split grille with inset bumpers, plus a wide scoop, gave an aggressive look.

As for the name, Ford added a pair of mid-year 1962 models to its line, called Galaxie 500/XL. The XL portion of the name has stuck around on various cars and trucks ever since.

Lincoln

1954 Mardi Gras

In 1954, Lincoln featured specially trimmed production models for auto show duties, just as it did the previous year. The Mardi Gras was based on a Capri two-door hardtop that had a special ice blue, gold, and red interior.

There was also a convertible called the Huntsman and a four-door sedan tabbed the First Nighter. Both featured special interiors and trim.

1955 Premiere

Lincoln was criticized for not including a wraparound windshield in its 1955 facelift for its production cars. They were only marking time until the radically all-new 1956 models came along. However, lack of window area was not a complaint on the 1955 Premiere show car. It featured a transparent top similar, but larger than, the 1954 and 1955 and Mercury production glass tops. Lincoln didn't share in the feature, but would get a glass top many years later. The Premiere name would appear on Lincolns, starting with the 1956 models. This example had a black body and white roof.

1955 Futura

1955 Futura

Imagine the amazed looks that people had when in 1955, the Lincoln Futura took its first public drive, cruising through Central Park, in New York. Compared to vehicles of that era, this space-age vehicle with the double-dome canopy roof and sporting huge rear fins, must have looked like a UFO to bystanders.

High-performance cruising came from the 300 horsepower engine, with push-button controls for the Turbo-Drive automatic transmission located on a functional arm rest.

Electronically operated, the plexiglass middle panel of the canopy would raise and pivot back when a door was opened, and the transmission interlock kept the car from moving with the top opened. Since the windows did not open, gill-like slits fed air into the interior. The large circular ornament on the rear deck lid was actually an audio-approach microphone that warned of oncoming traffic.

Instrument controls were located in compartments on the concealed instrument panel and covered by flexible roll-type doors when not in use. Warning lights for fuel, battery and temperature were located in a steering column binnacle, along with the speedometer and tachometer.

Futura had a starring role in the 1959 movie titled, "It Started With A Kiss." Starring Debbie Reynolds and Glenn Ford, the Futura was painted red and had many scenes in the film. Years later, George Barris turned it into the first Batmobile for the 1966 television show starring Adam West.

Lincoln

1955 Indianapolis

A shroud of mystery seemed to follow the Lincoln Boano or Indianapolis, as it is called today. Beverly Rae Kimes shed the light of day on the Italian-built sports coupe in Automobile Quarterly.

Inspired by the Indianapolis 500 and the other 1950s Italian Dream cars for U.S. automobile manufacturers, Gian Paolo Bonao built the Indianapolis on a Lincoln chassis for the 1955 Turin Auto Show. Styling bore no relation to Lincoln and the Lincoln name was applied at the show, before the opening. It was voted the outstanding car of the show and Henry Ford II was taken by the photos of the Indianapolis.

Ford bought the car, had it shipped to Dearborn, and reportedly liked it. However, he did not keep it and gave it away, thus beginning a long journey for the Indianapolis, which has been faithfully restored today.

The bright orange coupe carries smooth lines with the sides interrupted by false exhaust outlets from the front fender and false vents in the doors. Indianapolis name plates and stylized checker flags adorn the front fenders. The dash has a cover plate with Indianapolis flags and lettering showing when the car is not in use.

1965 Continental Town Sedan

Lincoln featured a contemporary version of the classic town cars of the 1920-30s, with its 1965 Continental Town Sedan. It featured an open chauffeur's compartment, with a window partition separating the rear seating from the front.

Though the exterior dimensions of the luxurious limousine were nearly the same as the standard Continental, its wheelbase and overall length had been increased five inches to 131-inches and 221.3 inches, respectively.

To move the large vehicle, the 430 cid Lincoln engine was used, with 320 horsepower.

1966 Coronation Coupe

Similar to the 1965 Thunderbird Town Landau, Lincoln's 1966 Coronation Coupe featured a padded roof that covered where the quarter windows would have been. For added privacy, the rear window was also reduced in size.

Other special features were the broad band of walnut running the full length of the lower body, and a new checkered effect grille. The design came from Ford Division's styling studio, with Chicago's Lehmann-Peterson doing the excellent coach work.

Shown above, on a raised turntable during the Chicago Auto Show, the Coronation Coupe appeared elegant, in a 1960s fashion.

1967 Continental Coronation II

Following up the previous year's Coronation Coupe show car, Lincoln introduced a sequel, the 1967 Coronation II.

As the photo shows, it was a mildly modified Continental two-door, with special paint job, retractable sunroof over the front seat, and concealed door handles.

Like the 1966 version, Coronation II had a padded roof that wrapped around and forward, omitting the rear passenger window. The body was painted a victorian gold, that was a murano pearl paint over a black lacquer, topped-off by a gold padded vinyl roof.

Ford designers created the look, and California-based Lance Automotive did all the custom conversion work.

Moving this nearly 5,000-pound coupe was the huge 462-cubic-inch Lincoln Continental engine, with 340 horses.

Lincoln

1969 Continental Town Sedan

Like the 1966 Town Sedan show vehicle, Lincoln once again offered a sophisticated version of the traditional chauffeured driven town car.

Though based on a Lincoln Continental four-door sedan, it showed a decided influence from the Mark III, including the concealed headlights and a strong central grille design.

The windshield on the Town Sedan was slanted rearward and the front side glass was removed from the doors. Separating the rear compartment from the driver was a divider glass partition and to provide even more privacy, the rear window was reduced in size.

Instructions to the driver from the rear seating were done via an intercom system, and the passengers could enjoy color TV and a multiplex stereo sound system.

The exterior was painted in antique moss pearlescent lacquer, and the interior was trimmed with moss green material accented with gold. Passengers enjoyed the use of a foldaway vanity.

1970 Mark III Dual Cowl Phaeton

Harking back to the classic automobiles of 1930s' millionaires and movie stars, Ford designers created the Mark III Dual Cowl Phaeton show car.

The 1970 version recreated the 1931 Lincoln KB, shown below, with its dual windshields, on a four-door convertible.

Additional features of the new version included red leather and corduroy interior, a prismatic silver flake exterior finish, and a unique Mark III grille that extended under the car.

Powering this large parade car was the standard Continental 460-cubic-inch V-8 engine. As fitting the Mark III Dual Cowl Phaeton heritage, it made its official public debut on Hollywood's Wilshire Boulevard, and then traveled to many major automobile shows.

194

1982 Continental Concept 90

When Lincoln unveiled the Continental Concept 90, it was a thinly disguised version of the coming 1984 Mark VII.

Concept 90 was 16 inches shorter than the Mark VII, which would be replacing, the Mark VI. It was also over two inches lower and had a six-inch shorter wheelbase.

Aerodynamics were important in the new design, and features like electronically controlled ride height, and thermo-statically controlled grille louvers helped lower the drag coefficient.

Design details like wraparound head and taillights, and doors that carry up into the roof, were glimpses of features that started appearing on 1983 FoMoCo products.

The Continental Concept 90 had the rare honor to have been the cover car for the June 1982 issue of *Motor Trend*.

1983 Continental Concept 100

The Concept 100 was believed to contain the largest number of functioning advanced electronic features ever contained in a single vehicle.

These items included satellite navigation, keyless entry and ignition, sonar detection system, electronically controlled air suspension, voice alert, and voice command capabilities.

In fact, the Concept 100 was nicknamed the "talking car" because the driver could verbally activate electronic wipers and headlights, and the car, through synthesized speech, could warn of pending oil, fuel level, and battery problems.

Sensors for the sonar detection system were installed in ports in the front and rear bumpers that warned of obstructions in the car's path, and displayed the distance between you and the car ahead and behind.

Under the sloping hood was an anemic 2.3-liter four-cylinder engine with multiple-port electronic fuel injection.

Exterior features included low-profile halogen headlights, with aerodynamic covers and bronze-tinted glass with compound curvature.

Lincoln

1985-86 Quicksilver

Ford developed the Quicksilver as a mid-engine four-door sports sedan that could transport five occupants.

When Ghia debuted this futuristic vehicle, it was painted silver, shown at the right. Later, the car was redone in a two-tone black cherry pearl and complimenting gray pearl. Quicksilver was mounted on an AC ME 3000 chassis.

The slick body shape used retractable headlights, flush belly pan, and skirted rear wheels. It also featured a new method of flush-glazing the retractable curved windows. Powertrain consisted of a transverse V-6 engine and five-speed transmission.

1986-87 Continental
Next Generation Mark

The Next Generation Mark was a design study created by Ford's Ghia operations in Turin, Italy. Though only a prototype without an interior, it was created to show a new direction for a personal luxury car.

Some of the styling features shown on the all-black concept were integrated bumpers, low-profile headlights, hidden wipers, recessed windshield that was radically raked, flush body surfaces, and side glass. The windshield used a special light transmittance control film that reduced harsh sunrays.

The female model shown standing next to the car illustrates the Next Generation Mark's low height of 53.4 inches. Overall length was 203.3 inches and overall width was 73.0 inches.

1987 Lincoln by Vignale

Originally called Vignale Gilda, the Lincoln by Vignale was a handsome two-passenger convertible. The sleek design was a combined effort between FoMoCo's North American Design Center and its Italian facility, Ghia SpA.

Sleek, low front-end height was partially achieved by small multi-beam headlight system. The front bumper used optimized air intakes and wide driving lights allowed a smooth transition from the front of the car to the sides. At the rear, the integrated bumper and sweeping taillights treatment emphasize the vehicle's overall width and highlights the large tires.

The hardtop roof was removable, with a convertible top stored under a one piece powered deck lid. The car included keyless entry, heated seats, and auto dim inside rear view mirror.

This would have been a handsome Lincoln sports car of the 1990s that might have competed with cars like Mercedes-Benz 300SL and BMW 325i convertibles.

1988 Machete

Adventures in styling shapes that flowed were prevalent in the Lincoln Machete concept car of 1988. While a machete is a sharp instrument, the vehicle named after it was anything but.

Airflow management was the key with front and rear lift control devices helping downforce and braking as well. A six window design flowed into the trunk. Controllable glass tinting was controlled via LCDs. Head and taillights were minimal in area, but were said not to lack in intensity.

The driver was surrounded by a flowing display area and console with fiber optic graphics, while the passenger had a smoothly sculptured safety bar.

Outside rearview mirrors were replaced by television cameras with a pair of screens on the dash completing the circuit.

Lincoln

1989 Ghia Continental

Prepared as an auto show display model, the Ghia Continental was modified by Ford's Ghia studio in Turin, Italy.

A front air dam that incorporated round driving lights, rocker panel cladding, and the electrically adjustable rear spoiler gave the stock Continental a more aggressive high-performance appearance.

The exterior was finished in veneto blue, with warm gray satin metallic grille and interior used platine beige leather seating and veneto blue wool carpet. Ghia also lowered the car's suspension and added special 17-inch wheels.

1992 Marque X

Ford Motor Company wanted to show its dedication to the growing popularity of cab-forward design vehicles, and the Marque X concept convertible was its latest idea in 1992. It was based on the Mark VIII, and under the hood was Lincoln's 32-value DOHC V-8 engine matched to a four-speed automatic transmission. To start the ignition, the driver needed a special coded credit card.

Further aerodynamic enhancements included a front electronically controlled, speed-sensitive spoiler, mounted underbody, that would deploy at 45 mph. At the same time, the air-spring suspension lowered the entire front one-inch.

Space efficient fiber-optic headlamps helped lower the front profile, and thin, full-width taillights used light emitting diodes (LED). The high-tech curved windshield was developed by Ford Glass, and incorporated liquid crystal display (LCD) sun-shield material.

This electronically controlled sun-shield had three sun visor positions that allowed the driver a choice of height adjustments.

Rear-seat passengers had use of an entertainment system that included a pop-up television and video player.

The beautiful Marque X was finished with Samoan orange pearl paint, and featured bold, asymmetrically designed chrome 19-inch wheels.

1995 L2K

Still in need of a convertible in its lineup, Lincoln floated the idea of a two-passenger roadster during the 1995 show season.

The L2K was kind of a shortened Mark VIII, powered by a Taurus SHO 3.4 liter, 250-hp advanced V-8. The rear wheels spun, thanks to an automatic tranny. A rear spoiler/mini-rollbar set off the outside and a set of trick analog gauges did the same for the interior.

To date, Lincoln is still waiting for open skies.

1996 Sentinel

Traditional Lincoln exterior styling, such as a crisp silhouette, blade fenders and high, linear beltlines were retained on the 1996 Sentinel concept. It showcased Ford's "New Edge" approach on a full-size, four-door, rear-wheel-drive luxury car.

Set in the Sentinel's metallic black exterior was a new interpretation of a 1940s-style Continental grille with its fine bar texture. Flush glass all round and compact vertically stacked projector headlamps added to the uncluttered look of the exterior. Massive 20-inch wheels were placed flush to the body to ensure a minimum of body overhang both front and rear, plus add to the Sentinel's aerodynamics.

The car's overall length of 218 inches was just one inch shorter than a 1996 Lincoln Town Car.

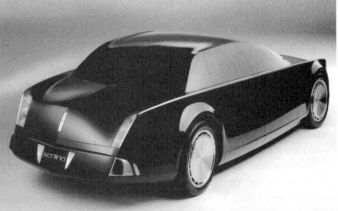

Lincoln

1999 Special LS

The special Lincoln LS Concept was first shown at SEMA 1999 and featured 18-inch HRE wheels, Pirelli P-Zero tires, an Eibach suspension kit, and Eaton supercharger.

Exterior modifications included dark-tinted windows, 18-inch wheels, chrome-tipped exhaust pipes, a rear deck extension, and Razzi ground-effects kit.

2001 MK 9

Envisioned as a new generation possibility in the Lincoln Mark series, the MK 9's exterior was low, wide, and sexy. It appears to be an update of the 1996 Sentinel concept, but is even more aggressive looking.

The body was finished in a gloss black paint that highlighted the crisp surfaces, and functional air vents which enhanced the elegant appearance of the MK 9's front fenders and hood.

Incorporated in the front design was an evolution of Lincoln's signature grille, flanked by twin xenon gas discharge headlights. Turn signal indicators were also integrated into each lamp unit.

Aluminum door handles were flush-mounted to the MK 9's door skin, and twin rectangular dual-exhaust outlets were neatly framed by the rear bumper fascia, and complement the horizontal emphasis of the red LED tail lamps.

Adding to the overall hot-rod look were enormous 22-inch, 10-spoke aluminum alloy wheels, fitted with P275/45/R22 Continental tires in front and P295/40/R22 tires in the rear.

Inside the MK 9, a combination of dark cherry red and Marlboro red leathers with accents of polished metal created a luxurious lounge environment. Dark cherry saddle leather was used for the flooring, and white leather for the headliner.

Lincoln

2002 Continental Concept

When first introduced, the 1961 Lincoln Continental, with its sheer body surfaces, center-opening doors, and chrome-accented bodywork, created a styling sensation.

Forty-one years later, that classic look returned on the 2002 Continental Concept, and again created a sensation with the motoring press and public opinion.

Many of the 1960s Continental characteristics were imitated, though redone in 21st century terms. The new Continental Concept used aluminum and composite body-on-frame construction with composite outer skin, finished in a color called silver sea spray. The grille, milled from aluminum, incorporated four round headlamps that were generated by a single source transferred to each lamp by fiber optic cable. The outer edges of the hood raised slightly to meet chrome bodyside moldings that accentuated the car's length.

The Continental's horizontal emphasis continued at the rear of the car, and a Lincoln star badge divided the large LED lamps.

But the show-stopper was the large luggage tray that slid out of the trunk by remote control and held Zero Halliburton luggage and golf club cases. Also triggered by remote control, or by simply touching the flush aluminum door handles, were the powered center-opening doors. These doors operated independently and with both doors open, the pillarless aperture was almost six feet wide.

Rectangular exhaust tips, integrated into the rear valence, hinted that this was a hot rod Lincoln. The high performance came from the 6.0-liter V-12 engine, with 414 hp under that long hood. Completing the powertrain on this rear-wheel-drive car was a six-speed automatic transmission.

Custom luxury featured on the Continental Concept included hands-free telephone functions, built-in laptop tables that stow in the console, a cabinet between the rear seats that housed crystal, and a drinks dispenser, a rear door large umbrella holder, and even cigar humidors.

1953 Bahamian

Before Mercury had its own full-fledged dream car, the 1954 XM-800, it exhibited custom variations of production models at early 1950s auto shows.

The *Bahamian*, shown on the left, was a Monterey hardtop with a tan body and a dark brown roof.

Two other '53 Merc specials were included in the display, one named the Contemporary and the other Kentucky Colonel.

The *Contemporary* was an all-black convertible trimmed with black leather and charcoal and white board-cloth material.

Painted mint green, the *Kentucky Colonel* four door sedan used white linen and Milan straw vinyl as upholstery, bound in mint green welting.

1954 XM-800

When the XM-800 made its debut as a 1954 dream car, it was billed as having a lower height than any production U.S. hardtop. It was more than just a dream car for Mercury, but a rolling laboratory.

The four-passenger coupe was developed far enough along that if public demand warranted, according to Benson Ford, it could have easily been placed into volume production.

In a sense it did happen, as the XM-800 turned into 1956 Lincoln. Compare the side view of the Lincoln with the profile of the XM-800.

Both featured forward-slanted hooded headlights, partially covered front wheels and tall, canted taillights that blended into the rear bumper/exhaust combination. Also, the 1957 Mercury grille was an interpretation of the concave thick and thin vertical bars from the XM-800.

The XM-800's pearlescent white and copper exterior matched the interior combination of white and copper vinyl. Individual-contoured seats were divided by stationary armrests that contained a variety of controls.

1956 XM Turnpike Cruiser

One of the most memorable Mercury dream cars ever was the XM Turnpike Cruiser. Noted stylist Don De LaRossa, then head of design at Mercury, is credited with creating the sensational XM Cruiser. It was developed to show the type of automobile that was coming to meet the enormous expansion in U.S. superhighways.

Though most people would assume that this car influenced the 1957 Mercury, it was actually the other way around. What the XM dream car did affect was the look of the 1959 production version, especially the larger concave-sculpted rear fenders, and larger V-shaped taillights. On the XM Cruiser, the bold 12-inch wide pearlescent coves made a nice contrast to the persimmon body color.

As shown above, transparent roof panels flipped-up when the doors were opened, allowing a no-stoop entry into the interior. These were similar to the ones on the 1956 Olds experimental Golden Rocket.

Driving visibility was excellent through large compound-curved front and rear glass, and the roof seemed to float, supported by thin, two-inch wide chrome pillars.

When the XM Turnpike Cruiser traveled the highways and turnpikes, it was transported in a trailer with large picture windows. During outdoor shows, those glass panels lowered, and the car shifted crosswise on the turntable.

Mercury

1962 Palomar

Though Mercury discontinued its two-door hardtop station wagon body style after the 1959 models, it made a reappearance in the 1962 Palomar show vehicle. It was not the hardtop style that was the focal point, but rather the third seat setup.

The rear section of the roof could be opened and the rear seat rose so that the passengers could look over the roof, yacht style.

A second windshield popped up to keep the bugs off of them.

Though interesting, the idea never caught on in Mercury, or any other domestic wagon. To call attention to the special seating to view the stars, planets and other things, the Palomar name was adopted from the Mt. Palomar Observatory in California.

1964 Super Marauder

George Barris and company customized a four-seat Mercury convertible and turned it into the two-seat Super Marauder. Wheelbase was shortened by five inches, and overall length was cut a total of eight inches.

Outside door handles were shaved off and the rear wheels were fully exposed. Four small air cleaners were exposed through the power-dome hood. Four Lucas headlights were used. Dual free-standing head rests were mounted behind the seats, the windshield was cut in half, and the magnesium wheels had knock off hubs.

Racing mirrors and the full length chrome side-mounted exhaust pipes added a hot-rod touch.

1964 Comet Fastback - See color section

1965 Comet Cyclone Sportster

With success of the customized versions of its production cars the previous year, Mercury continued with special versions for the 1965 auto show season.

Shown above is a Comet, converted into a two-seat, open cockpit car, called the Cyclone Sportster.

Popping out mid-hood was a custom supercharger air intake.

Directly behind is a nine-inch high windshield that was joined to the low cut door glass by thin pillars.

Lucas units replaced stock headlights, and a pair of four-inch driving lights was housed in the floating grille. Behind the bucket seats, was a highly stylish airfoil roll bar.

Comet Cyclone Sportster was also another of the Mercs that featured small circular pistol grips, instead of the conventional steering wheel. Also missing were the traditional floor pedals. They were replaced by an accelerator, power brake, and power clutch that were actually part of the floor and operated by foot pressure rather than foot travel.

Not in view is the large racing-type fuel-filler cap on the rear deck and bold taillights. Also very stylish, even if not practical, were the black vinyl padded rocker panels.

1965 Wrist Twist Park Lane

FoMoCo began featuring modern alternatives to the conventional steering wheel as early as the 1954 Ford Atmos dream car, and continued with new variations for the next dozen years.

In 1965, Mercury equipped five of its full-size convertibles with a prototype "wrist twist" steering system and allowed over 100 people to test drive them. The cars totaled over 100,000 miles when the evaluations were all completed. Ford continued the experiment during 1966, this time on 10 convertibles.

An energy absorbing crash pad was added between the Wrist Twist rings.

Press releases explained that a simple twist of the wrist was all that was needed to steer the car, but reports from those who drove them did not always agree. Turning the little hand wheels required the same lock-to-lock revolutions as a large steering wheel, which was no improvement. One thing the smaller wheels allowed was easier access to enter and exit the driver's seat.

Mercury

1966 Astron

For the 1966 model year, Mercury presented a concept idea that it featured on production 1954-55 models. That was a glass panel roof, but unlike the Sun Valley, the Astron's glass roof could change tint, automatically providing shade from the sunlight.

Actually the side, rear, and upper area of the windshield were all treated with the same light-sensitive material. Another feature from the past, redone with new technology, was the glass rear window, which retracted into the roof. Unlike the old rigid retracting windows, this glass had a bendable quality, which permitted it to roll upward in con-cealed channels and nest out of sight under the head lining.

Other external design changes to the stock Park Lane included rectangular lens covers over the quad headlights, a full-length textured band just above the rocker panel level, and small coach-type windows enclosed in the C-pillars.

At the rear, tri-color taillights gave indication of what the driver was doing. When accelerating, the lights shined green, then turned yellow for deceleration, and flashed red when braking.

Hess & Eisenhardt of Cincinnati, Ohio, built Astron from specifications provided to them by Ford stylists.

1966 Comet Escapade

Mercury's super hot-looking concept for 1966 was the Comet Escapade high performance roadster.

Ford stylists in Dearborn created the look, and Californian George Barris' Kustom City constructed it in a reported six weeks.

This open cockpit racer was shortened by 16 inches from a stock Comet, and featured a chopped windshield that connected with the side glass which flowed into the rear quarter panels. Sculpted sheet metal was thrust forward off the vertical dual racing headlights, and a new grille had a vertical divider. On the hood were twin tunneled air hood scoops that gave the Comet a personality all its own.

Headrests were built into the sleek roll bar. Running along the lower side panels, looking like chrome side pipes, were vents that cooled the rear brakes.

Racing wheels had anodized alloy spokes with a brushed finish and blue-white steel rims. The wheels were fitted with 14-inch blue line tires. Rear-end appearance included a floating panel of body color that was completely surrounded by taillight assembly. Sequential turn indicators were designed into the taillight unit, and a flush-mounted bumper molding framed the entire rear.

The interior was done in white leather and vinyl material, with black accent stripes, and the molded one-piece white bucket seats had diamond pattern inserts in the leather. Brushed stainless steel was used for the custom instrument panel, and the car was finished in 40 coats of deep pearlescent blue.

1968 LeGrand Marquis

For 1968, Mercury presented a unique idea for safer use of a car trunk. The trunk lid of the LeGrand Marquis, which included half of the right rear fender, swung up from the side, and opened like the cover of a book.

The idea was to permit loading from the right side, affording the advantage of curb-level access on city streets and protection from on-coming traffic on open roads.

Other innovations, which Mercury felt had production possibilities, included twin sunroof sections and unique quad rectangular headlights.

Mercury

1969 Cyclone Super Spoiler

What would you have if you took a Montego two-door hardtop, cut the roof off, and blended a roll bar into the pearlescent yellow body? When Mercury did exactly that, it was called Cyclone Super Spoiler.

Those were just some of the many design changes made. Both the grille and windshield profiles were lowered to reduce frontal area and improve aerodynamics. Housed on either side of the grille was an experimental modular lighting system that incorporated road lamps, turn signals, and directional lighting. Under the bottom of the front area was an airdam that was synchronized with the acceleration of the car, so that it extended forward and down to reduce lift.

Matching the bright exterior color, the interior was trimmed in yellow vinyl and psychedelic-type yellow velour. Bucket seats were used both front and back, but only the front had retracting headrests. Rear seating was nestled into the rear quarter panels.

Replacing the stock steering wheel was a leather-covered Moretti type Formula 1 three-spoke competition wheel, mounted on a tilt steering column.

Built into the rear spoiler were trim tabs that extended to increase the down thrust at higher speeds.

What's not seen in the above photos is how the rear sheet metal formed a ducktail spoiler around the taillight assembly. Those lights were modified Mercury Marauder X-100 units that gave full-width illumination.

1970 Cougar El Gato

El Gato (Spanish for "The Cat") was a futuristic-looking Cougar, with contemporary customized touches.

The roof was chopped and exterior door handles were removed. Unusual three-spoke 16-inch wheels were fitted to specially designed Firestone LXX tires. Up front, flat black striping ran from the bumper, over the hood, and ended inside the integrated hood scoop.

Subtle touches were the rolled front and rear pans.

Wall to wall taillights were accented by an asymmetrically placed racing-style gas filler cap. Center-placed exhaust tips were similar to those used on many recent concepts, like the 2001 Chrysler Crossfire.

1971 Montego Sportshauler

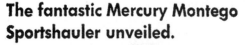

The Montego Sportshauler was a 1970s multi-use concept vehicle, created by Ford's Design Center. Based on a 1971 Cyclone, it was modified into a two-passenger vehicle that had a surprise in its trunk. It first was called the Cyclone Sportshauler, but soon the name was changed to Montego.

In the special rear compartment, behind the two passenger seats, a recreation vehicle like an all terrain machine, minibike, or snowmobile could be stored.

As seen in the images below, the rear window and deck lid opened electrically. When the rear was fully opened, a tailgate lowered to the ground to form a ramp and an electrical winch lowered the small vehicle.

Resembling a production fastback, the body was painted in pearlescent white, with candy orange on the rocker panels and the lower portion of the back panel. Special high traction tires for mud and sand had dual orange stripe sidewalls. The interior was also trimmed in orange metallic and brown. Power was provided by a 351 cu.in V-8, connected to a four-speed transmission.

The fantastic Mercury Montego Sportshauler unveiled.

Sleek and innovative was how Mercury termed its one-of-a-kind XM concept car. Designed by Ford Motor Company's world-famous Ghia Studio of Turin, Italy, the XM brought back the rumble seat. FoMoCo needed to develop vehicles that could average 27.5 mpg by the 1985 model year, so small designs like the XM seemed logical.

What made this concept unique was the reintroduction of the 1920-30s rumble seat. By raising the rear hatch window and flipping back the deck lid, the car converted from a two seater into a four-passenger vehicle.

Standing four feet tall, it had a 94-inch wheelbase, the same as the Bobcat compact, but XM was 10-inches longer.

Mercury

Painted red, with gold, black, and white accents, plus fabrics of a Buckingham Palace guard uniform, made this unique Capri show car a highlight at auto shows.

Model Lydia Hill was dressed in what could be the uniform of a female palace guard. Her outfit was similar to the car's all-red velour fabric interior, accented with white leather bands, gold buttons, and gold-embroidered crowns on black velour seatback bolsters.

The instrument panel and console had brushed gold aluminum applique. Special gold crown decals were on the rear fender, and 15-inch Gotti modular wheels were special details exclusive to this Capri.

1980 Anster

Weighing in at a mere 1,200 pounds, the Anster was a bold, aerodynamic electric car. About the size of a Mercury Bobcat, this concept body was made from injection-molded plastic and the large black front and rear bumpers contained energy-absorbing foam. Special features included electronically operated sliding doors, scientifically contoured inflatable seat cushions, and an on-board computer.

But the highlight of this fuel-efficient vehicle was the unique hybrid electric power system. Two power cells would provide DC power to drive all four wheels, and a compact power generator continuously recharged the energy cells.

As a safety measure, Anster's dash computer would continuously display the calculated average distance required to stop the car under current operating conditions.

Like today's cars, the Anster could help the driver pick the most direct route. But, unlike modern satellite technology, this computer was programmed via map cassettes.

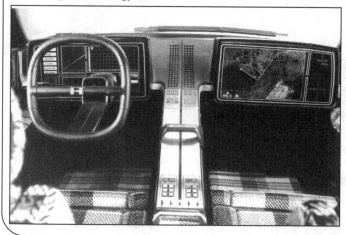

1981 LN7 PPG

Mercury Turbo LN7 was one of five specially prepared PPG pace cars which alternated in pacing the races in the CART-sanctioned PPG Indy Car World Series in 1981.

Shown here are two views of the modified Lynx coupe, which used a turbocharged version of the stock 1.6 liter four-cylinder powerplant.

Developed by Ford Design Center and Ford Special Vehicle Operations, this front-wheel-drive Lynx was constructed by Michigan-based American Sunroof Corp., (ASC). Jack Roush Performance Engineering prepared the engine and suspension.

Other cars in the 1981 series was the AMX Turbo, Chevrolet Corvette Twin-Turbo, Dodge Turbo Charger 2.2, and Oldsmobile Omega Turbo.

1989 Mercury One

Working in conjunction with Mazda, Ford created the Mercury One concept car. When people viewed this fiberglass Mercury One at the 1989 auto show, they were seeing a glimpse at the next generation Mercury Tracer and Ford Escort.

Ford was searching for a compact car with outstanding aerodynamics. Items like flush glass all around and integrated headlights were similar to the large Sable. The interior was highlighted by rich leather bucket seats.

Mercury

1988
Concept 50

Mercury stated that Concept 50 was a "concept for fun." The idea was to show the public what small-specialty front-wheel-drive vehicles of the future might look like. Concept 50 did have clean cab-forward styling close to the upcoming 1989 Ford Probe.

In fact, the 102.6-inch wheelbase, 177.4 length, and 50.6 height were nearly identical to the Probe sports coupe.

Created as a two-door hatchback, the car was targeted at young (18-30) singles or young, two-income couples.

Features include a small, multi-valve V-6 engine and all-wheel-drive. The five spoke wheels are similar in design to the 1989 Thunderbird SC wheels.

1990 Cyclone

1991 Mystique

Paving the way for the 1993 Villager, Mercury's first ever minivan, was the Mystique concept vehicle. It was distinguished by a unified, single design-form, flowing from front to rear. Helping to achieve that look were flush high-intensity wall-to-wall headlights and fiber-optic taillights.

Many of the styling cues would appear on the new Villager, but the Mystique used Ford's experimental T-drive powertrain configuration. The T-Drive system was a transverse V-8 engine with a centrally mounted transmission.

Flexibility of front-wheel, rear-wheel, or all-wheel drive was obtained with the T-Drive. Mystique also used an extruded aluminum space frame.

The roof was constructed with glass panels that had liquid-crystal technology to darken when in bright sunlight. Individual TV/VCR units were implanted in the passenger seatbacks.

While Mercury did not use the Mystique nameplate on a van, it did apply it to its coming 1995 compact car.

Sleek, aerodynamic cab-forward styling distinguished the Cyclone concept. Mercury described the car as having a mixture of dreams and performance. It also reincarnated the Cyclone name, used from 1964 through 1972.

Among the many features included was an electrochromic roof that allowed the driver to adjust for change in sunlight conditions.

Rear-view mirrors were eliminated and replaced by a camera that projected rear views on a television screen.

Mercury

1996 Fusion

Fusion was a mini-sport utility concept that combined style, with safety for inner city transportation. Developed by Ford's Concept Cars California outfit, Fusion offered diversity.

By removing the rear quarter and back glass panels, along with folding forward the canvas demi-top, you converted the closed vehicle into small pickup truck.

The high-tech interior was outfitted with lightweight bucket seats up front and a rear-folding split bench seat.

In September 2001, Ford introduced another Fusion concept vehicle, shown on the right, which further blurred the line between an SUV and a car. Ford also used the Fusion name on a Roush Racing prepared ZX2.

1997 MC4

One of the more handsome Mercury concepts was the MC4. With crisp, sculpted body panels, it blended sports coupe design into a vehicle that could be practical when it came to transporting passengers and their belongings.

A quad-door entry system was used, which combined two shortened front doors with two rear half-doors that opened out toward the tail of the car. These allowed the MC4 to have the look of a sleek sports coupe, yet provided easy entry to and exit from the rear seat area. The large interior accommodated four adults plus a child in an integrated youngster seat. Electroluminescent analog gauges were used, with the main gauges housed in a moveable cluster. This unit adjusted with the rake and

angle of the steering column, allowing the gauges to always be in easy view of the driver.

At the rear were the novel "gull-wing" trunk lids that raised from just above either rear wheel well to allow easy access to stored items.

In theory, the MC4, equipped with a V-8, could have been equipped by a variety of powertrains. Pushing a button located on the console would start the MC4's engine and activated three video-imaging cameras, designed to replace conventional mirrors, and improve rear visibility.

The MC4's 19-inch five-spoke cast wheels were combined with 255/40 R19 Goodyear low-profile tires, which were pushed to the corners of the body.

1997 MC2

Mercury fans were encouraged to hear that the Cougar brand was returning as a 1999 model, after an absence of two years.

What was startling was that the car would be front-wheel drive.

The MC2 concept gave a clear indication of the design vision customers would see in the new car. It was created by using computer-aided design technology at the Ford Small and Medium Car Vehicle Center in Germany as part of a global development project involving American and European designers.

Sheer surfaces and defined curves gave the overall impression of strength, which was emphasized by the satin-finish titanium paint and polished nickel-chrome trim details.

Five louvered glass panels were fixed to the windshield and the rear window to form what appeared to be a one-piece roof. The glass panels pivoted upward to let the fresh air in. At the rear were stylish neon-tube taillamps, and up front were halogen headlights with large auxiliary fog lamps. Unique 18-inch six-spoke alloy wheels fitted with low-profile 255x35x18 tires gave the MC2 a sporty stance.

The two front bucket seats were wrapped in light-blue leather and accented with a darker shade of blue leather.

1998 L' Attitude

The Mercury L'Attitude concept car combined the practical spaciousness and refinement of a family wagon with the robust off-road capability of a sport utility. It was based on the all new sable wagon for 1998.

The innovative tailgate design was one of the vehicle's most prominent features. A molded spare tire well designed into the center of the tailgate freed up cargo space inside the vehicle. The tailgate and window opened as a single unit from the side, providing drivers easier access to the spare, which stored about waist high.

Roof access was provided by exposed step wells built into either side of the lower bumper. Rear seat passengers could stand with the middle roof panel opened for photography. Camera mounts equipped with Nikon cameras were added to enhance the vehicle's versatility.

High-intensity discharge headlamps, marker lamps, and rear taillights increased visibility at night. For off-road use, additional projector beams, that directed high-beam light long distances, were located below the headlights. Sweeping neon turn signals consisted of two horizontal neon tubes in the rear and a U-shaped neon tube in the quarter pane.

L'Attitude's certainly could've had an attitude with its custom-tuned 3.4-liter, V-8 SHO engine. The 17-inch, six-spoke alloy wheels wrapped in custom-cut Goodyear tires improved off-road ability, and there was also a portable Apple Newton global positioning system on board, in case you got lost in the wilderness.

Mercury

1999 (MY)

(MY) concept was a Mercury design exercise for a multi-activity vehicle, combining maximum versatility with style. With the blurring of boundaries between a car, a truck, and SUV, this idea car was an adventurous new direction for the Mercury brand.

The five-door (MY) profile featured an arching roof, hard-edged rear hatch line, and flared wheel housings.

As illustrated in the photo on the right, the front doors opened conventionally, while the rear doors opened at the center, creating easy access to the interior.

All window glass had an amber-tinting, adding a nice contrast to the aluminum-like exterior and interior finish.

Hard to see in these images were the amber glass roof panels, one over the passengers and one over the cargo area. With the lower portion of the rear hatch in the opened position, the (MY) had over six feet to haul large objects.

Adding to the rugged looks were 18-inch, six-spoke aluminum wheels, and all-terrain tires.

1999 Gametime Villager

Beginning with a 1999 Villager minivan, Mercury designers incorporated a wide range of ideas to create the Gametime concept vehicle, and took tailgate activities to new levels. The most unique aspect was the built-in rear entertainment module, shown in the photo on the right. This system featured a plasma 21-inch flat screen monitor that had video feed from either a DVD player or the satellite dish connection. Also included were side-mounted stereo speakers, ice bucket, and humidor. Not shown are the dual sliding canvas sunroofs or the rear lift gate fitted tent canopy.

Exterior styling was altered with the addition of new front and rear fascias and bolder body-side cladding.

Gametime Villager was lowered with Roush Racing springs, and the vehicle was fitted with hand-cut 18-inch Michelin concept tires, mounted on TSW Hockenheim-R alloy wheels. Notice the notch in the rear bumper for dual DynoMax exhaust tips.

1999 Cougar S

1999 Cougar Eliminator

Mercury released quick follow-up concept cars after the introduction of its brand new 1999 Cougar.

First came the Cougar S, followed by the sexy Eliminator, both customized by Ford's Special Vehicle Engineering group.

Cougar S was all-wheel-drive, created to explore the growing modified front/all-wheel drive import vehicle market. It also had the muscles to take on competition with a 215 horsepower version of the 2.5-liter 24-valve V-6 Duratec engine, connected to a five-speed MTX-75 manual transmission.

The S sported a unique front fascia with integrated fog lamps and a lower brushed aluminum grille for improved cooling. Other custom touches included anti-splash wheel lips, a functional hood air scoop, and dual rear spoilers.

Deep-dish 18-inch three-piece alloy wheels were mounted with Goodyear Eagle GS tires. Recaro racing seats as well as unique alloy clutch, brake, and accelerator pedals spiced up the interior.

Eliminator was created to show what could be done to make the Cougar's appearance even leaner and meaner than the stock model. Its ride height was lowered nearly two inches by the addition of stiffer front and rear springs. Up front, the sheet-molded compound hood had an integral scoop, and the bumper included ground effects styling.

At the rear of the car were a deck lid spoiler, unique bumper and quad carbon fiber tip exhaust pipes. Those pipes were part of the stainless steel Borla exhaust system, which was tuned to emit a beautiful growl from the V-6 engine. In stock trim, the 2.5 liter, 24-valve DOHC powerplant produced 170 hp.

The bodywork was finished with a stunning coat of PPG Harlequin Chome-O-Flair paint, which changed hues depending on the light and angle of view.

Enkei VX-1 10-spoke alloy wheels were fitted to 18-inch Goodyear Eagle GS F-1 performance radial tires.

Mercury

1999 Marauder Sedan

2002 Marauder Convertible

Testing the waters for the demand for an old idea, a full-sized, rear wheel drive performance sedan, was on the to do list for the Mercury Marauder concept car, which played during the 1999 show season.

Using the name from its performance heritage, Marauder, Mercury fixed up a Grand Marquis sedan in similar fashion to the dear departed Chevrolet Impala SS, last made as a 1996 model.

The black Marauder featured a supercharged version of the 4.6 liter SOHC V-8 and claimed 335 horsepower from the steel block/aluminum head combo.

Added to the package were Edelbrock Performer IAS shocks, fat sway bars, Enekei SST wheels (17-inch front, 18 rears), Pirelli P-Zero tires, and the Marauder name embossed into the back bumper.

Bucket seats replaced the Grand Marquis' bench up front and the automatic shift lever moved to the floor, located in a console Shades of the 1960s S-55!

The reaction was immediate - build it! Of course, the chorus was made up largely of vintage hot rodders that remembered the 1963 1/2-64 Marauders, Parnelli Jones, and Pike's Peak, but then the Grand Marquis is one of the cult cars of the Geritol set anyway.

Mercury did announce production status, but wasn't in a hurry and promised the Marauder as a 2003 model.

To keep the faith, a Marauder convertible concept was announced at the 2003 Chicago Auto Show. While the sedan was a modification of a standard production model, the convertible looked like a member of the family, but had to be hand made.

Strangely, the convertible was at the press preview, but missing from the display when the public entered the doors.

The ragtop was done in black with a similar interior to the sedan. It featured 18-inch wheels all around, BF Goodrich G-force T/A tires, appropriate badging and a 140-mph speedometer. Mechanically, the beef-up process was similar to that which will be coming from the production Marauder sedan.

As of the time this was written, no word on convertible production has been made. Mercury was going through two life-changing experiences at the time, looking for a new image and adhering to the cost cutting ax due to Ford Motor Company's financial crisis.

After competitor Oldsmobile bit the dust, rumors abounded that Mercury was soon to follow. There has been lots of drum beating for the brand lately and Ford management insists that Mercury will be a survivor.

If the old hot rodders have any say, the Marauders (sedan AND convertible) will be part of that future.

Virgil Exner

DaimlerChrysler

Of all the domestic automobile manufacturers in the post World War II period, none have had the ups and downs of Chrysler Corporation.

It started the postwar period in second place in new vehicle sales, ahead of Ford Motor Company. It then went on a course of dizzying highs and abysmal lows that continues into the 21st century. Rather than chart them all, next time you look at or ride on a roller coaster, you'll get a pretty good idea.

For a company that under Walter P. Chrysler claimed to pride itself on engineering, it got into and out of its problems based on extremes of styling.

The dream/show/concept cars that are central to this book also had a range of styling, bounced around between outstanding and best forgotten.

Before World War II, Chrysler, still feeling the sting of the too-advanced Airflows, came up with a couple of right-on glimpses of the future, the Thunderbolt and Newport Parade Car.

After the war, perhaps encouraged by Harley Earl's fascination with dream cars, a series of dream cars were made, some in the U.S. and many by Ghia of Turin, Italy. Said to be inspired by styling head Virgil Exner, they showed up under the Plymouth, Dodge, DeSoto, and Chrysler banners.

Probably most folks remember Exner for his fascination with fins and some of the mid- and late-1950s' creations were so endowed.

As a point of clarification here, some years Chrysler Corporation displayed its dream cars under the Chrysler Corporation banner with no individual makes getting their own. They are listed under Chrysler here, as separating corporate and non-corporate Chryslers would only add to the confusion.

Exner's fascination turned more off-beat, as far as the public was concerned and perhaps the 1960 Plymouth XNR roadster, with asymmetrical styling, was an example.

Chrysler tired of Exner looking for a new theme and dismissed him, bringing in Elwood Engel from Ford, who brought the Thunderbird look with him.

From 1954 through 1981, Chrysler was involved in the gas turbine program and it started and finished with installation in production cars. However, a series of special turbine cars, designed by Engel and looking like T-Birds, was loaned to the public and tested. This added a new facet to the dream car history.

As its competitors shifted to production based show cars in the 1960s and '70s, Chrysler did too, but it turned out some pretty wild stuff, helped by outside customizers.

Like its competitors, Chrysler did mini cars and trucks as concepts, and when it was in one of its financial downtimes in the 1980s, it didn't do much at all.

Little American Motors was absorbed in 1987 and Jeep concepts were added to the Chrysler concept mix.

Perhaps the turning point (for the better this time) came when the 1989 Dodge Viper RT/10 concept was shown. An unabashed high performance sports car, it turned the spotlight on the pentastar. While others were doing 80 mpg safety cars, the Viper flew in the face on the notion that the future would be bleached dry of any fun.

Production status, no less significant than the 1953 Motorama Corvette, was announced for the Viper and the way was paved for a 1990s run of concept cars that easily led the industry in style, fun, interest, and speculation as to production.

The Plymouth Prowler, a (kind of) hot rod, went from concept to production, as did the Viper GTS coupe and Chrysler Cruiser.

Suddenly motorheads noticed that there were a bunch of car-loving guys running Chrysler, including designer Tom Gale and now legendary (and General Motors wizard) Robert Lutz.

Car enthusiasts weren't the only ones who took notice of Chrysler, as German luxury car and truck giant Diamler-Benz worked out a "merger of equals," ending the independence of Chrysler Corporation in 1998.

Early stages of the merger were not to the liking of the Chrysler leadership and departures of many, including Lutz and Gale, followed.

Plymouth was axed, concept cars took new directions, and the jury is still out regarding how much of a player Chrysler Group (as the U.S. operation is now called) will be. The Chrysler Crossfire has been approved for production, but it will take place at Karmann in Germany.

Hopefully the 2001 Dodge Super8 HEMI is not an indication, styling wise anyway.

In the sections that follow, as many Plymouth, Dodge, DeSoto, and Chrysler vehicles as possible are covered. Jeep, which came under Chrysler control in 1987, is covered in its entirety, going back to Willys, Kaiser, and American Motors ownership.

Thomas C. Gale

219

1941 Thunderbolt

The futuristic Thunderbolt shows where Chrysler might have headed, if not interrupted by World War II. Covered headlights and one-piece retractable hardtop roof were just two of the Thunderbolt's radical ideas.

Five Thunderbolts were built, each painted in a different color. The first were shown in 1940, as a 1941 model, and traveled along with the production Chrysler to the various auto exhibits. Notice the curved one-piece windshield, and grilleless front end. Fresh air was directed to the engine from openings under the bumper.

Hideaway headlight doors automatically lowered, when lights were turned on. Push buttons operated the doors, windows and trunk, along with the retractable roof.

Designer Ralph Roberts, shown with a scale model of the Thunderbolt.

1941 Newport Parade Car

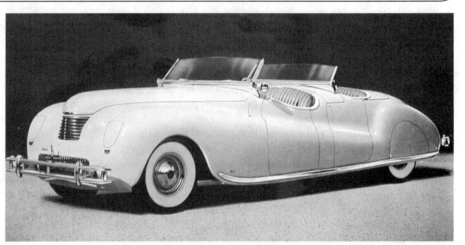

The significance of the Newport Parade Car in Chrysler and dream-car history cannot be underplayed. The four-door, dual-cowl roadster was designed and built by LeBaron and mounted on a 145-inch wheelbase Imperial chassis. The top folded out of sight when not in use. A straight flathead eight was used for power.

Smartly styled well ahead of the production cars, the Newport didn't raise resistance like the 1930s Airflows.

Like its stable mate the Thunderbolt, it had hidden headlights, but unlike it there were twin grilles.

The Newport held the distinction of being the only non-production car to pace the Indianapolis 500.

That continued until 1991 when the Dodge Viper pre-production concept was drafted to pace the 500.

Actually, there was a production, of sorts, for the Newport as six were constructed. They were assigned auto show and dealer display duties and proved a pleasant distraction in the unpleasant months leading up to America's involvement in World War II.

Chrysler

1951 K-310

Chrysler billed the K-310 not as a vehicle of the future, but the first practical dream car that explored innovative and workable design elements.

Based on a production chassis, with components from the Crown Imperial, the five-passenger K-310 was powered by a 310 horsepower FirePower hemispherical V-8. This was 130 more horses then a production engine.

It was also noted that this high performance engine performed on modern gasoline without supercharging.

Exterior and interior were color-keyed in lustrous blue, and debuting on this model were Virgil Exner's famous freestanding taillights suspended in chrome rings.

This element was used on several more of Virgil's dream cars and then on the production 1955-56 Imperial. The tire outline on the trunk lid was a styling cue that ended up on models like the 1957 Imperial and 1960 Valiant.

1952 C-200

The beautiful C-200, an Italian-built Chrysler dream car, arrived in New York City aboard the luxury liner *S.S. Constitution* early March of 1952. It was then displayed at the Parade of Stars Automobile Show in the Waldorf-Astoria Hotel.

Though the body was built and assembled by Ghia, Chrysler styling department did all the drawings, scale models, plus the trim and color details. Chrysler officials explained that the C-200 was a further example of how they were blending sports car styling with practical design and engineering features that would measure up to American drivers' demands.

Standing less than five feet tall, the C-200 had a long hood, short rear deck, and fully exposed wheel openings that were filled with true 17-inch diameter wire wheels. It was also pointed out that the dash had a leather-covered foam-rubber safety cushion. The freestanding taillights, like on the 1951 K-310, adorned the rear fenders of the C-200.

This model had direct influence on the 1998 Chrysler Chronos concept car.

Chrysler

1952 Parade Phaeton

Chrysler, not Ghia, built three dual-cowl phaetons on a slightly stretched Crown Imperial chassis.

Powering it was the FirePower engine. The car also had full-time power steering, Oriflow shock absorbers and Fluid-Torque Drive. The overall length of each of these special cars was over 20 feet.

The second cowl was the base for the rear-seat windshield. A tonneau top was concealed. The car's design was updated in 1955, reflecting the styling cues of the then current Imperial models.

Original seating was covered in pigskin, but later reupholstered cowhide leather.

1953 Special Sports Coupe

Designed in America and handcrafted by Ghia in Turin, Italy, the Special made its debut in Paris, where the French press labeled it the "sensation of the show." Only 55 inches high, the body featured the low sweeping lines found on that era's European sports cars.

The front had an integral grille and bumper unit, with vertical hydraulic bumpers that were set into the front and rear fenders.

Two-toning, which carried a dark color along the lower 10 inches of the body, gave the car an even lower-looking stance. Americans got to see the Special in the flesh on January 11, 1953, in the Chrysler Building in New York City.

Initially called the Thomas Special, it had a spare tire access door in the lower rear deck that opened to allow the spare wheel to roll out. This two-door hardtop was built for the President of Chrysler export division, C.B. Thomas , which explains the name. Built on a modified Chrysler chassis, the car had 17-inch wire wheels for better cooling of the disc brakes.

Traveling along with the Thomas Special to the various auto shows were several other unique Chrysler show cars. One in particular was the Coronation Imperial finished in royal purple with a white-crackle roof and gold plated trim.

1953
D' Elegance

The D'Elegance appears to be a fastback update of the 1951 K-310, featuring a grid-type grille, recessed headlights and free standing taillights.

Chrysler publicized these unique features as an example of how high-fashion styling and functional automobile design could beautifully blend. A further example was the design of the spare tire holder.

An electro-hydraulic mechanism raised the simulated rear deck wheel cover brought the tire out and down to bumper level for easy removal.

Not appreciated in black and white photos are the black and yellow leather seats and interior panels. Stored behind the seats in a rear compartment were four leather suitcases that matched the two-tone interior.

The 1955 Imperial owes much to the K-310, as did the 1956-74 Volkswagen Karmann Ghia coupe.

1954 La Comtesse

For 1954, a pair of production-based show cars highlighted the Chrysler brand's offerings to the public. A pair of Custom Imperial Newport two-door hardtops, the La Comtesse and La Comte, featured full-length plexiglass roof panels, continental rear tire mount, spoke wheels, and special trim.

The La Comtesse, shown here, was done in pink and white and was aimed at the feminine customer. For macho guys (a term of the future), the La Comte was done up in bronze and black.

Like the production cars, a 235-hp FirePower V-8 and PowerFlite automatic provided the motivation.

Since the 1954 models were the last using this body, new Chryslers would have to be readied for 1955, and indeed they were new.

Chrysler

1955 Flight Sweep Series

Two dream cars, the Flight Sweep I, a convertible, and the Flight Sweep II, a hardtop, were both predictors of the 1957 Chrysler models.

Breaking new ground, the "Forward Look" Flight Sweep siblings offered smooth, clean body lines, unmarred by seams and joints. This was accomplished by making the front fenders, cowl, and body all welded to the frame.

Both were four-passenger sports models, with front buckets and rear bench seat. Notice the return of the tire outline on the trunk lid, first shown on the 1951 K-310 and later featured on various Chrysler production cars.

Flight Sweep I

1955 Flight Sweep Series

Each Flight Sweep model featured two-tone paint treatments, which were emphasized by the downward thrust of the side chrome moldings and the upswept rear fenders.

Flight Sweep I was finished in vapor white with the lower half painted solar bronze. Flight Sweep II was airfoil green below jet-black. Extremely hooded headlights elongated the overall forward sloping stance, as did the shapely angled windshield.

Breaking away from the wire wheels on previous idea cars, these dream machines had full wheel covers designed to simulate exposed brake drum and cooling blades.

Flight Sweep II

Chrysler

1955 Falcon

Five model years before Ford released its first Falcon compact car, Chrysler used the title for a two-seat dream sports car.

This stylish roadster, painted in gauntlet black, used upward sweeping rear fins, and a windshield that sloped rearward, adding to the racy appearance.

Falcon featured special wire wheels with simulated knock-off hubs, but other wheel designs were shown at times. Like the 1989 Viper concept car, it used an externally mounted dual exhaust system.

The interior, including the bucket seats, was upholstered in red and ivory leather upholstery. Between those buckets was a floor mounted transmission lever connected to the fully automatic PowerFlite transmission.

This could have been a sensational reply to the GM Corvette and Ford Thunderbird, but Chrysler corporate management saw it only as a design exercise.

1955 New Yorker Coupe Special ST

Sporting many of the design elements from the production 1955 Chrysler model, this sleek two-door coupe was built by Ghia in Italy as a styling study.

Stock 13" tall taillights, peaked chrome headlight bezels, and floating bumpers are recognizable, but the grille is one of a kind.

1956 Norseman

To see the actual Chrysler Norseman, you would have to travel 200 feet under the Atlantic Ocean, off the coast of North Carolina. That's where this sleek, aerodynamic dream car, along with the SS Andrea Doria, settled when it went down in July 1956.

The Italian coach builder Ghia constructed this Virgil Exner design, using aluminum for much of the car's body panels. The cantilevered roof rested on thin grooved plastic for the wraparound front windows. The plastic replaced normal medal window posts.

The rear window was power operated, which enabled it to slide upward under the roof, for open skies above the rear seat.

Door handles were part of the upper fin, while the raised mid-body molding ran across the rear fender fuel filler door.

1956 Plainsman

One of the 1956 Chrysler corporate dream cars was the Plainsman station wagon. The eight-passenger wagon was mounted on a 115-inch wheelbase Plymouth chassis, but despite reports of the day, was not branded a Plymouth. The two-door wagon with significant styling advances was likely an answer to the 1954 Chevrolet Nomad dream car, also a two-door. The Plainsman provided several design advances and could have passed for a relative of the Packard Predictor.

Its third seat faced the rear, which would become a production setup for Chrysler products starting in 1957. Electric motors raised and lowered it. Steps for access popped out of the rear bumper when the tailgate was lowered.

The spare tire and wheel were hidden behind the right, rear wheel and was accessed by a lift-up panel, again like the 1957s would have.

The dream car had built-in jacks. Two-thirds of the palomino beige wagon's roof was covered by weather resistant white fabric. Inside the seating was accented with calf hide. A panel for controls extended out to the steering wheel, like the 1952-54 Mercurys.

Texas longhorn medallions continued the western theme.

The Plainsman made its public debut at the 1956 Chicago Auto Show.

No production version of the Plainsman followed, unlike the Nomad dream wagon.

Chrysler

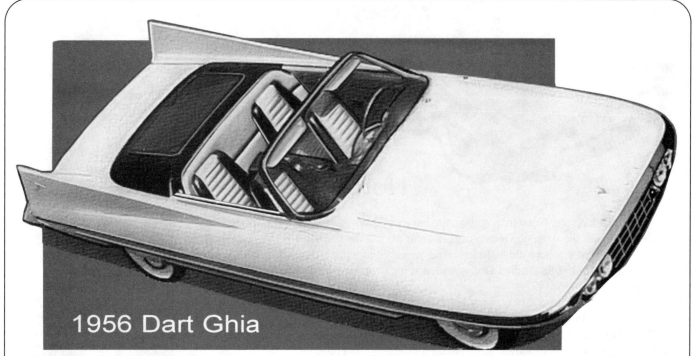

1956 Dart Ghia

This four-passenger car was Chrysler's approach to creating a super-streamlined automobile. The fluid shape was determined by mathematical analysis of the vehicle traveling through 200 mile-per-hour wind.

Large, razor thin tail fins gracefully flowed out from the rounded aluminum body, and a full-body underpan added to the wind cheating design.

The car, which was nearly 19 feet long, featured a roof that could slide back into the rear storage compartment, making the hardtop into a convertible.

Propelling the Dart was the MoPar FirePower V-8 with fuel injection that developed an incredible 400 horsepower. The body structure was welded to the experimental chassis, which featured a torsion bar front suspension.

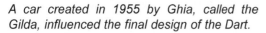

A car created in 1955 by Ghia, called the Gilda, influenced the final design of the Dart.

1957 Special K-300

Ghia created the K-300 on a modified Chrysler chassis, and powered it with a 331-cubic inch, 300 horsepower V-8 engine.

The interior was furnished with short-wave radiotelephone, mini-bar, refrigerator, and trimmed in leather and gold-plated trim.

More than just a concept car, the K-300 went to the Shah of Persia.

Chrysler

1958 Imperial D'Elegence

Chrysler reused the D'Elegence name from its 1953 dream car on this curvacious four-door hardtop.

Painted metallic blue, the 1958 D'Elegence foretold design elements that would appear on future Imperials. Features included hidden headlights, but there was no powertrain.

1961 TurboFlite

Chrysler Corporation showcased its gas turbine engine development in production cars, while rival General Motors did the same in radically designed Firebird dream cars. With the 1961 TurboFlite, things changed.

Mounted on a Plymouth 118-inch wheelbase chassis with a body built by Ghia, the TurboFlite was home to the 140-horsepower CR-2-A turbine, but likely few people noticed. The roof rose for access to the inside, the grille took the center of the front end and left the leading edge of the front wheels exposed. In the back was a wing/air-brake that rivaled the 1969 Dodge Charger Daytona and 1970 Plymouth SuperBird. More specially constructed turbine-powered cars were just around the corner for Chrysler.

"Streamlining is the greatest variable in automobile design." W.H. Korff, aerodynamic engineer, 1963

Chrysler

1963 Turbine

When Chrysler lured designer Elwood Engel away from Ford in 1961, his first design was the 1963 Chrysler Turbine - or "Englebird."

Built to test reaction to his design and the effectiveness of a gas turbine engine, only 50 of the 1963 Chrysler Turbines were manufactured. A total of 200 motorists from 48 states actually drove the car for short periods of time. Those participants were selected from a list of over 30,000 applicants submitted to Chrysler .

The body was hand-crafted by Ghia of Italy as a four-passenger two-door hardtop, painted in a metallic bronze color with a black vinyl top. Cleverly designed headlight/taillight bezels were styled with a rotary-blade motif to emphasized the unconventional power source.

Inside the car, an aluminum tubular console extended from the front to rear between the copper-colored leather bucket seats. A twin-regenerator gas turbine engine, that developed 130 horsepower, was the heart of this limited-edition concept vehicle.

The turbine had only a fifth of the moving parts of a piston engine, making it run smoother, quieter and more vibration-free. There was no radiator, since no anti-freeze was needed, as the engine was self-cooled.

There were no pistons, no valve gear, and just a single spark plug for igniting the fuel in the combustion chamber.

This turbine could operate on various fuels, which included white gas, diesel oil, kerosene, JP-4 jet fuel, or any mixture of them. Also, the exhaust ran cooler and cleaner. The turbine engine was about 200 pounds less than the traditional engine.

1966 300X

The 300X was a Chrysler research car, with emphasis on advance ideas in interior environment and driver controls. Based on a modified 1966 Chrysler 300, it was constructed by renowned custom car builder Gene Winfield.

A front passenger seat, which rotated to face the rear, was unique, as was the absence of a normal steering wheel. In its place were adjustable handgrips, allowing the driver, with a light hand twist action, to steer the car. Designed into the steering unit were push-button controls for lights, wipers, door locks, and turn signals. Since exterior door handles were gone, a key-punch card was inserted in a vertical slot that would pop open the doors. That card also started the ignition.

Treadle-operated brake and accelerator were adjustable to suit requirements of the driver. All seats had adjustable rubber diaphragm suspensions, replacing conventional seat springs.

Scanning the road behind, a truck-lid mounted TV camera replaced the old-fashion mirrors. On the dash panel, a television screen informed the driver on traffic conditions to the rear.

Among the unusual convenience items were the push button emptying of ashtrays by vacuum action and an audible clock which gave the time by tape-recorded voice.

The AM/FM radio used punch cards to pick-up a range of stations, and the rear seat passengers could watch television on a small set, which was stowed away when not in use.

1969
Concept 70X

Concept 70X, a fiberglass-bodied dream car, was created by Chrysler's advanced styling group to showcase many new safety ideas. Notable features included doors that would open and slide parallel to the car, replacing the conventional swing-out version. These doors used parallelogram hinges, allowing the doors to open a mere 15 inches from the side of the car - great for tight parking spots.

The center console doubled as a rear-facing child's seat, and the headrests were a see-through mesh. Even the rearview mirror was different, as it had a red light that would warn the driver of danger from following traffic.

As strictly a design study, the passenger side had a single door, but the car had double doors on the driver's side. The right side's door was 71 inches long, giving easy access to the rear seat without folding down the front seat.

Note that in the photo below, the car's various controls were housed directly behind the steering wheel, closer to the driver.

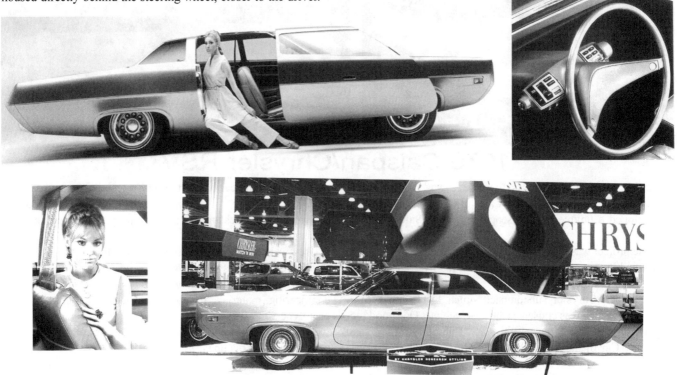

Chrysler

1970 Cordoba de Oro

Elwood Engel headed the design department that created the four-passenger Cordoba de Oro. Masterfully utilizing a smooth yet sharp-edge fuselage shape, the luxury hardtop featured pillarless monocoque design.

Four rectangular openings at the front of the car contained experimental headlights and thermostatically controlled air intakes for the engine.

Cordoba de Oro was equipped with several special instruments, one that showed the condition of the road surface being traveled, a monitoring system that detected vehicle malfunctions, and a sequence-locking mechanism for the doors and ignition.

Four specially constructed seats, anatomically crafted to fit body contours, were included. Not seen in the above photo is the brake spoiler over the back window that raised, like an airplane flap, when the brakes were applied.

1976 Calspan/Chrysler RSV

In cooperation with the National Highway Traffic Safety Administration (NHTSA), and Calspan Corporation, Chrysler developed a unique five-passenger Research Safety Vehicle (RSV).

The project was part of a program to help develop practical, producible, energy efficient, and safe family transportation for the mid-1980s.

A French Chrysler subcompact Simca 1308 with a four-cylinder engine was chosen as the base vehicle. One good reason was that the Simca 1308 was "Car of the Year" and "Safety Car of the Year" for Europe in 1976. The body was modified and the car was fitted with special advanced safety features. Up front, the reconstructed body was designed to offer front and back impact protection up to 50 mph and 45 mph for side collisions.

Tires were the new "run flat" design. Inside the car, and inflatable restraint system was featured, along with energy-absorbing interior trim panels. Chrysler provided design, engineering, materials, cost analysis, and construction of the prototype vehicles.

Calspan ran tests of the various components and aided in the development of occupant protection.

1977 LeBaron Turbine

A different look was achieved for Chrysler's new LeBaron coupe to attract attention to the gas turbine power plant that was still being developed, thanks to help from the U.S. Department of Transportation. However, the program was nearing an end.

A chiseled, sloping front end with upright center section, done in soft polyurethane, provided a home for hidden headlights and adequate cooling for the turbine.

Other body modifications included a T-bar roof, formal rear-quarter windows, and special trim.

The 1977 LeBaron Turbine would be the last Chrysler turbine show vehicle with special bodywork.

1982 Stealth 2+2

The front-wheel-drive Stealth 2+2 was based on a Plymouth TC3 L-body platform.

This steel-bodied concept included flush window glass and retractable headlights. The side windows did not roll down, but pushed out. Popular Recaro leather bucket seats up front, a rear jump seat, and super sound system filled the interior.

When first shown, it had a 1.7-liter turbocharged VW engine. Later it was upgraded to the 2.2-liter 4-cylinder, which was also turbocharged and connected to a 5-speed manual transmission.

Dodge used the Stealth name for its 1991-1996 stylish sports car.

1985 Stealth

During the 1985 season, the Stealth was modified, and used to demonstrate a scale model of a U.S. NAVSTAR satellite which promised to provide future drivers a space-age navigation system.

Chrysler

1983 LeBaron Turbo Convertible

Long before DaimlerChrysler existed, Mercedes-Benz had an influence on mid-1980s MoPar designs.

For 1982, Chrysler introduced a 2.2-liter turbocharged, five-speed manual tranny concept convertible that was a clone of the Mercedes 380SL.

The 90-inch wheelbase prototype featured bumpers and side treatment that would ended up on the 1988 LeBaron production models.

1984 Concept Wagon

Nearly 20 years before the 2002 Chrysler Pacifica lit up the auto shows, this aerodynamic Chrysler concept wagon, minus any fancy name, appeared at select gatherings.

Crossover wagons were unheard of then, but this one featured impressive interior room and styling.

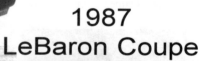

1987 LeBaron Coupe

For the 1987 auto-show circuit, Chrysler tricked up a production LeBaron coupe.

Stylists added lower front fascia, front air dam, a rear spoiler, driving lights, side body skirts, and a rear spoiler.

Monochromatic cars were popular during this period, so the body, bumpers, and special wheels were all the same shade of ruby red pearl paint. The interior featured two-tone leather with wide diagonal burgundy seat pads.

1987 Portofino

Portofino was the first MoPar concept to feature the new cab-forward body design. This advanced aerodynamic shape was the basis behind the styling success of future Chrysler automobiles.

Powered by Lamborghini's 3,485 CC V-8, this mid-engine touring sedan had true sports car performance and handling. The engine was all-alloy construction, used chain driven dual overhead camshafts, and delivered 225 horsepower. The transmission was Lambo's 5-speed manual.

Scissors-style doors did not translate to the production cars, but added an exotic element to the concept. These four rotational doors pivoted up and out of the way to allow for ease of interior entry/exit. Traditional center pillars were eliminated by the special unibody design.

Driver's cockpit resembled an airplane with high-tech features. For example, the cockpit had a fully adjustable instrument pad, steering wheel, and headlight/windshield wiper-switch gear.

Feature for feature, the 1993 Dodge Intrepid most resembled the Portofino concept.

Chrysler

1989 LeBaron PPG

Doing double duty was what the CART PPG Indy Car World Series pace car program was all about. It was meant to showcase the products of the domestic auto industry, which was a major customer for series sponsor PPG Industries, which supplied paint and glass.

The cars then were displayed at auto shows, helping PPG, and at race tracks, to the benefit of the manufacturers.

This highly modified LeBaron PPG open pace car was Chrysler's entrant for 1989. Redone with new grille and minimal headlights, modified doors and a roll bar/airfoil, the LeBaron was at home on the turntable and at speed on the race track.

1989 Millennium

Showcasing Safety

Millennium showcased Chrysler's styling cues coming on the 1993 cab forward LH sedans. It also was an idea car filled with the latest technology in safety.

Enter the car and your personal ID number automatically adjusted the pedals, steering, driver's seat, and rearview mirror to preprogrammed settings.

Starting the car was voice-activated, and head-up display projected a complete self-diagnostic check of the vehicle.

Voice command also activated the car's head-up display satellite navigation system. The forward-looking radar system, when in effect, detected poor visibility. It also told when something either slowed or stopped up ahead and suggested a safe speed.

Rear proximity radar warned of possible dangers and impending accidents to the rear of the vehicle.

Millennium also was equipped with rain-sensitive wipers and a heated windshield.

Chrysler

1991 300

The 1991 300 sport sedan concept car traced its lineage back to the Chrysler 300 luxury performance series of the 1950s and '60s.

Built on a 126-inch wheelbase, with Viper under carriage, the rear-wheel drive four-door sedan was equipped with a "Copperhead" 8-liter V-10 engine mated to a four-speed automatic transmission.

Functional rear-hinged doors, as well as the no fixed B-pillars, allowed for easy interior entry/exit. As a safety feature, the front doors had to be opened before the rear doors would open.

The curvaceous rear end featured an active aero spoiler. Front tires were 19-inch with even larger 20-inch tires for the rear. A dark silver exterior color complimented the black and tan interior, with wood trim highlights.

Special features included air conditioning vents in the driver's seat, a combination video cassette recorder/TV, a contoured steering wheel, cellular phone, and separate headphones for rear-seat passengers.

1992 Thunderbolt

Chrysler Thunderbolt was seen as a possible flagship for the corporation, borrowing the full-fender look of the 1941 Thunderbolt concept vehicle. The car's striking proportions incorporated the cab-forward architecture with wheels placed at the corners of the vehicle. This allowed greater space for the car occupants, as well as providing extremely stable handling.

As a rear-wheel luxury coupe, Thunderbolt used the Chrysler-designed 4-liter 32-valve aluminum DOHC modular V-8 that was mated to a 4-speed electronic transmission.

The new engine boasted a healthy 270 horsepower and the car came equipped with four-wheel disc anti-lock brakes, all-wheel independent suspension and traction control. Front wheel size was 19-inches, with 20-inch rear wheels.

Thunderbolt's interior featured room for four, with a front passenger side combination navigation system and entertainment center, which included video and computer capabilities.

Chrysler

1992 Cirrus

The Cirrus was shown to the public as a preview to the cab forward design, which would evolve into the 1995 JA-body Cirrus production car. Size-wise, concept Cirrus was smaller then the coming mid-size Dodges and Eagles. B-pillars were absent, and rear doors were hinged at the back, allowing very easy access to four-seat interior. Thin lighting strips replaced conventional headlights.

Power came from an alcohol-burning two-stroke turbocharged 3.0-liter, V-6 engine that could have met California's tough low-emissions standards for 1996. Even though it was a clean burning powerplant, it was able to put out 400 horsepower. Underhood package volume was approximately one-half that of an equally powered four-stroke engine, with corresponding weight and complexity reductions.

Cirrus, with its exaggerated cab-forward styling and highly sculpted exterior, showed just how far Chrysler designers reached for exciting new levels.

1995 Atlantic

During the mid-1990s, MoPar designers were exploring modern cab-forward look, but with the Atlantic, they went retro, resembling the classic 1930s Bugatti Atlantique.

It featured a 4.0-liter straight-eight engine with dual overhead cams and 32 valves; this mockup engine was made from two Neon fours and was reported to generate 325 horses. It was connected to the front-drive four-speed automatic transaxle.

Size-wise, Atlantic was over half a foot shorter than the 1995 LHS, but used a 13-inch longer wheelbase to achieve the near perfect proportions.

Adding to the powerful expression of the Atlantic were the enormous 21-inch front and 22-inch rear wheels mounted with Goodyear tires.

Chrysler

1996 LHX

For 1996, Chrysler's show focus was to provide sneak previews of the next generation LH production sedans. Carrying out the task were the Chrysler LHX and Dodge Intrepid ESX.

Perhaps more was promised than delivered as the concepts had a 124-inch wheelbase compared to 113 on the real thing. Styling was kind of squashed compared to the current LH cars of 1996, but the production all-new 1998 models were more aerodynamic than their predecessors.

An egg-crate grille and a 19/20 inch wheel combination did give a concept look to the LHX. Power came from Chrysler's 3.5 liter V-6, still mounted north-south like the first generation.

1997 Phaeton Dual-cowl

Inspired by Chrysler's dual cowl 1941 Newport parade car, the 1997 Phaeton version embraced and contemporized the famous original.

Beautiful two-tone champagne pearl paint brought out the flowing lines and richness of the hand-crafted body. The four-door all-steel body Phaeton had a retractable roof that folded and stored in the trunk area. There was also a retractable rear compartment windshield. Cream and brown-colored leather trim, woven cream leather inserts, satin metal details, and Zebrano wood gave a richness to the interior.

Both front and rear passenger compartments were separate and had their own radio, climate controls, and luxurious seats.

Speedometer and tachometer gauges were also featured in both compartments, which allowed rear passengers to monitor vehicle performance.

Phaeton's imposing size was supported by impressive performance. Its 132-inch wheelbase and 22-inch wheels were powered by a 48-valve 5.4 liter aluminum V-12 engine.

Chrysler

1998 Chronos

Reaching a new level in contemporizing a classic form, the beautiful Chronos was a large concept automobile with an overall length of 205 inches.

Notice from the side view how the front wheels were moved forward, the rear wheels back, and the cabin placed rearward, which gave the car similar proportions to many of Virgil-Exner 1950s creations.

In fact, Jack Crain, head of Chrysler Design Studio C, stated, "This car really owes its inspiration to Exner's 1953 Chrysler D'Elegance dream car."

Inside, luxury features included custom wood trim, a hand-sewn center console housing an in-place humidor with storage and lighter, plus a steering wheel hand wrapped in leather.

Under the long, tapered hood was a 6.0-liter, V-10 engine producing 350 horsepower.

1999 Pacifica

"Our Pacifica concept minivan was inspired by the luxury and convenience offered in executive jet travel," said Neil Walling, DaimlerChrysler's V.P of design. "We wanted to bring the benefits of executive jet travel down to earth, into the minivan and on to the road."

The most notable feature was the raised roof that provided space for interior overhead storage bins, and a separate passenger-side exterior storage compartment for large things like snow or water skis. Built into the rear of the cabin was a special golf bag rack system that allowed storage for up to four sets of golf clubs. In the rear seating were fully-reclining, adjustable power leather seats with power foot rests, like those on first-class airlines. It also featured airline-inspired overhead storage bins, overhead lighting, and drop-down video screen. Two sky lights ran the length of the roof.

Pacifica was painted light pewter pearl coat, and featured the winged medallion inside the egg-crate grille with chrome edging similar to the 1999 LHS. Front lighting came from the compact projector beam head lights and fog lamps were housed in the lower fascia.

The Pacifica concept was also a preview of the coming new 2001 MoPar van.

In 1999, Chrysler celebrated its 75th anniversary and marked the 15th anniversary of the Chrysler minivan.

1999 Pronto Cruiser: See Color Section

PT & GT Cruiser Series
(PT stands for Personal Transportation)

2000 Cruiser GT

PT Cruiser concept vehicles have been coming on a regular basis since Chrysler's popular retro car/truck went on the market for 2000. Early in the chain was the Cruiser GT, which featured a turbocharged 2.4-liter four-cylinder engine, rated at 200 horsepower. With complaints as to the output of the Neon-based engine, this setup had market potential and would lead to a production version.

Not all the tricks were under the hood. A revised front fascia and two-inch wider tread gave the GT a more aggressive look.

2000 Panel Cruiser

Of the first three PT Cruiser concepts shown here, the Panel Cruiser is the only one not committed to production, at least at the time of this writing. Recalling the hot rod days of sedan delivery and the departed panel truck, the Cruiser Panel was an open invitation to customizing and classy light hauling chores.

Apparently cries of "build-it" from auto-show goers and the possibility of only limited-production demand have kept it off the new vehicle market.

2001 PT Convertible Cruiser

If there was doubt as to whether the PT Cruiser was a car or a truck (federal government agencies disagree), a vote for the car label was made quite loudly by the convertible version.

Shown as a 2001 concept, the two-door had a roll bar and an elevated rear seat.

It was painted deep shadow blue pearl, with a dark taupe and light pearl beige interior. The 19-inch wheels aided its exit from truck duties or designation.

As of this writing, all signs are go for a production version of the convertible to be in the pipeline.

"The distinct personality of the Chrysler PT Cruiser is unmatched by any vehicle on the road," Tom Gale

Chrysler

Described as a true hybrid breed of crossover vehicle, the Citadel blended cargo room with a futuristic powertrain.

A 3.5-liter gasoline engine with 253 horsepower drove the rear wheels and electric motors power the front ones.

Art deco-influenced interior featured black jade leather, brushed aluminum, and dark wood accents.

The gauge indicators were 3D.

2000 300 Hemi C

In a thoroughly modern way, the 2000 Chrysler 300 Hemi C design paid homage to the legendary 1957 300-C. Beautiful proportions, a monocoque profile with pronounced wheel flares, and a seemingly endless hood were some of the convertible's characteristics.

The concept's rear-wheel drive set-up allowed for a minimal front overhang, while the front fender air exhaust ports and the centrally placed chrome twin exhaust pipes hinted at what was the heart of the car - the V-8 Hemi engine.

Though only a prototype, the all-aluminum 353-cubic-inch (5.7 liter) pushrod engine featured hemispherical combustion chambers and two spark plugs per cylinder. This engine delivered 353 horsepower and 353 lb.-ft of torque to the rear wheels. Completing the powertrain was a robust four-speed automatic transmission. Reflecting its Hemi heritage, the 2000 300 Hemi C could sprint to 60 miles per hour in 5.9 seconds and clock a top speed of 160 mph.

The body was finished with a custom paint job of frosted mocha pearlcoat, and the concept rolled on Goodyear tires, 19-inch front wheels and 20-inch rear wheels.

An understated monochromatic taupe-based color interior featured a wedge California walnut molding that linked the instrument panel to the hard-cover tonneau.

2001 Crossfire

The Crossfire harkens back to Virgil Exner's 1953 D'Elegance fastback concept car, with long hood, full circle wheel wells, and an elegant grille.

Unlike the cars of the 1950s, the Crossfire was built with a one-piece carbon fiber body on an all-aluminum frame. Part of the car's chiseled appearance came from the center peak line, or "spine" that ran over the hood, roof, and boat tail rear-deck panels.

The body was painted in sapphire silver pearl, and the wheels featured an eight spoke design that Chrysler stated, "reinforces the vehicle's sure-footed, grounded look."

Those are 19-inch tires up front and 21 inchers on the rear. Powered by a supercharged 2.7 liter, 275 horsepower V-6 engine, coupled to a five-speed manual, it was estimated to achieve a top speed of 148 mph (238 kph).

2002 Pacifica

DaimlerChrysler clearly intended the 2002 Pacifica concept car to be a preview of an upcoming production model. It needed a crossover wagon in its lineup, especially with minivan sales starting to soften.

First shown to the public at the 2002 North American international Auto Show in Detroit, it employed now traditional Chrysler themes and non-controversial styling. Built on a 116.3-inch wheelbase, its overall length was 198.8 inches. Power was Chrysler's OHC 3.5 liter V-6. No lightweight, it tipped the scales at nearly 4,500 pounds.

Public reaction was favorable, but the decision to produce the Pacifica (named after DaimlerChrysler's California design studio) was made before the car went on display. It is slated to become a 2004 production model.

1954 Adventurer

Billed as a forward-looking concept, the smoothly-contoured Adventurer was a four-passenger sports coupe, designed and built in Detroit.

A bold exposed side exhaust system, and a racing-style-fuel filler just below the wraparound rear window indicated that the Adventurer was a high-performance automobile.

Matching the car's glamorous appearance was the famous 170-horsepower Fire Dome V-8 engine. Other 1950s high-

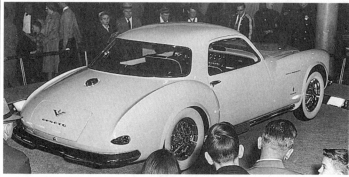

tech options included full time power steering, automatic transmission, and power brakes.

The four bucket seats were upholstered in black top-grain cowhide with white piping. Etched and burnished aluminum plate surrounded the seven dials of the recessed instrument panel.

DeSoto went on to offer a series of performance cars with the Adventurer name starting mid-year in 1956 and continuing through 1959. The Adventurer was the top of the line for 1960. Dodge used the name on trucks for many years.

1954 Adventurer II

Adventurer II was introduced to the American press June 16, 1954, during ceremonies for the new Chrysler proving ground near Chelsea, Michigan. The car was first exhibited at the Turin Auto Show.

Larger than its predecessor Adventurer, to which it bore little resemblance, this sports coupe was mounted on a standard DeSoto chassis, and used the Fire Dome V-8 with 170 horsepower. Ghia of Turin, Italy, handcrafted the body.

The front hood was extremely long, with a downward slope. The low roof flows smoothly into the rear deck with a slight notch back bump. A large rectangular grille featured a "beehive" pattern, with headlights inset deep into the front fenders. A jet-shaped after-burner cone taillight housing gave the effect of blazing jet exhausts at night. The rear window, formed of tinted plastic, could be raised and lowered electrically from the driver's bucket seat.

Black and white cowhide was used in the interior, with an etched and burnished aluminum plate that highlighted the seven dials of the recessed instrument panel.

"We are pleased to debut the Adventurer II to the press, so that we can get test reaction of Chrysler's new theories of design by professionals whose job is to interpret, as well as observe and report significant events." L.I. Woolson, DeSoto President

1959 Cella I

Cella I was DeSoto's three-dimensional prediction of future 1960s automobiles, though it was only a plaster-like 3/8-scale model. It was part of DeSoto's 30th anniversary, celebrated in 1959.

Its power source was to be based on new scientific developments. This referred to electrochemical cell, which transformed hydrogen and oxygen into silent electrical energy to drive four lightweight, high-speed motors located at the wheels.

Braking energy would be recaptured and stored in reserve batteries for future use, which would have contributed to the car's fuel savings.

A rear wall refrigeration compartment was to include beverage dispenser and pop-up storage. A swing-into-position television receiver with fingertip controls would have been offered.

A canopy-type roof would lift to provide easy entrance. Periscope rear-view mirror would have eliminated the need for a rear window. Also proposed was a telescoping instrument panel, which would provide maximum crash protection and that would give or slide forward under body impact. Vertical fins were added to the rear fenders for directional stability.

No full-sized Cella I was built, for DeSoto was in trouble. In November of 1960, the last domestic DeSoto, a 1961 model, was built.

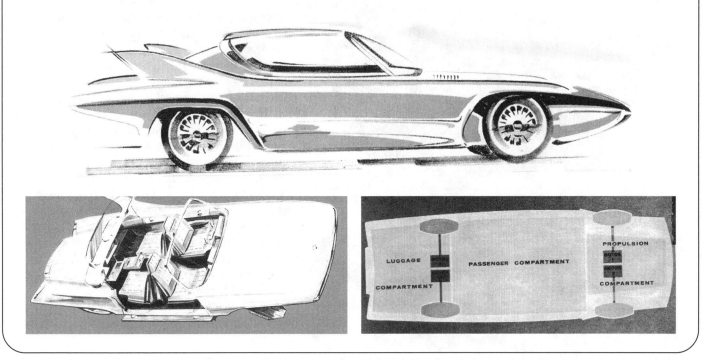

DODGE

1954 Firearrow Roadster I

The Firearrow was a bold, new approach to auto designing for Chrysler Corp. Simplicity was the key to the car's styling. Low and smooth body-lines of the two-seater was almost completely unadorned, even external door handles eliminated. Most notable body feature was the thick grayish-tan side molding that completely encircled the body and formed part of the grille. Also up front were the deeply recessed dual head-lights.

Twin chrome exhaust tailpipes were boldly mounted externally, along side the rear fender. At the rear, the sloping deck contained two hatches, one for luggage and the other for the spare tire.

Yellow-buff leather with maroon piping upholstery was used on the buckets, with matching door panels. The dash was color-matched to the metallic red exterior.

Two of these roadsters were constructed, both shown above. They differed in color, front end, and trim details.

1954 Firearrow Coupe

Continuing the design concepts embodied in the ear-lier convertible model, the two-seat coupe blended American tastes with a European accent.

Again a V-shaped side rub rail was used, but it did not flow into the larger airscoop grille like the ragtop. Two pairs of small vertical bumpers, cushioned in rub-ber, were mounted at both front and rear. Twin chrome exhaust tailpipes poked out the rear fenders, and the large wrap-around front and rear windows were emerging trends in the early 1950s.

Bucket seats were finished in pleated opal blue leather with white leather inserts. Luggage space was behind the twin seats, with parcel bins covered by chrome rollback tops. Deep blue carpeting finished the floor and luggage compartment. The gas filler cap was located inside the trunk.

Handcrafted by Ghia from Chrysler designs, the coupe was painted in metallic opal blue.

Built on standard Dodge 119-inch wheelbase, it used the 150 horsepower V-8 with PowerFlite automatic transmission.

1954 Firearrow Convertible

Another Firearrow in the form of a four passenger convertible was unveiled last minute at the 1954 Chicago Auto Show. Visual differences between this car and the hardtop were grille pattern and altered rear deck design.

Bold harlequin-patterned black and white leather filled the interior. Same as the coupe, the convertible used the 241-cubic-inch V-8, pumping out 150 horsepower along with the PowerFlite auto transmission.

Dodge

1954 Granada

Granada was described as the first car ever built on conventional chassis with one-piece, all-plastic body. Previous plastic cars were assembled from many separate parts. Even the bumpers, structural body members, and body-attaching brackets were made of fiberglass.

The upper chrome side molding was a preview of what appeared on the 1956 production model.

Built on a conventional Dodge chassis, Granada's total overall body length was 211-inches. It was powered by the 241.3-cubic-inch Red Ram V-8.

1961 Flitewing

Flitewing looked more like a styling exercise for a Chrysler 300 than a Dodge dream car. The front grille, bumper and quad headlights were similar to the 1963-64 Chrysler, and the 1960-62 compact Valiant.

A press release from 1961 informed that it cost Dodge $125,000 to construct the experimental car. Actually Flitewing was described as "a design of practical features, not a way-out dream car."

The opening and closing of the doors automatically activated the "flip-up" window-roof canopies. They could be controlled by push buttons in the left door panel.

Providing the flight in Flitewing was a muscular 330-hp, 383-cubic-inch, ram-induction V-8. The unusual speedometer used a series of 13 elliptical windows, and push-button controls placed in the full-length console and door panel replaced normal dials and knobs.

Dodge

1962 Turbo Dart

Continuing its gas turbine program for 1962, Chrysler installed the power plants in a pair of Dodge Dart and Plymouth Fury two-door hardtops. A Turbo Dart and Turbo Fury made a 3,100 mile cross-country test to publicize the advantages of the power plant.

The Turbo Dart, shown here, used diesel fuel (turbines can use many types of fuel) and averaged more than 19 miles per gallon when driven at constant speeds. The average speed for the test was 52 miles an hour.

Chrysler would continue to experiment with gas turbines, but after starting with a series of production based cars in 1954, would switch to more exotic vehicles in which to install them.

1962 Turbo Power Giant

After primarily showing off standard passenger-car versions of its gas turbine power plant, Chrysler adapted one to a medium duty Dodge truck in 1962.

The Turbo Power Giant boasted a savings of 400 pounds over a comparable piston engine, with 80 percent less moving parts. An automatic LoadFlite transmission was used. To dress up the package, a special grille and generous bright trim was added.

Later in the decade, Ford and Chevrolet introduced specially built gas turbine-powered trucks, but both were futuristic designs that bore no resemblance to the production models.

1964 Charger

Called a specialty show car, the Charger used basic Dodge panels, combined with wild custom modifications. Special Charger features included a large hood scoop, unique headrest-rollbar combo, and competition-height windshield, which deflected the air flow over the driver.

Under the hood scoop sat a 426-cubic-inch, 365 horsepower V-8, featuring a single , four-barrel carburetor. It was mentioned at the time that the drag-strip Ramcharger engine, with 425 hp and twin four-barrel carburetors, would also fit under the lower hood.

Long, rectangular exhaust ports were placed at the rear of the doors. They closed off the exhaust headers for street use, deflecting the exhaust through twin mufflers. On the drag strip, the cover plates were removed, reducing back pressure and improving engine breathing. Featured magnesium wheels were made by Halibrand, fitted with Goodyear Wingfoot high performance tires.

The charcoal-gray leather interior included a novel cockpit divider that carried the body surface through from the hood to rear deck.

"Movement is the function of an automobile. Our job is to make that movement as attractive as possible."
Elwood Engel, Vice President and Director of Styling, Chrysler Corporation (1964)

Dodge

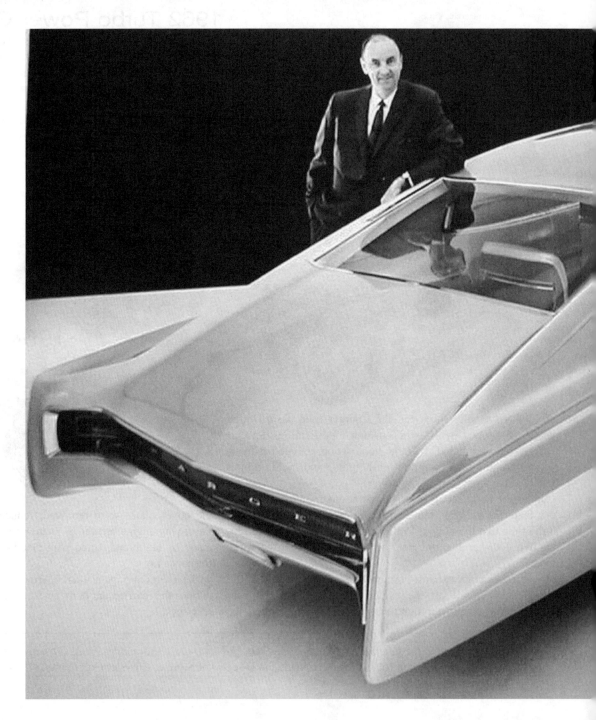

Mid-summer 1965, the Charger II "idea car" gave the public a big clue of how the upcoming 1966½ Charger would look. Painted pale silver metallic, the ultra-sleek fastback styling accentuated the 17-foot-long body, as did the extended rear fenders.

What is not visible in these photos is the thin striping along the full length of the car in colorful delta vermilion. This striping was repeated along the roofline, and also on the side walls of the tires. Up front, horizontal chrome bars filled the grille, flanked by custom rectangular headlights. At the rear was a wall-to-wall taillight. Door handles were absent and the opening mechanism was set flush with the door.

Halibrand magnesium wheels were equipped with special Goodyear high-performance tires.

At the time, Charger II was only equipped with a 318 cubic inch V-8, but the engine bay could've handled the 426 Hemi.

The interior featured a full-length console that ran from the front to the back of the rear seats.

Four bucket seats, trimmed in a pale silver vinyl, had horizontal open slots, designed for better air circulation and passenger comfort.

The large concave rear window was set behind the two rear bucket seats so there was no direct sunlight on the passengers.

Proudly standing along side of his creation on the previous page is VP of design, Elwood Engel.

1965
Charger II

251

Dodge

1967 Deora Van

It was hard to believe that this futuristic vehicle started as a Dodge A-100 van. This was an early step into the then unexplored field of the true sports-pickup.

All metal body work was handled by the famous Detroit-based Alexander Brothers, from designs by Harry Bradley. The windshield was hydraulically raised and the single front door swung open. For easier entry/exit, the steering wheel would swing out of the way. The power plant was the 170-cubic-inch Slant Six engine, located in the covered truck bed. Dodge mentioned that there was room to fit a 318 V-8.

Speedometer and tachometer were floor mounted on the drivers right and other gauges were in the sidewall panel.

1968 Charger III

Charger III went further than the 1964 and 1965 editions, and Dodge claimed it was the most aerodynamic car it ever built.

This low-slung candy apple red two-seater was only 42 inches high and included a jet-aircraft-type canopy, elevating bucket seats, swing-away steering wheel, and air brake flaps.

The spoiler-type air brake flaps were synchronized with the regular braking system.

Lower side scoops fed air to the rear brakes. At the rear, twin quick-fill gas caps and stop lights, which supplement the full-width taillight, were located under flaps.

With no rear window, a pop-up mirror was used for rear, wide-angle vision. A service hatch permitted routine checks of battery and fluids, without raising the hood.

Charger III was designed by Dodge and built by Vince Gardner of Detroit.

1968 Charger IV

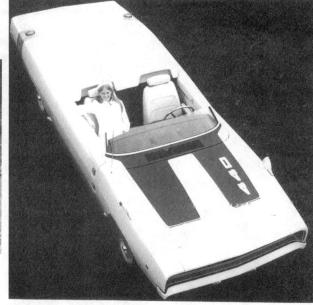

Another fun experimental creation from Elwood Engel and associates was the no name Charger R/T. Engel's crew took the stock Charger design to the extreme by chopping the top off and cutting down the windshield.

The body was painted white with blue trim, and bumpers were de-chromed and painted white. Non-glare black panels accented the hood and trunk lid. Shaved door handles and two large competition gas caps were added touches.

Custom rear deck cowls were contoured and recessed to fit the headrests on the white vinyl bucket seats.

A perforated stainless steel steering wheel and stainless exhaust pipes added bright accenting.

As the large numerals on the hood advertised, there was a 440-cubic-inch engine to power the Charger R/T. Since it had no official name, it was later known as the Charger IV.

1968 Super Bee Convertible

Dodge's Super Bee, based on the Coronet from mid-year 1968 through 1970, was always in the shadow of the more popular Plymouth Road Runner. To attract some much needed attention, this special Super Bee convertible was put on the show circuit in 1968.

Even though the Super Bee never came in ragtop form, that didn't mean it didn't make an attractive package. Notable features included a flat black accented hood (complete with a raised center/scoop), black-out grille exterior side exhaust pipes and Charger-like bucket front seats and console.

Bumble bee rear stripes let you know it was a member in good standing of the Scat Pack.

1968 Scat Packer

Occasionally in the 1960s, trucks were modified and featured as special show vehicles by the manufacturers.

For 1968, Dodge grabbed attention with its D-100 Scat Packer pickup truck. Bumble-bee stripes ran vertically on the rear fenders, and deep-dish chrome reverse wheels were custom touches.

Dodge

1968
Darool

Daroo Series

Toward the end of the 1960s, Dodge designers came up with a pair of hot-looking Dart GT-based show cars that nicely blended many contemporary custom ideas with futuristic features. Their performance-oriented styling typified the division's increasingly youthful image.

Both versions were named Daroo (dar-u), which was derived from early Anglo-Saxon meaning "dart or spear."

Shown on these two pages are various views of Daroo I and II, along with descriptive information on their individual characterizations.

1969
Daroo II

Daroo I sliced the top off a Dart GT Sport, extended the front by 17 inches, and chopped another 10 inches off the rear. Barris Kustom City did the job.

A "V" design theme started at the front and flowed rearward, encompassing the windshield and side door glass. At the rear fender line, it "kicked-up" and joined tapering windsplits, which swept from the back on the tonneau and down the rear deck.

Painted a one-of-a-type pearl honey yellow that emphasized the "Dart-in-motion" design, it was off-set by charcoal smoked tint, non-glare window glass that appeared almost black. The front grille was made up of non-reflecting brushed and satin horizontal bars, which secretly hid the headlights.

The power plant was Dodge's newest engine, the 340 CID V-8, with a single four-barrel. To compliment the 275 hp Scat Pack engine, curved, tuned, ram thrust tubes on the hood forced cold air to the carburetor for added performance. As seen in the interior photo, the transmission was a four-on-the-floor manual. A deep-dish steering wheel, and special gauges canted toward the driver, finished off the black vinyl interior.

Daroo II was created from design suggestions, supplied by Ron Perau's Imperial Kustoms of Tulsa, Oklahoma. Like Daroo I, it also had a 340-cubic-inch 275 hp V-8, but it was hooked up to an automatic transmission, with steering column gear selector.

The body was re-proportioned, with a lengthened hood and shortened rear deck, yet kept within the production Dart's 196-inch overall length. Rear springs were relocated, lowering the car's overall height by nearly 10 inches. A 15-inch wide streamlined airfoil-type molded roll bar had sail panels the length of the rear fenders and merged into a functional air spoiler that was sculptured into the rear of the body.

Painted frosted fire, a combination of arctic orange and pearlescent gold fleck, Daroo II also displayed the familiar black Scat Pack Bumble Bee racing stripe.

Running the length of the hood and rear deck lid were dual, two-inch polished aluminum channels. Honeycombed aluminum grille covers concealed rectangular headlights.

Striking silver-trimmed tufted vinyl upholstery and tangerine tone nylon carpeting were color keyed to the glowing exterior.

Dodge

1969 Custom Swinger 340

The Custom Swinger 340 indeed had a 340 cid V-8, four-on-the-floor, dual exhausts, and wide-tread tires. A unique hood scoop was actually functional, as were the chrome hood pins.

Painted a bright red, with Cibie headlights, grille-based dual driving lamps, and a rear spoiler, the vehicle was a popular Dodge attraction at the annual new car and custom vehicle shows.

1970 Super Charger

George Busti of Creative Customs built the missile-shape Super Charger from designs by Dodge stylists.

This topless two-seat roadster featured a Charger Daytona tapered nose cone, and a windshield cut down to 10-1/2 inches. All window openings were filled and door handles removed. Two sets of vacuum-operated louvers were incorporated in the hood for engine cooling.

Under that mile-long hood was a 440 cubic inch V-8 Magnum engine.

Finned aluminum exhaust pipes were located along both rocker panels, and functional fender top air scoops allowed hot air to escape for cooler brakes.

1971 Diamante

Diamante was a custom blend of a winged Dodge Charger Daytona and the stylish 1971 Challenger. The design was developed by Dodge engineers in wind tunnel studies and tested on the high-banked ovals of the NASCAR circuit.

A sculptured sloping front end added to downward air pressure and included pop-up headlights. Side intake scoops and side-mounted exhaust pipes helped the 426 cubic inch Hemi breathe better. A removable roof panel revealed the integral chrome roll bar. The rear window raised and lowered by a switch on the control console.

Some of the features on the Diamante concept were available on the production models. They included the Hemi, wide F-60 x 15 tires, heavy-duty suspension and brakes, manual four-speed tranny, and Rallye instrument cluster.

Dodge created the look, and Ron Mandrush of Synthetex, Inc. of Dearborn, Michigan was credited with the superb Diamante conversion.

1976 Charger XS-22

Dodge stylists customized a 1976 Charger SE to illustrate where they could take the design.

Special features included T-top roof with removable tinted glass panels, padded vinyl roof with stainless steel trim, and covered rear quarter windows. Large cast aluminum wheels finished the unique look.

Dodge

1978 Truck Series

Street Van

Big Red

Rawhide

Adventurer SE Classic

Termed "adult toys," Dodge displayed a quartet of special show trucks during the 1978 model year.

Street Van had striking exterior graphics, painted in red, orange, and yellow. It also used color-keyed flared wheel wells, front ground effects air dam, and deep-dish chrome wheels to complete the custom look.

Adventurer SE Classic pickup sported a custom pearlescent white color that was tastefully complimented by the maroon hood, cab, and tonneau cover. Fenders were flared and flowed into the air dam. Adding to the elegant appearance were chrome spoked wire wheels.

Big Red was a Utiline pickup that thought it was a heavy-duty semi-cab truck. It had plenty of chrome on the massive bumper and grille treatment. Chome exhaust stacks, dual air horns and deep, ribbed wheels were macho touches. In a way, it was an early experiment that might have lead Dodge in the direction of the 1994 Ram.

Rawhide, the fourth in the group, was based on the Ramcharger. It used a one-way, mirrored designer rear window, had rugged sheepskin seats, and fleece carpeting.

1979 Big Red - See Color Section

1980 Mirada Turbine

A rather ordinary-looking 1980 Mirada marked the end of the line for Chrysler's gas turbine passenger car program. Containing the seventh generation turbine, it returned to the format of the first public turbines in 1954, when they were installed in a pair of 1954 Plymouths.

Despite high hopes and extensive public interest, the turbine had a difficult time meeting present and future emission standards.

In the "energy-crisis" era, the government was more interested in high economy than high tech. Chrysler's federal subsidy for the program was cancelled and with Chrysler in financial trouble, the program could not be carried on.

1980 Mirada Magnum

A show version of the Mirada, the Magnum featured a front section, including grille, that echoed the classic 1936 Cord coffin-nose design. Added were a T-bar roof, concealed headlights, turbo silver body paint that was accented by a black grille, moldings, vertical front fender vents, closed quarter windows, special wheels, and tires. The interior was done in black leather.

1980 St. Moritz Diplomat

St. Moritz previewed the T-bar roof that was a coming option on the 1980 Diplomat. It had a two-tone exterior paint scheme of iridescent red on top and a pearlescent sand with pearl silver mist, from mid-side panels down. Grille and wheels were color-keyed to the upper-body paint.

A convertible look was added to the rear window and the quarter windows were reshaped.

1981 024 Turbo Charger 2.2

Developed under the guidance of Chrysler Corporation Product Design Office, the Turbo Charger 2.2 was one of five official pace cars for the 1981 PPG Indy Car World Series.

Based on a Dodge 024, the highly modified front-wheel-drive car had a turbocharged 2.2 liter four-cylinder engine. Special body panels, flush-mounted windows, tall rear spoiler, and special paint scheme were all the work of Synthetex, Inc., Romulus, Michigan.

Dodge

1982 024 PPG

It didn't take long for the pace cars for the CART PPG Indy Car World Series to stray from their stock beginnings. For its share of the 1982 track duties, Dodge showed off its entry. Based on 024 underpinnings, the result was well disguised with completely different body work.

Gullwing doors, skirted rear wheels, and an aggressive rear spoiler all caused the race track gentry to take notice. Just so there was no misunderstanding where this sleek vehicle came from, a big pentastar was proudly displayed on the hood.

1983 Shelby Street Fighter

The Street Fighter Rampage was based on the 1983 Rampage 2.2 compact pickup. It was also an adaptation of a 1983.5 Dodge Shelby Charger, from designer and builder Carroll Shelby.

A special four-color version of Dodge truck's ram's head logo dominated the hood scoop. A custom air dam, ground effect skirts, spoiler, full-moon racing wheel discs, unique paint, and tape treatment gave the Street Fighter an aggressive, threatening appearance.

1985 Direct Connection "P"

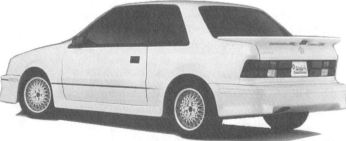

The Dodge-Direct Connection Project "P" car featured an aerodynamic front air dam with integrated fog lights, headlight covers, and a functional hood scoop for the inter-cooled turbo 180 horsepower engine.

Mechanically, brakes were enhanced and quick ratio rack and pinion steering upgraded handling. Styling added aerodynamic ground effects, along with low profile V-rated tires and wider aluminum three-piece modular wheels.

Dodge

1986 M4S

Dodge's M4S was one of those concept cars that had more than one life.

Starting back in 1983, Chrysler and PPG Industries combined their efforts in creating an exotic-looking pace car. The result was the short front overhang, long rear tail section, and a mid-mounted 4-cylinder (M4S) dream machine. Specialized Vehicles Inc. in Troy, Michigan, built it.

Though the transversely positioned 2.2-liter engine was small, it was equipped with twin Bosch L-Jetronic electronically managed fuel-injection systems, and cranked out a healthy 440 horsepower.

After appearing at the PPG Indy Car World Series races and auto shows, the car had a starring role in the 1986 low budget B movie, "The Wraith."

Press releases inform that the swoopy design was inspired by contemporary racecars that ran in the World Endurance Championship and IMSA GTP events. At the rear, adjustable wings between the extended fenders provided down force for high-speed stability.

1986 Dakota Sport V-8

Dazzling the auto show crowds was this unique Dakota concept truck. Based on the then all new mid-size Dakota 4x4 pickup, the truck featured rich candy turquoise paint, integral six-lamp light bar, black-out bumpers, stone guards for the headlights, and driving lights and special road wheels and tires.

The interior was quite special with sling-type seats that were trimmed in buckskin leather and Colorado fabric.

1987 Daytona 199X

Based on a 1987 Daytona platform, this idea car had a full-length glass roof panel, hidden headlights, and bumpers that were integrated with the body.

Under the hood was a 16-valve, turbocharged, inter-cooled, 2.2-liter four-cylinder overhead cam engine that pumped a healthy 225 horsepower. Zero to 60 mph was clocked at 4.5 seconds.

Note the dual instrument panels, one freestanding on top of the dash, the other seen through the steering wheel. Placed to the left of the wheel was a satellite navigational map system.

To unlock the steering wheel and start the car, a key card was supplied instead of the normal metal key.

Dodge

1988 Intrepid

Intrepid was an aggressive, aerodynamically shaped sports car that illustrated a possible Dodge of the future. Developed by Chrysler design studio off the Daytona chassis, Intrepid's flowing, wedge-shaped body, was topped off by an aircraft-inspired all-glass canopy.

Power was provided by Dodge's Turbo III, a 225 horsepower 2.2 liter 16-valve four cylinder engine, that was paired with a five-speed manual transmission.

Intrepid's sheet metal body panels were painted in a shaded radiance of candy red multicoat and orange red. Dual NACA air ducts, vented the mid-engine layout.

The interior was ergonomically designed and finely tailored in deep blue glove leather and harlequin fabric. V.D.O. analog gauges filled the dash.

1989 Viper

If a list of the most significant cars in this book is made, at or near the top is the Dodge Viper. Shown in 1989 by a Chrysler Corporation just getting back on its feet after a drubbing in the market that nearly cost its existence, the RT/10 Viper was an unabashed high-performance sports car.

It was shown at a time when America was finishing up a decade of energy crisis, federal government threats to the auto industry, and a fear we would all be stuffed into micro cars by the time the century was over.

The open two seater didn't apologize for bulging fenders, side exhaust, and, most of all, not for having a new aluminum V-10 engine, with a six-speed manual transmission.

Lee Iacocca and his buddy Carroll Shelby had a hand in the snake, just as they did the Ford Cobra. However, something came to notice, there were a bunch of car guys at Chrysler. When a Japanese Dodge Stealth ran afoul of public opinion when it was to pace the 1991 Indianapolis 500, a Viper stepped in, the first non-production car since the 1941 Chrysler Newport Parade Car.

"Build it" cries were answered, much to America's surprise, and the first of the limited production 1992 Vipers were snatched from showrooms.

A coupe version, the GTS was shown in 1993 and it, too, made production as a 1996 model.

Racing programs, Corvette stompings, and even a much newer 2003 Viper followed, but books would have to cover all the developments - and they have.

1993 GTS

1990 Dakota Sport V-8

Bringing a new dimension to the phrase, "the more the merrier," the Dakota Sport V-8 showcased many off-road elements into one complete aerodynamic package. It also featured the extended cab model that was new to the Dakota truck model line up. Poised beneath a fully integrated brush guard, was a front air dam and halogen driving lights.

At the rear, topped by a fixed spoiler, a honey-combed "Baja" tailgate looked great and improved the airflow.

Complimenting the body's advanced aerodynamics on this Dakota concept was a 5.2-liter V-8, that was electronically fuel injected, and delivered 170 horsepower and 260 pound-feet of torque. Another unique feature was the power-operated retractable cab back and "rumble seat" versatility of two rear seats. The exterior was finished in gloss black multicoat and matte silver protective paint.

1990 Daytona R/T

This slick all-wheel-drive concept featured a low, aggressive stance that indicated the high-performance engineering packed inside.

Power was supplied by Chrysler's 174 horsepower, multipoint fuel-injected, single overhead cam, 2.2-liter engine with variable nozzle turbocharger. Wrapped around the muscle was a taut skin highlighted by an integrated whale tail, flush glass, a glass roof, and aggressive ground effects.

Daytona R/T rode on Goodyear experimental 17-inch tires mounted on alloy wheels.

1991 Neon Concept

Versatility was the key to the Neon concept car, but the styling was what caught the public's attention. Though this was a one-of-a-kind vehicle, it indicated the look that led to the production Neon. Cab-forward design did a great job of maximizing passenger space, while minimizing mechanical space.

Wind flowed up and over the sharply inclined hood, windshield, and integrated rear spoiler for improved ground-hugging performance. Sliding electric doors opened to a five-passenger interior, with seats that were removable for easy cleaning. Stereo and headrest speakers were also removable.

When the sun became bright, the special opaque glass was designed to absorb the ultraviolet rays and keep the interior cool. A fabric sunroof could be pulled back and the rear window lowered for a convertible feel.

Neon's concept car's power came from the External Breathing A direct injection, three-cylinder, two-stoke, 1.1-liter engine that ran on alternative fuel was used. It weighed 40 percent less than a traditional engine, but produced over 100 horsepower.

Virtually every component used on the concept could be recycled into reusable components. It even came with a trash compactor built into its trunk.

Dodge

1994
Venom

This sexy-looking muscle-car concept was built on the Neon platform. The body was formed of light-weight aluminum panels and had styling cues from muscle car-era Dodge Challenger and Chargers.

Unlike the front wheel drive Neon, Venom was a rear-drive coupe that used a version of the LH 3.5-liter V-6 engine, with 245-horsepower.

Venom was another of the exciting vehicles created at Chrysler's Pacifica Advanced Product Design Center in Carlsbad, California.

1994 Aviat

Another concept based on the Neon was the radical Aviat creation. Outrigger-style rear-quarter fenders were designed to cool the engine and house the rear wheels.

Much of the shape of Aviat was generated in a comput-er, to redefine the basic vehicle shape for the best coeffi-cient of drag.

The engine was a DOHC 16-valve 2.0-liter inline 4 cylinder, which produced 145 horses. Even though the engine was front-mounted, the cooling system was moved to the rear.

1996 Intrepid ESX

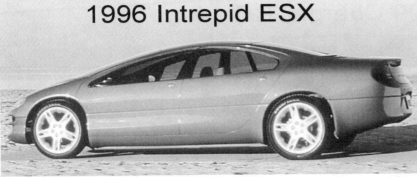

There is no question that this vehicle led the way for the second-generation 1998 Intrepid. The goal was to create a sexy looking four-door sedan that would obtain 80+ miles per gallon.

This required radical new engineering, which led to a hybrid-propulsion system of a 1.8-liter three-cylinder diesel engine and electric wheel motors. The diesel engine provided 135 hp and the two electric motors turned out 55 horsepower each.

The Intrepid ESX body was all aluminum and the custom-designed suspension was built and constructed by Reynard Racing Cars.

"Good design is lasting, not faddish." Thomas C. Gale

1997 Copperhead

Dodge added another snake in its exotic car pit with its Copperhead concept. This two-seat roadster would have made a perfect stablemate for the Viper V/10.

Copperhead was finished in a copper fire orange, featured front engine, five-speed manual transmission and rear-wheel-drive. Compared to Viper, its older sibling, Copperhead had an extra 12 inches of wheelbase, was eight inches shorter, and three inches narrower.

The car's shape looked fast with its minimal overhang, achieved by pushing the wheels way out to the front and rear corners.

The sinuous design offered an air scoop grille, deep-set rectangular headlights, elongated hood with dual side air scoops, drastically sloped windshield, and scaled-down dorsal fin on the rear deck. All this was enhanced with cast aluminum wheels, 18-inches up front and 20 at the rear.

Under that curvacious hood sat a 220 horsepower, 2.7-liter V-6 engine.

The interior featured contoured bucket seats with an unconventional deep amethyst snakeskin-like finish. Note that when viewed in its entirety, the center console and instrument pod had an uncanny likeness to the head of a copperhead snake.

Dodge

1999 Charger R/T

Along with the name, Dodge brought back the heritage that made the 1960s Charger R/T a legend. This advanced four-door went into an entirely new dimension.

True to the original muscle-car form, Charger R/T, with its low, thrusting hood, was powered by a supercharged, 4.7-liter SOHC, 16-valve V8, matched with a five-speed manual transmission that drove the rear wheels.

The sloping front grille and headlights looked menacing, and the body had a taut appearance. The rear-deck spoiler, and fascia, with sly-looking taillamps and twin exhaust outlets, all signify a vigorous departure from the past.

One look at the radio knobs and three-spoke steering wheel will confirm that. The pistol-grip shift lever adds to the feeling.

Throughout this interior past and future, street and racing are balanced. Exposed metal is emphasized, but the front and rear bucket seats are made of carbon fiber and have red leather accents. The Charger R/T has the kind of ferocity that results in 325 horsepower.

But Charger R/T is environmentally gentle: its compressed natural gas (CNG) fuel produces negligible emissions at the tail pipes.

1999 Caravan R/T

Caravan R/T was a Radiant Viper red minivan with an attitude. Harkening back to its 1960s' muscle-car heritage, Dodge stuck a high-performance 225-horsepower 3.5-liter aluminum block multi-valve V-6 under the hood. The engine was hooked up to the AutoStick transaxle and the Caravan rode on 18-inch wheels.

Two Viper hood scoops were added to the hood, a rear spoiler to the roof, and chrome exhaust tips at the rear.

The interior continued the Viper influence with a brushed aluminum instrument panel, racing accelerator, and brake pedals. Seats were finished in Viper black leather with red R/T logo embroidered into each headrest. The entire floor was made of black rubber, with a raised tread texture.

The year 1999 was the 15-year anniversary of Chrysler Corporation's minivan, introduced in 1984.

1999 Power Wagon

Not only did Dodge resurrect the Power Wagon name for its 1999 concept truck, it wasn't afraid to borrow a bit of the rugged shape from the World War II veteran Power Wagon WM-300 pickup, last sold domestically in 1968.

The rugged front styling, separate fenders, and running boards all gave the Power Wagon concept a combination retro and high-tech look. At 77 inches high, it towered above the conventional Ram pickup. It was of four-door design with the rear doors opening only after the fronts were ajar. Inside it was anything but bare metal like the original. Leather bucket seats, a console, and ash wood accents were strictly upscale. Multi-purpose storage areas were located behind the seats.

Power came from a turbocharged 7.2 liter in-line six diesel, hooked to an automatic transmission. The four-wheel-drive Power Wagon was mounted on 35-inch tires that looked like the military tread on the early Wagons.

2000 ESX3

Following up the 1998 ESX hybrid concept car was the 2000 ESX3, again a hybrid. Like the 2, it had an aluminum direct injection 1.5-liter diesel as its primary propulsion and an electric motor when a boost was needed. The electric was driven by a lithium ion battery that the diesel kept charged.

Weighing in at 2,250 pounds, it claimed 72 miles per gallon, while providing all the roominess and comfort of the day's sedans, in compliance with federal safety standards.

A thermoplastic body cut weight, just as in the ESX2.

Styling was well integrated from the crosshair grille in front to the chopped rear deck.

To help define the ESX2 and ESX3, Chrysler group called them "mybrids," standing for mild hybrid.

Dodge

2000 MAXXcab

Dodge engineers accomplished what seemed to be the impossible by creating a truck that made passengers a priority. One gaze at this powerful concept vehicle from Dodge and you'll realize that it's different.

Dodge MAXXcab turned the traditional upside down by providing plenty of comfort, and was nicknamed "Passenger Priority Pick-up." MAXXcab utilized cab-forward design to provide uncommon interior spaciousness. It even accommodated kids, with three built-in child-safety seats, and a power seat in the middle of the back row.

An overhead camera allowed the driver to monitor the kids' Edu-tainment center including the Internet, a sketch pad, and DVD player Infotronic system with a plug-n-play laptop computer, e-mail, and voice recognition for phone, navigation, laptop functions, and vehicle diagnostics.

The 4.7-liter V8 engine provided the horsepower and torque - 238 horsepower and 295 pound feet of torque to be exact. Making the loading and unloading easier, the MAXXcab featured an elevator tailgate.

Exterior sheet metal had a "semi-truck" appearance, which was painted butane blue pearl, with navy leather seats and trim

2001 Super 8 Hemi

Perhaps a way to acknowledge Tom Gale's retirement as design chief for DaimlerChrysler's Chrysler Group was the controversial Super8HEMI concept car of the 2001 season.

Gale's designs were noted for being tuned to the public's taste. The Super8 seemed to be following a (very) different drummer. Freeman Thomas, vice president of Advanced Product Design and a brave soul, took credit for the combination of retro, edge, and jukebox styling.

A wraparound windshield, best left in the 1950s, green plastic side spears, and squashed roof styling were all in the styling mix for the carbon fiber-bodied four-door. A bold cross-hair grille and large sunroof were also part of the circus.

Inside, reached by center-opening doors and no B-pillar, styling was of the same persuasion as the exterior. Matching the retro windshield were push buttons operating the automatic transmission and a turbine car-like driveshaft tunnel cover.

If you dwell only on the visuals for the Super8 HEMI, you miss the real significance as it was rear wheel drive and a showcase, so to speak, for the new Hemi 353 cubic inch V-8 engine. Chrysler Group had committed to both production of the Hemi and converting some of its future models to rear drive. The Hemi would be announced in 2002 as a production engine for the 2003 Dodge trucks.

As of this writing, it looks like a win-win situation. We won't see the Super8 HEMI again and rear drive Hemi V-8 MoPars are coming our way.

2001 Powerbox

As a follow-up to its 1999 Power Wagon concept pickup, Dodge showed off the Powerbox concept wagon for 2001. It featured similar frontal styling, separate fenders, and running boards like the pickup, but was an eight-passenger four-wheel drive SUV. Side doors were center opening to give plenty of room to those who climbed up to get in.

Styling was only part of the story. It was powered by a supercharged 2.7 liter V-6 that produced 250 horsepower and ran on compressed natural gas (CNG). But that's not all.

A 72-horsepower electric motor drove the front wheels, while the CNG engine took care of the back. There was no mechanical connection between the front and rear drive systems.

A 0-60 mph sprint took seven seconds, miles per gallon claims were pegged at 25, and the whole setup was billed as zero emissions. As yet, the Power Wagon/Powerbox theme has not translated to a production version, but there is a feeling that it isn't over yet.

2002 SRT-4

Needing a player in the street racer sweepstakes for young buyers, a Neon was modified and assigned duty on the show circuit in 2002. The Dodge SRT-4 featured a "combat styled" front fascia, hood scoop, projector beams, and bold rear spoiler.

Body height was dropped and 17-inch aluminum wheels have the needed hunkered down look.

A supercharged four-cylinder engine cranked out 208 horsepower, but the potential buyers were likely more interested in the amps cranked out by the Alpine CD system and an array of speakers.

At press time, no production version was announced, but several potential competitors were already on the market.

Dodge

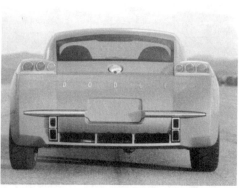

2002 Razor

In reaction to the growing number of modest priced sports coupes, like the Hyundai Tiburon, Dodge let loose the Razor concept car on the show circuit for 2002.

Co-opping the name with Razor USA L.L.C., the close coupled coupe features a 2.4 liter DOHC turbocharged, inter-cooled four, combined with a six-speed manual transmission and rear-wheel drive.

Claims for the Razor include 0-60 in six seconds flat and a top speed of 140 mph.

Basics are emphasized with exterior chrome restricted to lighting, rear view mirrors, exhaust tips, gas cap, and minimal bumpers. Inside are racing-type buckets and four-point seat belts. Seating is for two, with storage space behind the seats.

While Razor kick scooters are popular with the younger set, the Razor would have given them something to shoot for, if it had been produced. As of this writing, that is not in the cards.

2002 M80

Following up its rugged-looking Power Wagon and Power Box concept trucks, Dodge applied the bold retro-look styling to the smaller Dakota-sized pickup and came up with the M80 for 2002.

Prominent PET-plastic exposed fenders and storage boxes gave an off-road flavor to the four wheel drive truck and contrasted with the yellow painted body. The rear window flipped up like 1950s station wagons, so objects longer than the five foot bed could poke into the passenger compartment.

Speaking of the insides, the seats and cooler enhanced center console were removable for carrying and other activities.

Powering all this was a 3.7-liter Magnum V-6 and attached five speed manual gearbox.

Production was considered, for the M80 would have been an answer to the Chevrolet SSR retro truck, but DaimlerChrysler came up with a 100,000-unit limit for new models during 2002 and with that, the M80 looks like it will stay just a concept.

1951 XX-500

Plymouth's first venture into the dream-car arena was not a particularly impressive nor futuristic one. The XX-500 was built by Ghia of Italy, on a 118½-inch Plymouth wheelbase with a stock Plymouth six-cylinder engine and driveline.

Of six-window design, its slab sides, semi-fastback styling and bold central grille all were in conflict. Reportedly, Chrysler got a deal on the price and no one was particularly upset

A Bedford cord and leather six-passenger interior, plus good-looking spoke wheels, were a step up from the usual Plymouth low price fare.

1954 Belmont

Belmont was an early MoPar experimental car constructed in reinforced fiberglass. It was very stylish for Plymouth at the time, with long fenders and low, flat hood.

It rode on a Dodge chassis, used the Dodge 241 cid V-8 with 150 horsepower, and Plymouth's Hy-Drive transmission.

A special instrument grouping included a tachometer and the radio controls were located in the center armrest, with an adjacent electrically controlled antenna. The car's removable fabric top and spare tire were stored in the rear compartment.

Exterior finish was azure blue (a light green metallic) that contrasted with white-leather-covered bucket seats. Taillights appear to be a version of the units that were on the 1953 Chrysler models.

Plymouth

1954 Explorer

Plymouth's Explorer sport coupe was a sister car to the two Dodge Firearrows. Explorer's 114-inch wheelbase was five inches shorter than the Firearrow. A large air-scoop shaped grille slanted forward.

Explorer combined the taillight and exhaust pipe assembly, with the lights set into the fender. Chrome rings encircled the combination. The exterior was finished in a light green metallic. The large rectangular grille, with its vertical chromed ribs, was similar to the Firearrow coupe, but the Plymouth had two large headlights instead of quads on the Dodge. Placed in the forward ends of the V-shaped rub rail was the parking light/turn signal combo.

Heavy bumpers wrapped around and ended up at the wheel openings.

A press release informed that while the car was only four and a half feet high, there was over 34 inches of headroom.

The steering wheel was polished natural wood with aluminum spokes, and the radio controls slid out of sight and could be covered by a panel. Behind the twin bucket seats was a compartment that contained matching black and white luggage, similar to the car's upholstery. A small console between the seats was for maps and an ashtray.

Classic 15-inch chrome wire wheels had simulated knock-off hubs.

1954-1962 Turbine Specials

1954   1955

1956   1959

1960   1962

In the mid-1950s, both Chrysler Corporation and General Motors were showing off their development work on the gas turbine, which dated back to World War II. The difference was General Motors showcased its turbine power for the road in radical dream cars like the Firebird series, while Chrysler installed them in standard production passenger cars. In the 1950s and beyond, Chrysler wanted to show the application for the everyday driver and chose Plymouths.

With development led by George Huebner Jr., the first public showing was in a 1954 Belvedere two-door hardtop. It was first displayed at the Waldorf-Astoria Hotel in New York City on April 7, 1954. The turbine fit under the hood, was attached to a standard manual transmission (using only third and reverse gears), and weighed some 200 pounds less than the six-cylinder powered Plymouth. Heat exchangers aided in output. A second 1954 Plymouth was also constructed.

Turbine Plymouths followed in 1955, 1956, 1957, 1959, and 1960. In 1962, both Plymouth and Dodge Dart turbines were built.

Belvedere four-door sedans were used in 1955, 1956, and 1957 and a Fury four-door hardtop got the call for 1959.

There were no new turbines for 1960, but a 1960 Plymouth four-door hardtop was modified for a turbine in 1961, as was a 1960 Dodge truck.

For 1962, a pair of Dodge Dart and Plymouth Fury two-door hardtops got turbines. A cross-country run was made and garnered much publicity.

From 1955 on, the turbine Plymouths got non-stock exterior and interior trim, noting their unique power. The twin exhaust outlets in the back were another giveaway.

The first generation turbine was only good for 100 horsepower, about the same as the Plymouth flathead six. When a second turbine was built for 1956, it carried a second generation power plant and rating of 200 hp. The third generation turbine bowed in 1961. Though production Plymouths were no longer the brand of choice for turbines, Chrysler development continued with the run of 50 cars for public testing in 1964 perhaps a high point.

Despite decades of development and concept vehicles, regular gas turbine mass production still is in the future.

Plymouth

1960 XNR

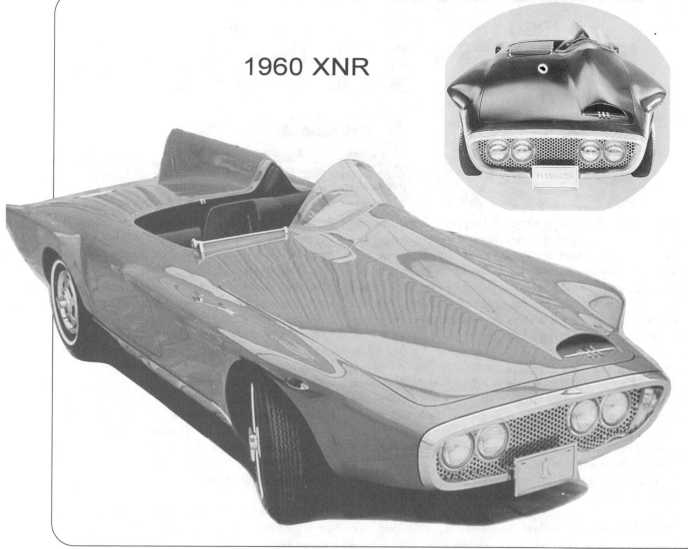

1958 Cabana

Stretching the limits of station wagon design (and maybe good taste) was a dream car for 1958, the Cabana. Designed by Chrysler and built by Ghia, the nine passenger wagon was of four-door hardtop design, something Plymouths never had or would have.

Though the styling looked on the radical side, the purpose behind the Cabana was adequate access for not only the hauling customers, but ambulance and hearse operators as well. Sliding rear plastic panels in the roof and center opening side doors aided in getting to the inside and vice versa.

Below the beltline, styling was not strongly Plymouth, save for the fins, which had a bit of a 1960 look. A concave grille with the bumper partially surrounding it would look like a number of cars to come, but not Plymouths.

No small car, the Cabana was built on a 124-inch wheelbase Plymouth frame, with an overall length of nearly 216 inches and width of 80 inches. There was no driveline; it was a roller.

1960 XNR

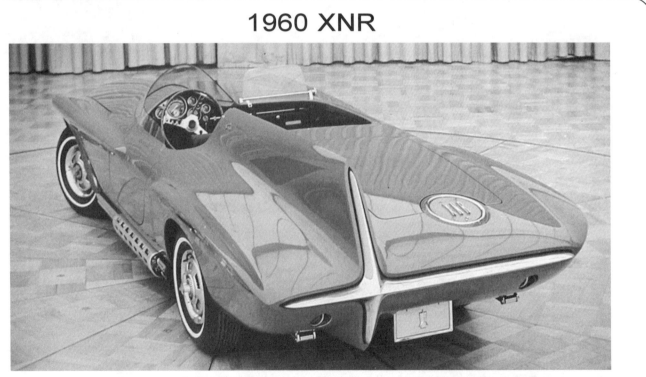

The XNR was a tribute in name to designer Virgil Exner. The sleek roadster featured off-center styling. A single fin, in the form of a graduated plane, ran the length of the car, and concentrated around the driver. Lines of the lean car's airscoop continued back through the entire length of the car, becoming a functional single fin on the driver's side of the car. The frame for the grille was actually the front bumper.

Body was hand made by Ghia in Italy, and powered by a standard Chrysler Corporation six-cylinder engine.

The artistically modern chrome "X" at the rear of the car blended into the fin and served as the bumper. On the rear deck was a large circular gas cap cover, with large XNR letters.

There were two cut-down windshields, the passenger's side was designed to fold flat, and the driver sat four inches higher than the passengers.

Most influenced by the XNR, was the 1962 Plymouth. It adopted the slopping hood, wingtip front fender line, and the vertical fin theme on its rear deck.

The body was hand made by Ghia in Italy.

Plymouth

1964 Satellite II

A closer look at the 1964 Satellite II show car revealed a removable front roof panel that connected to the windshield header and landau rear canopy. Outside there was an altered grille and trim, while inside were four bucket seats and a full length center console.

The Satellite name would be adapted to a line of intermediate Plymouths for 1965, which were based on the 1964 standard-sized Plymouths, which were intermediate size anyway. Got that?

1965 V.I.P.

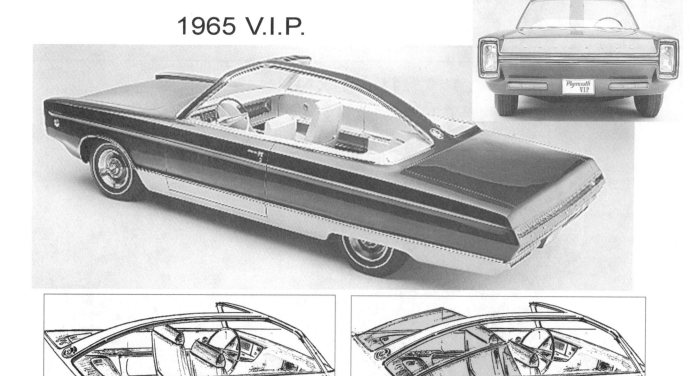

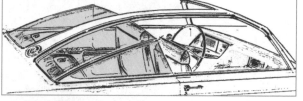

Plymouth promoted its V.I.P. idea car as the ultimate in comfort, convenience, communication, entertainment, and safety. As stated by Plymouth General Manager P.N. Buckminster, "The V.I.P. is a necessary exercise in preparation for the future."

The most outstanding feature was the longitudinal roll bar, which acted as the guide for the upper portion of the flexible glass top. Each glass section retracted into the trunk area when passengers wanted an open-air ride. A new photochromic glass darkened when exposed to light and then cleared again when the light faded. The handsome body used a base magenta color, but the paint was iridescent and would change in various shades from pink to brown, according to the angle of light. This was possible because of many tiny transparent crystals contained in the murano pearl paint.

Inside the car, the driver had a rear-vision scope on the dash panel, which was a compact closed-circuit television that showed pictures of the road behind. A second TV set could be viewed by all passengers, but was shrouded from the driver's eyes.

Interestingly, when information on this car first appeared in newspaper articles, it had no name and was just referred to as Plymouth's "Idea Car," but by showtime in Chicago, it was finally titled V.I.P. Plymouth used the V.I.P. name on a luxury line of production cars starting in 1966.

Plymouth

1967 Barracuda Formula SX

Plymouth designers had fun when they created the Formula SX, a variation on the then current Barracuda Formula S performance sports compact.

The body was constructed of fiberglass, with modifications that included a restyled fastback roof, and new front features. The grille, headlights, and turn-signal lights were recessed behind the chrome bumper. This made the bumper an integral part of the overall deep metallic red body.

Formula SX was built on a 108-inch wheelbase with an overall length of 190 inches and height of 51 inches.

Black triple racing stripes ran from the front grille, over the roof, and down the deck lid. The deep-dish wheels were like nothing else shown by Chrysler Corporation.

1969 Duster I Road Runner

Plymouth created a wild concept version of its popular Road Runner muscle car, designed to maximize the car's stability in high-performance situations.

Called Duster I, it was converted to a two-passenger model that was equipped with a 426-cid Hemi engine. A functional roll bar, which contained adjustable airflow spoilers, was integrated into the rear quarter panels. Aircraft-type "dive brakes" were included as part of the fender sides, which were activated as a part of the braking system. Adjustable air dams in the front stone shields reduced frontal lift at high speeds.

The aerodynamically squared rear profile minimized drag at high speeds, and the wheelbase was shortened by six inches for increased weight transfer to rear wheels. Details included dual racing fuel fillers in both rear quarter panels, for rapid fill-ups, and H.60 x 15-inch prototype tires.

Plymouth began using the Duster name on its new 1970 compact coupe.

Plymouth

1970 Rapid Transit System 'Cuda 440

The 'Cuda 440 was the most extensively altered of the vehicles traveling in Plymouth's 1970 Rapid Transit System Caravan.

Lower by two and a half inches, it sported a new grille that covered rectangular concealed Cibie rallye-type headlights. Rear-end styling was modified to accommodate the two wheelie bars and a drag chute, and notice the reinforced steel braces over the rear window. All door handles, trunk, and hood latches were removed and replaced by electric solenoid openers.

The exterior colors were Plymouth Lime Light and two shades of gray all covered in marano pearlescent.

Custom details, included the geometric-shape and stripe designs that covered the body. Note the faint "440" numerals that are wrapped over the rear window.

1970 Rapid Transit System Road Runner

For the third model year of the Road Runner, Plymouth commissioned Roman's Chariot Shop in Cleveland, Ohio, to construct the "Rapid Transit" show car.

Major customizing included the enlarged rear wheel wells, rear quarter fender scoops, and a large rear spoiler. The spoiler was installed four inches above the deck lid, and though it blended into the rear fenders, the trunk could open and close normally.

In the new plastic honeycomb grille were nine-inch rectangular Cibie headlights, and the modified taillights connected and stretched across the entire width of the rear panel.

The hood and deck were flat black with a white pearl roof and candy gold sides. Oversized Road Runner cartoon birds were illustrated on the body sides, kicking up dust as they sped out of the air scoops.

Muscle power came from the mighty 426-cubic-inch Hemi, connected to a beefed-up TorqueFlite transmission, and a 4:10 axle.

1970 Rapid Transit System Duster 340

Plymouth featured the Duster name on the previous year Road Runner show car, and for 1970, it was applied to its new Duster compact model.

Not missing a beat, Plymouth immediately had a custom version of its production model on display at the auto shows. The completely restyled front on the Duster 340 included four Lucas headlights, rectangular parking lights and a rolled-under pan. The entire car was lowered three inches, with the radiator cut the same to accommodate the styling changes.

Very subtle design touches included the addition of chrome moldings along the rocker panels, which accented the low stance, and a unique spoiler built into the rear of the roofline.

With a name like Duster 340, the obvious engine was the MoPar 340 cu.in. V-8, which was mated to a four-speed manual transmission and a 3.91 axle.

Duster 340 was painted candy red, with flat black and hues of pearl, and was finished with deep Universal Regal wheels shod with on Goodyear Y-7 Speedway tires.

1980 Turismo Spyder

Chrysler built this two-seat concept version of its subcompact Plymouth Horizon TC3, targeted at young married couples and singles, looking for a fuel-efficient sporty car. One of the car's designers, senior product planner Bob Marcks remarked, "This isn't just a show car. We're looking for public reaction."

The car started out as a four-passenger model, with nearly the same dimensions as the production TC3. A non-production T-bar roof, louvered quarter windows, and black moldings gave the show car more exotic styling.

Suggested power at the time was the new 2.2-liter 4-cylinder engine that was coming in the 1981 Plymouth and Dodge K-cars. Finishing touches were the addition of dual exhausts, 14-inch cast aluminum wheels, oversized tires, lower suspension, and a recessed rear window.

Plymouth

1986 Concept Voyager

Concept Voyager was Chrysler's answer to family boredom during long driving trips. Everything, including the kitchen sink, was built into this minivan. When taking a break from driving, snacks or even a light meal was possible with the propane stove and a small refrigerator. The sink was for clean-ups, and there was even a portable vacuum cleaner. Entertainment included a pop-up video screen for rear passengers.

As seen in the photo, the roof was raised about 10 inches, creating storage space in a bin with a convenient slide-out tray. Blended together were the bubble windshield and tinted moon roof, for maximum visibility and increased headroom.

The driver's job was made a bit easier with the dash-mounted global-positioning navigation system. The interior also featured experimental molded-foam fabric covered seating.

An added safety feature were Goodyear dual-section tires.

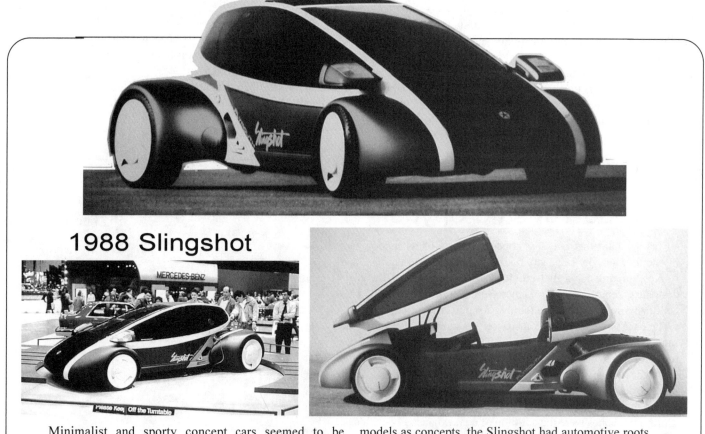

1988 Slingshot

Minimalist and sporty concept cars seemed to be Plymouth's forte. For 1988, showgoers got a look at the Slingshot, a two-passenger runabout that featured entry via a raised canopy, covered wheels extending past the body, and radical styling.

While Ford and GM had motorcycle-based high mph

models as concepts, the Slingshot had automotive roots.

It was powered by a turbocharged, twin cam 2.4-liter four and had a six-speed transmission with a ratchet shifter, which gave outstanding performance and economy.

With wheels near the corners, the wheelbase was a long 103 inches, while overall length was a short 148.9 inches.

1988 X2S

While traveling the auto shows, this concept was known as X2S. That was a code name for the show car version of the future production Plymouth Laser.

Painted a vivid red, this front-wheel-drive sports specialty car was Plymouth's attempt to bring some fun to its model line-up and project a more contemporary image.

The X2S had a full-glass moon roof and the car's bright finish, including the targa band, was done in a rich, three-tone iridescent red.

Propulsion was via a 2.0L double overhead cam 16-valve engine with five-speed manual transmission. Rounding out the equipment were a unique sports interior, 16-inch wheels, and performance tires.

1989 Speedster

Inter-crossing a high-performance motorcycle and open sports car resulted in Plymouth's futuristic Speedster. MoPar engineers were proud of the fact they used advanced computers to design this fun car.

Front fenders and hood were combined to form a motorcycle-type faring that wrapped around the front of the vehicle to the doors. Inside this faring were pop-up upper and fixed lower light bars. Speedster's low wrap-around windscreen was a blend of a motorcycle air deflector and a cut-down roadster windshield.

The interior had molded plastic tub with fixed seating that was upholstered in a unique "wet suit" material, with removable foam pads.

Basically, you could hose out the cockpit and have dry seats in no time.

Since the seats didn't move, the steering and foot controls were adjustable. A normally aspirated 2.0-liter four-cylinder Mitsubishi-built engine enabled the Speedster to live up to its name.

Plymouth

1990 Voyager III

Plymouth's vision with the Voyager III concept was a possible answer to congested urban traffic and air pollution. It was two vehicles in one.

The front micro-car seated three and was powered by a 1.6-liter propane-fuel engine. When attached to the detachable rear-modular section, an added 2.2-liter four-cylinder powered the rearmost wheels. When the two-piece commuter vehicle was connected, it was only slightly longer than a production Grand Voyager, yet could carry eight passengers.

Voyager III also gave an early look at the design direction of the future 1996 MoPar minivans.

1993 Prowler

Chrysler Corporation was right on in coming up with concept-car designs that hit the hot button for the fantasies of the motoring public. Following in the tire tracks of the Dodge Viper was the Plymouth Prowler, which bowed at the 1993 North American International Auto show in Detroit.

Prowler was a modern rendition of the old-fashioned hot rod of the 1940s and 1950s, more often than not a Ford. With open front wheels and "cycle" fenders, running boards, fendered rear wheels and plush seating for two, the aluminum body's flowing lines produced a vehicle thought unbuildable in the 1990s.

Modern touches included free-standing twin front bumpers, small built-in composite headlights, and a curved windshield.

Underneath it all were current mechanicals, which turned out to be the one sore point in Prowler's prowess. An OHC 3.5 liter V-6 sat where the free world knew a V-8 was supposed to be. Despite claiming 240 horsepower and producing decent performance, it was two cylinders short of being right. The driveshaft headed toward a rear-mounted automatic transmission, aluminum enhanced four-wheel independent suspension, and aluminum frame produced balanced handling.

Public reaction was gangbusters and production commenced with the 1997 models. A neat trailer with styling like the Prowler trunk was offered and several color combinations came and went (the first ones were purple), but Prowler only generated a slow, steady sales stream after the initial impact.

With the Plymouth name set to die, Prowler became a Chrysler branded car midway through the 2001 model year, but in 2002 DaimlerChrysler announced the end.

1999 Howler

To answer the critics that said the Prowler should have a V-8, Plymouth unleashed the Howler at the SEMA show in 1999. A Jeep 4.7 liter OHV PowerTech V-8 and a Borg-Warner T-5 manual transmission showed that it could be done if Plymouth wanted to.

Not just an engine transplant, the Howler also had an extended rear trunk, which could be converted into a mini pickup truck.

With Plymouth now under a less than understanding DaimlerChrysler ownership, cries to build it went unheeded.

1994 Neon Expresso

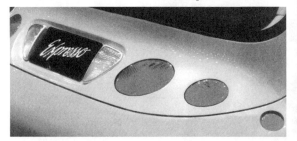

Like a car from Toonsville in the movie "Roger Rabbitt," Neon Expresso was a show stopper during the 1994 season. There was nothing else quite like its tall greenhouse and bubble windows. Both body and wheels were painted banana yellow and the door handles were tinted blue.

Constructed from a shortened Neon platform, Expresso was a full two feet shorter than the production Neon, but was also 15 inches taller.

A Neon 2.0-liter four-cylinder engine powered the front drive concept, with 132 horsepower. Built into the rear of the driver's seat was a laptop computer along with an entertainment center. Also on board was a satellite navigation system. Under the tall bucket seats were large storage areas.

Plymouth offered an Expresso edition of the production Neon as an optional package with "Expresso" graphics, but nothing like the concept version. Other Plymouths also got Expresso option packages.

1995 Backpack

Stretching the limits for small, fun vehicles seemed to be Plymouth's mission in concept life in its final years. Another example is the Backpack, a show circuit traveler in 1995 and beyond.

A small pickup truck with 2+2 seating, it had Neon underpinnings and was not short on gimmicks. With an overall length of only 142 inches, but height close to a minivan, it used vertical room to its advantage.

The back of the passenger seat folded down to create a work table and the driver seat turned to face it. There was additional storage space under the rear jump seat.

The small pickup bed and a roof rack were for carrying what could stand up to the elements.

Off the parts shelf came the Neon 2 liter OHC 4, good for 135 horsepower and no doubt a good time.

Plymouth

1997 Pronto

With the 1997 Pronto concept car, Plymouth was after unique, affordable transportation.

The Pronto differed from traditional four-passenger sedans by tall architecture, spacious interior, roll-back fabric roof, and distinctive stand-alone blow-molded bumpers. The windshield was moved forward and body utilized minimal front and rear overhang. Interior storage pockets were built into the C-pillar.

Pronto had a Prowler-like face. Body panels were to be made with acrylinitrile/styrene/aceylate (ASA) plastic and had a single molded-in color. The suggested engine was the 2-liter SOHC with 132 hp, and a three-speed automatic transmission. Cast aluminum wheels were 18 inches.

1998 Pronto Spyder

"This kind of car has kinetic energy," said Tom Tremont, design director for Pacifica, DaimlerChrysler's California design studio. "We toyed around with naming it 'Gator' because it looks like an alligator ready to strike."

True enough, viewed from any angle, this car, with its low-slung body and "machine-like" lines, had a sort of bared-fang animal force about it. But the styling also spoke of a futuristic sophistication. That's partly because the Spyder's body was made from an advanced injection-molded plastic that allowed designers to do razor-sharp edges, precise intersections and details. It also meant that the Spyder could sticker for half the price of the typical high-end sports car. Mated to a five-speed manual, the rear-wheel-drive Spyder's supercharged, 225-horsepower 2.4L 4-cylinder transverse mid-engine was configured for breath-taking performance, while the interior featured "romantic" detailing that hints at an earlier classic racer era.

Plymouth concept cars soon came to an end as the Plymouth brand was axed by DaimlerChrysler. The final Plymouth produced was the 2001 Neon.

1950 Alcoa Coupe

Looking like a customized Jeepster with a Studebaker roof, the Alcoa coupe was a proposal for an enclosed passenger car-like version of the Jeep roadster.

Alcoa Aluminum built the coupe to propose a modification that could widen the sales appeal of the Jeepster.

Aluminum body work made the Alcoa Jeepster a two-passenger vehicle with a large conventional trunk in back. A modified horizontal grille and side trim added passenger car-like accents. Reports of how many were made vary between two and three.

No matter how many Alcoa turned out, it was all for naught as sales of the Jeepster was not sufficient to continue production past the 1950 model year. Leftover unsold 1950 models were retitled as 1951s until the inventory was cleared.

1969 Jeep XJ 001

Not realizing the Jeep styling would become classic, there were constant efforts to modernize it with some form of contemporary styling. One such effort that was shown all over the country was the XJ-001, done by Kaiser Jeep Corp. shortly before Jeep was sold to American Motors.

In 1969, Kaiser came up with a fiberglass stylized body, open doors, semi-open rear compartment, modern front clip, racing stripes, hood scoop, and other non-off road gingerbread. The body was set quite low on a Jeep CJ-5 Universal chassis.

Public reaction was underwhelming and neither Kaiser nor AMC could afford, or was inspired to try, a production version. While out on display, the XJ-001 was destroyed in transit.

Jeep/Eagle

1978 Concept Jeep II

Part of American Motors' Concept 80 caravan was a downsized version of the Jeep flat fender CJ-3, called Concept Jeep II. The idea behind Concept 80 was to show vehicles that could render outstanding economy and get America through the next "energy crisis."

AMC kept the Jeep proportions intact, but all dimensions were smaller. Only when standing next to a full-sized Jeep CJ-5 did the difference become apparent. The II had a 76-inch wheelbase, eight inches shorter than the real thing. Overall length dropped 20 inches and height fell nine inches. The downsized seats were done in Levis trim, like the production interiors.

With budget restrictions and Renault's approaching control of the company, miniature Jeeps never got out of the concept stage.

1985 Cherokee Targa

American Motors' Jeep Cherokee hit the market for 1984 and revolutionized the SUV field (though it wasn't called that at the time). To get some attention for the 1985 show season, this Cherokee Targe two-door without a roof was fielded, shown here at the Chicago Auto Show.

A rollbar behind the front seats set off the mostly stock Cherokee bodywork.

In a way, it looked a little like the Jeep Commanche pickup, which bowed as a 1986 model.

The Cherokee went on to survive takeovers by Chrysler Corporation and Daimler-Benz and stayed in production through the 2001 models.

1987 Comanche Thunderchief

While still under the American Motors logo, but shortly before Chrysler took over, the 1987 Commanche Thunderchief was shown. This macho, one-of-a-kind shortbed Comanche was described by American Motors as "A Jeep with thunder."

Three slots at the front of the Thunderchief's hood allowed cool air into the engine compartment area for American Motors new fuel-injected Power Tech six.

The exterior was finished in bright red, with rear quarter "aero"-enhancing panels, all keyed to the red body color. Other custom touches were the addition of a roll bar with top-mounted off-road driving lights, front brush guard with two more driving lights, lower air dam, and running boards with recessed step plates.

1989 Concept I

The Concept I was nearly completed by American Motors when Chrysler Corporation took over. It was one of the attractions of the deal. It took until 1992 for the Concept I to evolve into the Jeep Grand Cherokee, which went on to become one of the most popular Jeeps of all time.

Concept I featured a flush front end, including lower protective cladding, which continued around the entire vehicle. The flush slide glass eliminated exterior wind noise and contributed to the aerodynamic design.

Unique 17-inch cast wheels and custom designed Goodyear all-terrain radial tires completed the fresh appearance.

1990 Cherokee Freedom

Similar to the 1985 Cherokee Targa, the 1990 version was a top-down concept built from a Cherokee Limited station wagon.

Painted a color called Viper Red, the Freedom 4x4 featured a power-actuated top, plus a "sport bar" behind the front seats.

Jeep's Power Tech six, with 177 horsepower, was the moving force behind this proposed fun in the sun vehicle.

1990 Eagle Optima

With the Eagle Optima, Chrysler showcased the design direction of its future automobiles. Featuring a dramatic treatment of the cab forward design, this concept provided optimal visibility, combined with excellent interior and cargo space.

The exterior was finished in a three-coat pearlescent white color, which exhibited a beautiful iridescence under various lighting conditions. Interior color was quartz gray with blue accents.

Configured as a rear-wheel-drive and operational vehicle, power was supplied by an experimental, 32-valve all-aluminum V-8, positioned north/south. Built on a 112-inch wheelbase, Optima used 17-inch tires.

Jeep/Eagle

1993 Jeep Ecco

Jeep Ecco blended the simple, go-anywhere trademarks of earlier Jeep vehicles with ideas to meet the concerns of the more environmentally aware generation.

Ecco was constructed of recyclable aluminum and plastic components and powered by a lean burn, two-stroke engine. This little 91-cubic-inch (1.5-liter) powerplant was Chrysler's "Series Three" all-aluminum design, that was placed midship in the vehicle, and put out 85 horsepower.

While lightweight, this two-door, four-passenger, full-time four-wheel drive vehicle used lower plastic "rafts" to support and protect the upper body.

Wheelbase was longer than the 1993 Wrangler, but the overall length was 10 inches shorter.

High ground clearance and a very wide track, due to placing the wheels to the corners of the vehicle, gave Ecco great stability and maneuverability under any road condition.

1991
Wagoneer 2000

Debuting in January 1991, Chrysler exhibited the Wagoneer 2000 to illustrate the future of the Grand Wagoneer.

Radical styling incorporated a low-slung hood that swept back into the long, sculpted fenders.

An innovative flush-mounted roof rack popped up to accommodate extra luggage, and built-in steps dropped out of each door sill, when a door was opened.

With the tailgate opened, there were removable stadium seats.

The interior used two leather bench seats that easily converted into 2+2+2-bucket seating, and for fun, there was a moveable entertainment center, with built-in TV/VCR/CD player.

Wagoneer's aggressive design, along with oversized 20-inch tires, indicated that there were serious horses, 220 of them, under the sloping hood of this all-wheel-drive dream machine.

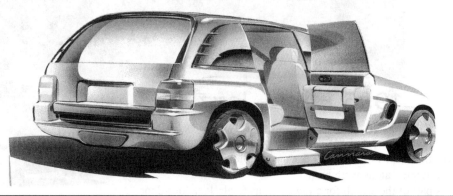

1993 Jeep Ecco

"Jeep Ecco looks a bit like a turtle - its smooth underneath, has rounded upper roll cage and its wheels stick out sort of like legs." Chrysler designer Trevor Creed

Jeep/Eagle

1995 Eagle Jazz

When Chrysler bought American Motors, it snatched the Eagle nameplate and put it on a variety of cars that were all over the map. Finally, Chrysler gave up after the last of the 1998 Eagle Talons were built.

As part of the search for an image, this Eagle Jazz four-door hatchback concept car made the rounds in 1995. Based on a somewhat abbreviated LH platform, the Jazz only stretched 175.8 inches from front to back. A try for a European look brought mixed results on this side of the Atlantic.

Power came from a 2.5 liter V-6, connected to an AutoStick transmission.

Chrysler was hinting that a short LH model was in the offing, but it never materialized.

1997 Icon

Jeep Icon was a creative exploration for a next-generation Jeep Wrangler. This was a major challenge to create a 21st century Wrangler, which is an automotive and American icon.

Traditional Jeep Wrangler design cues were updated, including the long dash-to-axle proportions, classic grille face, exposed hinges, folding windshield, and roll cage.

Icon's muscular appearance was achieved by increasing the size of its bumper, tires, and wheel arches.

Icon designer Robert Laster said that this overall concept was inspired by design elements found on today's high-end mountain bike.

Where the old and new Wranglers differed was Icon's unibody construction and integrated aluminum roll cage. Also new was the double-wishbone suspension.

Behind the famous vertical bar grille was a 2.4-liter four-cylinder engine, connected to a five-speed manual transmission; 19-inch tires were used at all four corners, and the spare.

1998 Jeepster

Chrysler asked, "What if you had the power and fun of a sports car, coupled with the capability and rugged nature of a Jeep Wrangler?" The answer for 1998 was the Jeepster concept, a take off on the original 1949 Jeep Jeepster.

Raw power for the two-plus-two seater came from a 4.7 liter V-8, with an estimated 275 horsepower. A version of this engine debuted on the 1999 Grand Cherokee. The drivetrain was the four-speed automatic Quadra-Trac II with four-wheel drive.

A dual exhaust system with three-inch diameter pipes showed that Jeepster meant business.

Like the Prowler, the vehicle was dropped lower in the front and was higher at the rear. Jeep's traditional seven-vertical intake slotted grille was flanked by uniquely detailed headlights

The rollbar cage and soft-top cover worked like the 1997 Jeep Icon concept . Jeepster's bright red steel unitized body was offset by deep blue fender flares and side panels. Cognac-colored seats were made of the same weather-resistant leather as rugged hiking boots.

There was no spare, but the 19-inch Goodyear Extended Mobility tires would maintain their shape even after a flat. These tires first appeared on the Plymouth Prowler.

The Jeepster had a unitized body.

1999 Commander

Jeep Commander combined two of the brand's highest ideals, that of off-road prowess, along with environmental responsibility.

With the addition of an alternative power source to this Jeep, dual electric motors (front and rear) with fuel cell battery pack, this concept vehicle commanded respect in any environment, while making minimal impact on it.

Off-road aerodynamics were aided by a special heat-exchanging cowl panel that improved wind flow over the windshield and drew hot air out from under the hood to keep the fuel cell system cool. At highway speeds, a rear spoiler deploys from the roof.

Painted Starbrite Silver, Commander offered an innovating "on-demand" roof rack, available when needed for luggage,

but stayed flush with the roof in its normal position. Aluminum/composite frame, carbon-fiber body, and dual electric motors (front and rear), made the Commander like no other Jeep prototype or production model.

Twenty-inch cast aluminum wheels were finished in a sterling silver tone.

Navy blue interior made a nice contrast to the Cognac leather trim inserts on seats.

Sterling silver tone 19-inch cast aluminum wheels finished the exterior. Internet and vehicle diagnostic information were provided by a small laptop computer that could dock into the center console. A small microphone embedded in the steering column received voice commands, which then was translated into data.

Jeep/Eagle

2000 Varsity

Category busters were big at the end/start of the millennium in 2000 and Jeep's contribution to the confusion was the Varsity, a sedan-like hatchback SUV that wasn't supposed to look like an SUV.

"We once again challenged ourselves to invent a new vehicle category," said Tom Gale, executive vice president, design.

Not shy on rugged looks, the Varsity combined all the Jeep styling cues with four wheel drive. Power came from a 3.5 liter V-6, pegged at 300 horsepower. An automatic transmission kept it under control.

The interior was a combination of leather seating, aluminum accented instruments, and black rubber inlays.

2002 Compass

DaimlerChrysler has been itching to replace the Wrangler with a more contemporary design for some time and the 2002 Compass concept is the latest test balloon.

The enclosed hatchback two-door is based on a shortened Liberty platform. The spare tire was mounted outside in a stylized mounting. Off-roaders will be interested in, but not thrilled with, the independent front suspension. In back, a live axle on coil springs is not controversial.

Power comes from the 210-horsepower 3.7 liter OHC V-6 in the Liberty.

What direction the Compass points for future Jeeps remains to be seen.

2001 Willys

2001 Willys 2

Acknowledging the contributions of Willys Motors to its heritage, DaimlerChrysler fielded a pair of concept Jeeps with the Willys' name. Both appeared during 2001.

Bowing at the North American International Auto show in Detroit was the Jeep Willys, an open two-door with a carbon-fiber body on an aluminum frame. Independent suspension coil-overs held down front and back wheels. Power came from a supercharged 1.6 liter four, rated at 160-hp. An automatic tranny and two-speed transfer case dispatched full-time power to all four 22-inch wheels. Styling, at least up front, previewed the Liberty.

In late October, a second version of the Willys was shown at the Tokyo International Auto Show. The Willys2 basically added a hardtop to the Willys. A rather large roof rack, complete with off-road lighting, upped carrying capacity for the 95-inch wheelbase vehicle. It weighed about 3,000 pounds and had a top speed of 90 mph.

The Willys series (which may not be ended) and the 2002 Compass concept all may be hints of an eventual replacement for the Wrangler that has styling that (more or less) dates back to the Willys' era and birth of the Jeep as a light transportation vehicle for World War II.

Independent Makes

AM Styling VP Richard Teague
and Javelin girl Judy Rockley.

Despite their near-constant financial problems, the independent automobile manufacturers of the United States made significant contributions to the dream/show/concept car arena.

Covered in this segment are some of the offerings to the public from American Motors, Nash-Kelvinator Corp., Hudson Motor Car Co., Kaiser-Frazer Corp., Packard Motor Car. Co., Studebaker-Packard Corp., and Tucker Corporation.

There were, of course, many more independent manufacturers, before and even after World War II, but not all played the auto shows like those above. Nash and Hudson merged to form American Motors and there was a continuum of dream/concept cars from 1950's Nash NXI right into the 1980s, when AMC was swallowed by Chrysler Corporation. Notable were two concept car groupings, Project IV of 1966 and Concept 80 of 1978.

After significant styling contributions to Packard, Richard Teague went to American Motors after a brief stint at Chrysler Corp., and had a hand in some of the outstanding cars of their times, like the 1966 AMX, 1969 AMX/2 and 1970 AMX/3.

Teague's forte, both at Packard and AMC, was working miracles with limited finances. It is mind boggling to ponder what Teague could have accomplished with a budget like that of the Big Three.

American Motors was the custodian of Jeep from 1970 into 1987. Some concept vehicles were produced under AMC, but all Jeep vehicles are listed under DaimlerChrysler, the current owner of the brand.

Hudson's foray into dream cars was brief, despite having styling under the brilliant Frank Spring. Conservative management and dollar doldrums kept the Hudson tally to one vehicle shown here, the 1953 Super Jet, which became the Italia. Limited production followed, but Nash-dominated AMC was not about to put further Hudsons in the spotlight.

If realities of the new car open market hadn't bitten Kaiser-Frazer after the postwar shortage was quenched, the corporation might have turned out some spectacular dream cars.

Styling of the 1951 Kaisers was well advanced over the competition. However, our Kaiser coverage is limited to some specially trimmed show cars and a pre-production example of the Kaiser-Darrin, which became a reluctant show car in the battle between noted stylist Howard "Dutch" Darrin and K-F management.

Packard was a dream-car player, right to the end of its life as a true luxury marque in 1956. Edward Macauley loved style and loved to flaunt it, much like GM's Harley Earl, but lacked the dollars. A string of 1950s Packard dream cars belied the financial troubles that lied beneath, but sure garnered plenty of interest. Teague's tenure at Packard can be remembered by (among others) the 1955 production-based Request and the 1956 Predictor, one of the most spectacular dream cars of them all.

Studebaker Corp., which merged with Packard to form Studebaker-Packard Corp., was not a major player in the dream car competition. Despite having some of the best looking and most advanced production cars of all time, like the 1953 coupes and 1963 Avanti, it did not tease the public with dream/show models ahead of production. A 1958 atomic powered vehicle is the best we can do.

Controversial Tucker Corporation started its public campaign with the Tucker Torpedo coupe to show how way out the new Tuckers were supposed to be. The fact it was a scale model was not publicized. Since scale models served several roles in our dream/concept scenario, it is covered here.

Independent domestic manufacturers are gone today. In fact, it is debatable if there are two or three major manufacturers left of domestic origin. Despite their departure, the vehicles that were generated by the independents remain significant to the history of dream/show/concepts over the past 60 or so years.

1955 Nash Pininfarina Speciale

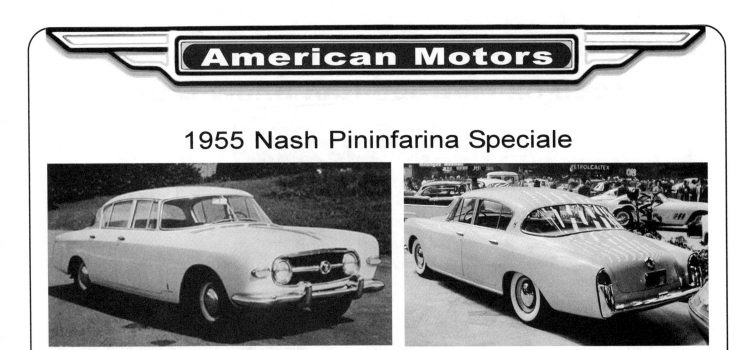

With Pininfarina badges affixed to its production cars due to a styling contract, Nash's association with the Italian firm was well known. How much of the 1952 and up Nash's design came from Pininfarina is subject to debate.

Looking for a replacement down the road, for the 1955 or 1956 model year, Nash ordered a prototype from Pininfarina. It got back a well smoothly styled replacement for the Ambassador, in running form.

Featuring reverse-angle C-pillars like the production models,

it added a wraparound windshield, inboard headlights, and a Nash-inspired dashboard.

Nash merged with Hudson to become American Motors before the Speciale (as it was badged) arrived, and an all-new full-sized car was out of the question, especially with an all-new Rambler in the works.

Normally a prototype does not qualify for dream-car status, but Pininfarina, in hopes of getting approval from AMC, displayed the Speciale and got photos published worldwide.

1956 Nash/Rambler Palm Beach

Shown extensively here and abroad, the 1956 Palm Beach by Pininfarina could well have been a prototype for the next generation Nash-Healey sports car. Early appearances carried a Nash badge and wheel covers, but that changed to Rambler before long.

American Motors ordered the car to be built, but did not follow up with a production program, even a limited one like the 1951-54 Nash-Healey had. The failure to progress was for financial reasons, not the styling of the Palm Beach, which was one of the better looking dream cars of the decade.

While the greenhouse carried the Nash theme of reverse angled rear pillars, the rest of the Palm Beach looked more

European. Up front, a jet-intake grille was flanked by two more openings and the headlights were encased in plastic bubbles. A pair of rear fins looked like the 1958-59 Ramblers would have and set off the rear cove.

While the Palm Beach looked exotic, its underpinnings were anything but. A Rambler flathead six produced just 90 horsepower and was joined by a standard Rambler three-speed manual transmission.

1960-62 Metropolitan Show Cars

1961 Westerner

1960 Station Wagon

American Motors was launched from the assets of Nash-Kelvinator Corp. and Hudson Motor Car Co. on May 1, 1954, with Nash being the strong partner. About the same time, the British-built Metropolitan was launched to compete in the sporty small car market.

It first carried the Nash badge and later Hudson before it became an independent make in 1957. Unfortunately, production ended in 1960, but with a large inventory on hand, it was marketed into 1962. Coinciding with the year of its production curtailment was the start of it being used as the basis for show cars. Show versions continued into 1962.

Four show cars, all convertibles, with regional themes and varying paint and trim, made the rounds at auto shows.

There was the 1960 Fifth Avenue, 1961 Westerner (shown), Palm Beach, and Cape Cod. For 1962, a trio of Royal Runabouts were fielded, a convertible and two hardtops. The show cars were successful in helping clear inventory.

A pair of Metropolitan station wagon prototypes were constructed and photos were released, but it is likely they were not seen by the public at auto shows.

1964 Rambler Cheyenne

Tarpon wasn't the only auto show attraction for 1964 at the Rambler display.

American Motors did lots of specially trimmed, production-based show cars in its day and seeing how many station wagons it sold, the Cheyenne got its own turntable. Anodized aluminum side trim on the Classic Cross Country was similar to the gold trim on the 1957 Rambler Rebel.

Signage for another Rambler show car, the Carrousel, is in the background.

1964 Rambler Tarpon

American Motors created a surprisingly sporty show car and later a controversy when it introduced the 1964 Rambler Tarpon. It was first shown at the Society of Automotive Engineers (SAE) convention in Detroit in January and to the public in February at the Chicago Auto Show.

Basically, a stylish fastback was grafted onto the all-new compact 106-inch wheelbase Rambler American; much like the Plymouth Barracuda was derived from the Valiant. With semi-boat tail styling and a vinyl swath down the middle of the roof, the Tarpon fit right in to the coming sporty compact wave, which the Barracuda and Ford Mustang would expand in spring.

A convex grille, chrome wheels with knock-offs, and redesigned taillights dressed up the outside, while four bucket-type seats did the same for the inside.

The controversy was not with the Tarpon, but rather what followed.

With favorable public reaction, producing the

Tarpon would have no doubt helped counter the sales slide AMC was about to experience.

Instead, the design was super sized and put on a Rambler Classic 112-inch wheelbase intermediate platform and called the Rambler Marlin. It appeared mid-year in 1965 to a less than enthusiastic reception. The Marlin died after a small number of 1967 models were sold.

1966 Vixen

To garner some much needed attention, American Motors announced a series of four concept cars in June of 1966, Project IV. The cars toured the country to test public reaction, much like the 1950 Nash NXI (which became the Metropolitan).

The quartet provided a decent preview of some upcoming new products from AMC. Filling the sport coupe role was the Vixen, featuring a landau roof, wrap over doors, and a front clip, complete with scoop, that was mighty close to that on the 1970 Hornet compact.

Vents were angled at 45 degrees to increase visibility when the car backed up. A sliding rear quarter window gave flow-through ventilation.

Like three of the four cars in the series, the Vixen was a roller. It had no power train.

American Motors

1966 AMX

The most significant member of American Motors' Project IV of 1966 was the AMX, a name that would stick with the corporation for many years.

A two-passenger sports model, it featured a cantilever-type top and no front A-pillars. An old feature was revived with the "Ramble Seat" with two more passengers seated in the trunk area. The lid flipped up for access and the rear window rose as a windbreak. Mounted on a 98-inch wheelbase and 179 inches long, the AMX closely previewed the production model, which would bow as a 1968 ½.

The first AMX was a fiberglass-bodied roller, like the other Project IV entries, but public reaction at the shows was so

strong, AMC had Vignale of Italy produced a steel bodied example with a new AMC thinwall 290-cubic-inch V-8.

The engine would have plenty of room to grow and would reach 401 cubes in due time.

1966 AMX II

Applying the AMX name to a two-door hardtop that had little resemblance to the original begot the AMX II member of the Project IV family.

The stylish II was more a preview of the forthcoming 1968 Javelin in size, but not in design, which was closer to the 1967 Mercury Cougar. It had an overall length of 187 inches and 110-inch wheelbase and taillights with red, amber, and green lenses.

It, too, was a roller.

1966 Cavalier

Most innovative of the Project IV vehicles was the Cavalier four-door sedan.

It featured interchangeable fenders and doors with left front the same as right rear, etc. Hood and deck were also the same stampings. It was 175-inches long and had a 108-inch wheelbase. Styling proved another tip-off for the 1970 Hornet, but that car did not feature the switchable tin.

The Cavalier was another roller. Chevrolet would take over the name in the 1980s for its long-lived subcompact line.

1967 AMX III

Previewing the 1968 Javelin's frontal styling and to some extent the 1971 Hornet Sportabout lines was the AMX III concept wagon, which bowed to the public at the 1967 Chicago Auto Show.

While sporty crossover wagons were decades away, the idea of a Javelin-based wagon got show goers to take notice. The rear hatch rose and then slid forward to rest on the roof.

When the 1968 Javelin sporty compact arrived in the fall of 1967, the public had been prepared for its arrival with the size and basic package shown in the 1966 AMX II and the styling in the 1967 AMX III.

1968 AMX/GT

The AMX/GT answered the question, What if you cross an AMX with a Gremlin?

The reason nobody asked it was that the AMX/GT was first shown at the 1968 New York Auto Show and the Gremlin was not introduced until mid-year 1970.

With the AMX production car a mid-year 1968 model, this show version was quite striking.

It leads one to wonder what if the truncated style had bowed on the AMX first.

American Motors

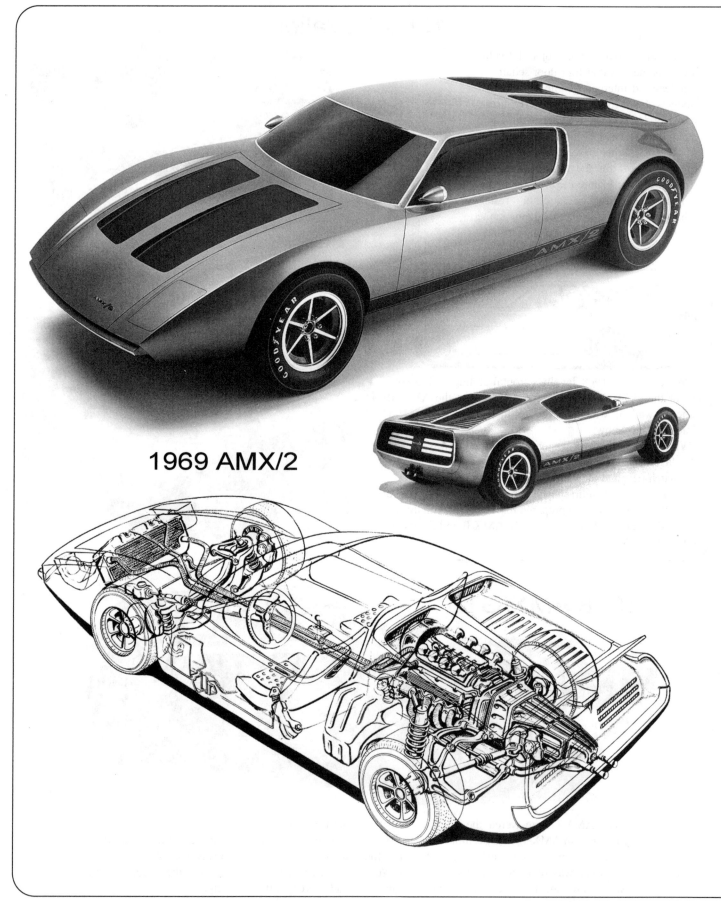

1969 AMX/2

1970 AMX/3

Like General Motors and Ford Motor Company, American Motors tried its hand at designing and building mid-engine sports cars. Ford's designs got into production in the UK, GM's Corvettes never got out of prototype stage and AMC fell somewhere in between.

The first step was a non-powered concept car, the AMX/2 (not to be confused with the 1966 AMX II of Project IV fame). Designed by the AMC staff, it was done in fiberglass, with hopes of installing an AMC V-8 mid-ship. The AMX/2 had a 105-inch wheelbase, length of 171.5 inches, width at 70.4 inches, and overall height a low 43 inches.

On display at the 1969 Chicago Auto Show for the first time, it generated public support encouraging American Motors to go further. The next step was the AMX/3, which retained the intended engine and chassis design, but featured a sleeker four window body, compared to the two window AMX/2. A prototype was built under the direction of Giotto Bizzarini of Italy. It was followed by five running examples. There are reports of a sixth being made after the short production run ended. Dimensions were close, but not identical to the AMX/2.

A 340-horsepower 390-cubic inch V-8 provided power and transaxle design varied. It was shown in Europe in March of 1970 and debuted stateside at the New York Auto Show in April.

Plans called for production of the AMX/3 to continue, but roblems and cost overruns closed the project before it could mirror the civilian Ford GT-40 production.

The AMX name would bounce around the AMC vehicle lines into 1980, but the rear engine experiments for AMC ended with the AMX/3.

American Motors

1971 Gucci Sportabout

AMC was quite adept at dressing up its products with various designer themes, something Lincoln would dwell on for many years.

American Motors had a fling with Dr. Aldo Gucci. He designed modifications to the 1971 Hornet Sportabout wagon and the result was a one-off show model. Outside there were Gucci emblems and a grille with the lights covered by a wraparound transparent cover. A restyled grille and separate side marker lights were added. Inside was a special upholstery pattern, picnic tables, vanity and set of fitted luggage.

Show reaction was positive and a toned down Gucci option for the Hornet Sportabout was available for 1972 and 1973.

1972 Gremlin Voyagaur

To remedy a complaint about the Gremlin, AMC showed it got the message about the limited rear access, at least when it came to a show car, thus the 1972 Voyageur. Highlighting it was the "Grem-Bin," which was a sliding tray that included the rear panel and extended the cargo area, or provided a place for tailgate parties and the like.

The Voyageur also featured special side trim for sporting outdoor types. When it came to production Gremlins, they had to make do with the small rear window/hatch through the 1976 models. A slightly larger window/hatch finally arrived for the 1977-78 Gremlins and Spirit sedans, which replaced them.

1973 Hornet GT

Using different styling on each side of a car was common in styling studios, especially when money was tight, but showing such an example to the public was a bit unusual. American Motors wasn't afraid to try and the Hornet GT idea car of 1973 contains several elements from the styling studios.

On a short Gremlin wheelbase, it had a Hornet front clip with a modified grille. The rear quarters featured a large window on the left side and more formal smaller one on the right.

The first views came at the annual shareholders meeting in early 1973.

1974 Gremlin G/II

From our vantage point today, the 1974 Gremlin G/II idea car doesn't look all that unusual; save for the details, it was a long-lead preview of the 1979 Spirit from AMC.

The hatchback gave a different perspective to the abruptly chunky regular Gremlin. It appeared for the first time in the fall of 1973 at the Detroit Auto Show. It utilized a Hornet front clip, which eventually was adapted to the Spirit.

A different grille set it apart from the Hornet.

1974 Gremlin XP

An advanced styling experiment to evaluate a possible next generation Gremlin look was one of several idea cars American Motors fielded in the first half of the 1970s.

The Gremlin XP featured a wraparound rear window that attacked the massive C-pillar that Gremlin had since its inception as a mid-year 1970 model. It was three pieces so that the center could be opened for access to the area behind the rear seat. It kind of resembled the 1950s Nash and Rambler trademark of a reverse-angled rear pillar. A two-toned rear cove held a quartet of round taillights.

As it turned out, the Gremlin would run to the end of its production in 1978 with the wide rear pillars.

1976 Pacer Stinger

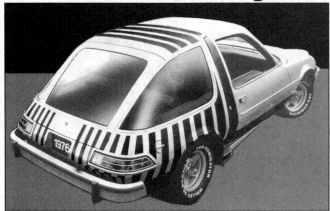

Few remember that the Pacer was a hot seller for AMC in its early months on the market in 1975. However, when the number of buyers who wanted something different began to be satisfied, sales dropped and the final years were not popular ones for the Pacer. Production ended mid-year in 1980.

An early show model during the popular era was the Stinger for 1976. It went on a national tour at custom car shows.

Yellow pearl paint with bumble bee stripes, exterior side exhausts, road lights, fender scoops, and special wheels were part of the setup. Inside, black and yellow vinyl seats and sporty options completed the package. No production version was to follow.

American Motors

1978 Concept I

1978 Concept II

American Motors unveiled six concept cars for the 1978 show season that illustrated the company's vision for more fuel-efficient cars for the 1980s.

Under the banner of Concept 80 were the Concept I, Concept II, Concept Grand Touring, Concept AM VAN, Concept Electron, and Concept Jeep II. Concept I and II were similar in size with a 96-inch wheelbase, overall length of just over 153 inches, and width of 68 inches.

They were not production-based. Slim roof pillars, minimal front and rear overhang, and thin door panels helped AMC claim they could sit three people across, front and back.

Large glass area gave the interior an open feel.

The Concept I had a quasi-continental rear tire mount and spoke wheels. The Concept II featured a built-in rollbar/B-pillar which divided the roof in segments. It also had aluminum wheels. Rectangular headlights were used on the Concept I, while headlamps in the Concept II were hidden. Both had no driveline and therefore were rollers.

1978 Concept Grand Touring

Most production based of the AMC Concept 80 vehicles was the Concept Grand Touring. Based on the Gremlin platform, its purpose was to infuse luxury features into a small car.

With a wheelbase of 96 inches and overall length, it turned out to be the longest of the Concept 80 group. The metallic green hatchback featured a dark green part vinyl roof and formal rear quarter window, special grille and spoke wheels. Inside was leather and cord texture seating.

General Motors/GM Corporate

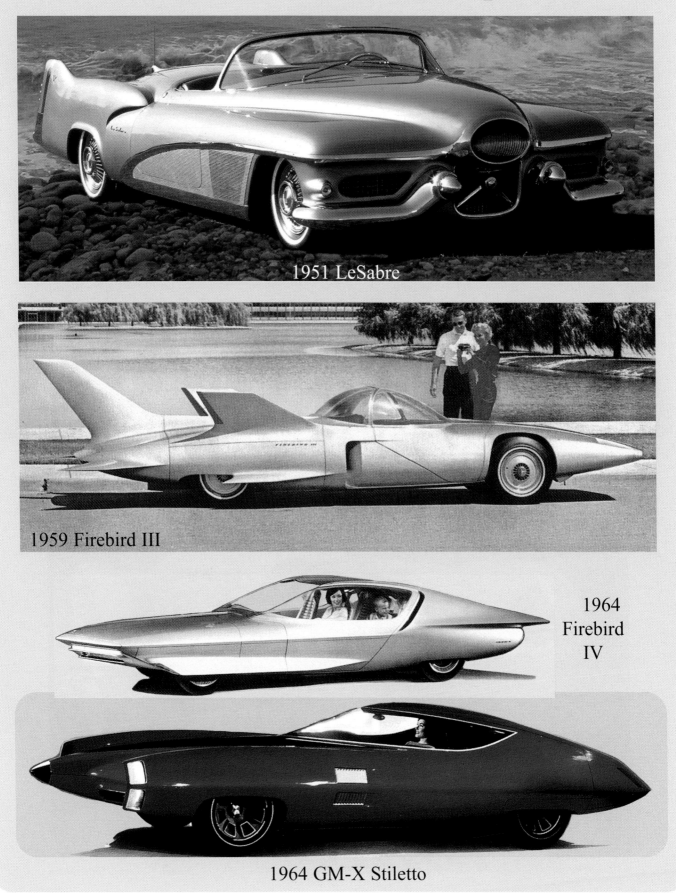

1951 LeSabre

1959 Firebird III

1964
Firebird
IV

1964 GM-X Stiletto

General Motors/GM Corporate

1981 Aero X

1991 HX3

1992 Ultralite

2000 Precept

2002 AUTOnomy

General Motors/Buick

1939 Y-Job

1954 Wildcat II

1972 Silver Arrow III

1956 Centurion

1983 Questor

General Motors/Buick

1985 Wildcat

1999 Cielo

2000 Blackhawk

2001 Bengal

2000 LaCrosse

General Motors/Cadillac

1953 LeMans

1959 Cyclone

1985 Cimarron PPG

1905 Osceola

1989 Solitiare

1990 Aurora

2002 Cien

General Motors/Chevrolet

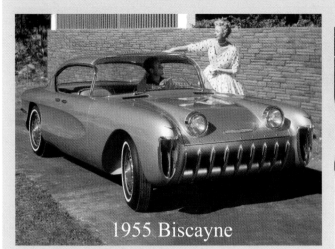

1955 Biscayne

1956 Impala

1960 Corvette XP-700

1963 Monza
Super Spyder

1962 Corvair Monza SS

1967 Camaro Waikiki

1962 Corvair Monza GT

General Motors/Chevrolet

1972 Corvette 2-Rotor

1978 Malibu Black Sterling

1981 Turbo Vette III

1985 Camaro GTZ

1986 Corvette Indy

General Motors/Chevrolet

1987 Express

1993 Highlander

2000 SSR

1999 Nomad

2002 Bel Air

General Motors/Oldsmobile

1953 Starfire X-P Rocket

1955 Delta

1954 F-88

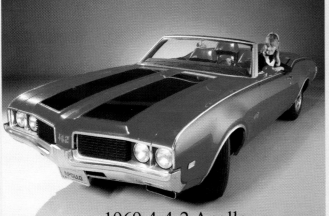

1969 4-4-2 Apollo

1964 4-4-2

General Motors/Oldsmobile

1971 Contessa

1990 Expression

1992 Anthem

1999 Recon

2001 O4

General Motors/Pontiac

1956 Club de Mar

1979 Grand Prix Landau

1984 Fiero

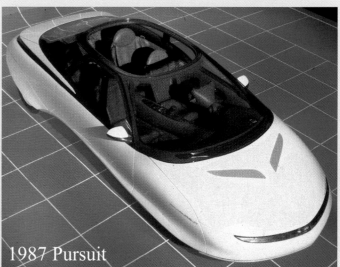

1987 Pursuit

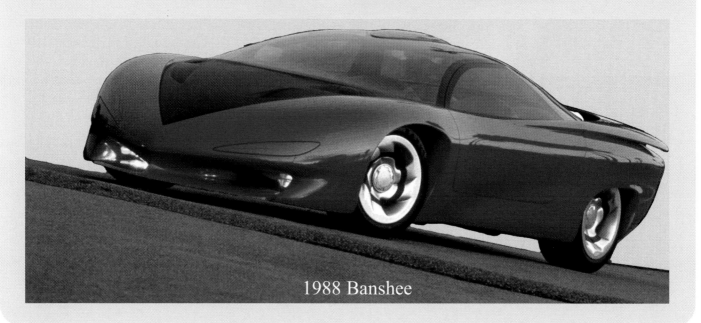

1988 Banshee

General Motors/Pontiac

1989 Stinger

1990 Sunfire

1992 Salsa

1997 Rageous

1998 Montana Thunder

General Motors/Pontiac

1999 GTO

2000 Piranha

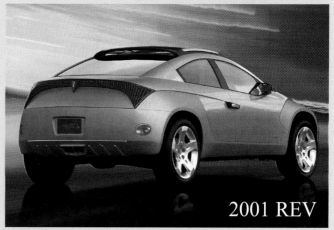

2001 REV

2002 Soltice Coupe

General Motors/GMC Trucks

1988 Sierra CART/PPG

1990 Transcend

1991 Sagebrush

2000 Sierra Street Scene Special

2002 Terra4

Ford Motor Company/Ford

1953 Muroc

1954 FX-Atmos

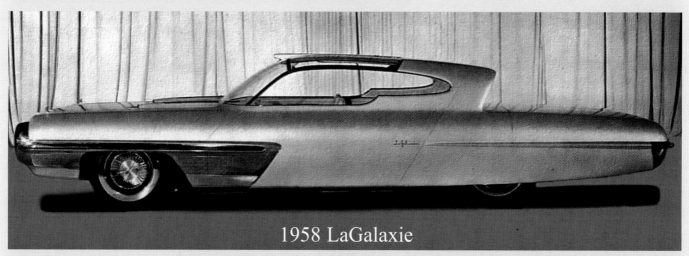

1958 LaGalaxie

1958 Volante

1962 Cougar 406

1973 Explorer SUV

Ford Motor Company/Ford

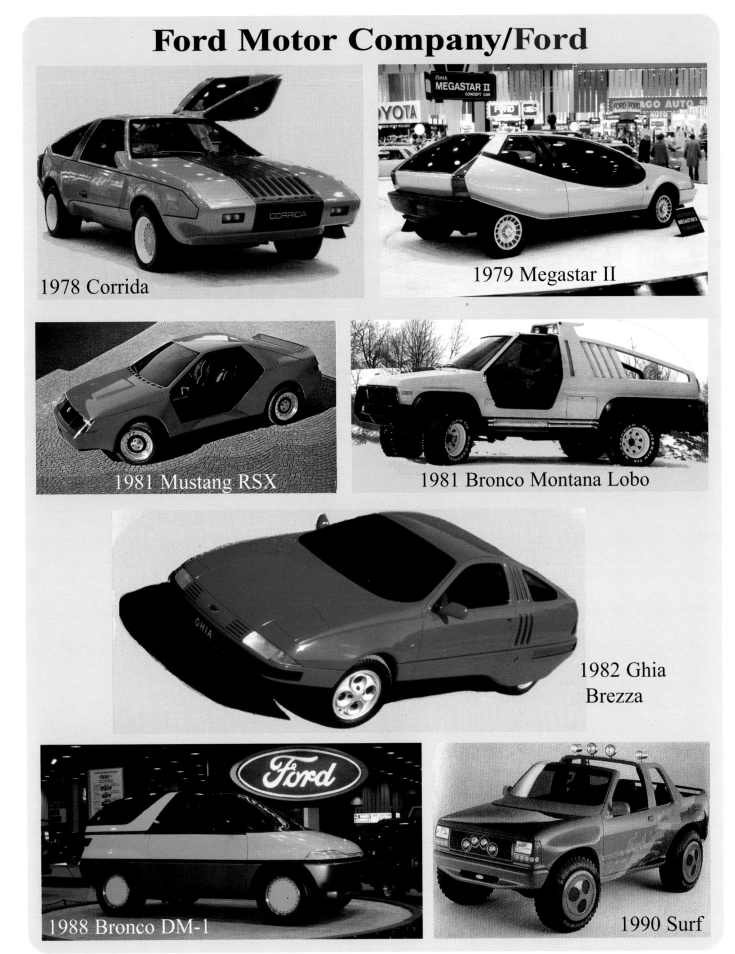

1978 Corrida

1979 Megastar II

1981 Mustang RSX

1981 Bronco Montana Lobo

1982 Ghia Brezza

1988 Bronco DM-1

1990 Surf

320

Ford Motor Company/Ford

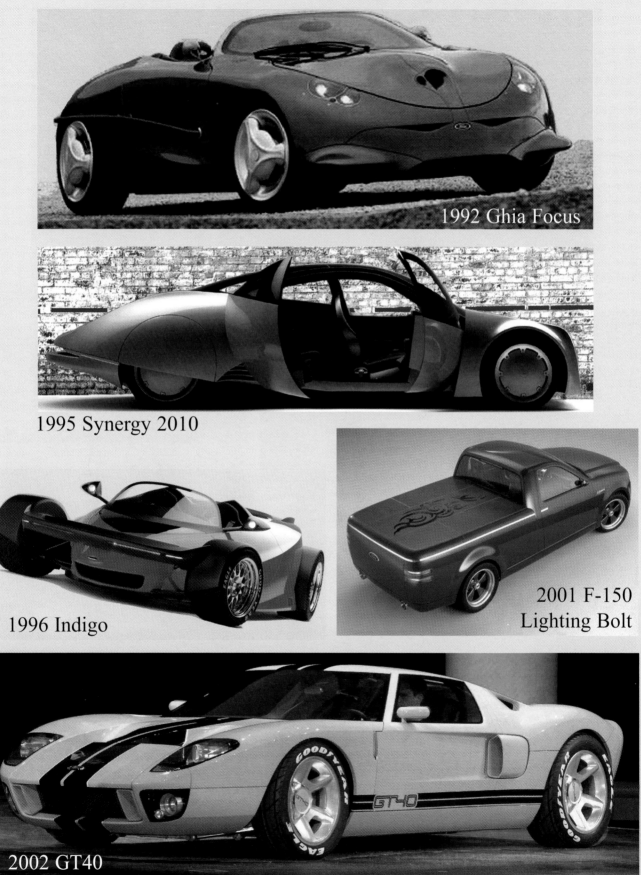

1992 Ghia Focus

1995 Synergy 2010

1996 Indigo

2001 F-150 Lighting Bolt

2002 GT40

Ford Motor Company/Lincoln

1966 Coronation Coupe

1992 Marque X

1995 L2K

2001 MK9

2002 Continental Concept

Ford Motor Company/Mercury

1954 XM-800

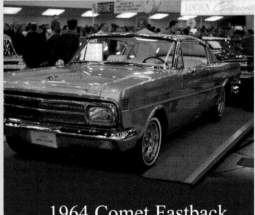

1964 Comet Fastback

1964 Super Marauder

1956 Turnpike Cruiser

1966 Escapade

1970 Cyclone Super Spoiler

Ford Motor Company/Mercury

1979 XM

1997 MC4

1990 Cyclone

1999
Cougar S

1999 (MY)

DaimlerChrysler/Chrysler

1941 Thunderbolt

1941 Newport Parade Car

1963 Turbine

1961 TurboFlite

DaimlerChrysler/Chrysler

1966 300X

1995 Atlantic

1997 Phaeton Dual-Cowl

2001 Crossfire

DaimlerChrysler/DeSoto

1954 Adventurer II

1959 Cella I

DaimlerChrysler/Dodge

1954 Firearrow Roadster I

1979 Big Red

1967 Deora

1982 024 PPG

1986 M4S

DaimlerChrysler/Dodge

1989 Viper

1987 Daytona

1990 DBX

1994 Venom

VENOM YESTERDAY'S POWER, TODAY'S SOPHISTICATION!

DaimlerChrysler/Dodge

1999 Charger RT

2000 MAXXcab

2000 ESX3

2002 Razor

2002 M80

DaimlerChrysler/Plymouth

1960 XNR

1965 V.I.P.

1966 Barracuda

1969 Duster I Road Runner

1980 Turismo Spyder

DaimlerChrysler/Plymouth

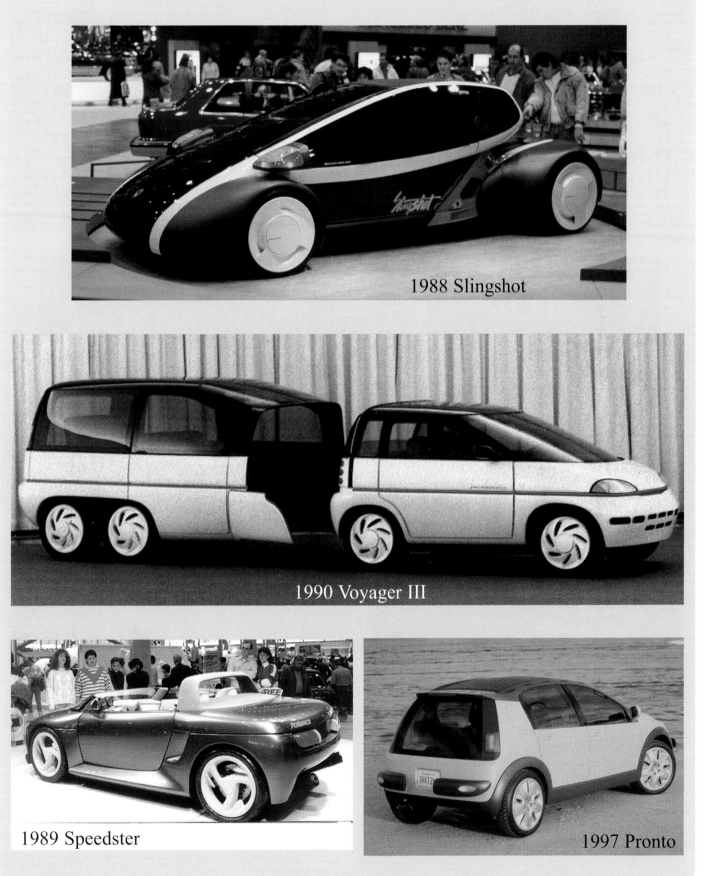

1988 Slingshot

1990 Voyager III

1989 Speedster

1997 Pronto

DaimlerChrysler/Plymouth

1993 Prowler

1994 Neon Expresso

1998 Pronto Spyder

1995 Backpack

1999 Voyager XG

DaimlerChrysler/Jeep

1985 Cherokee Targa

1990 Cherokee Freedom

1991 Wagoneer 2000

1993 Ecco

1997 Icon

DaimlerChrysler/Jeep

1998 Jeepster

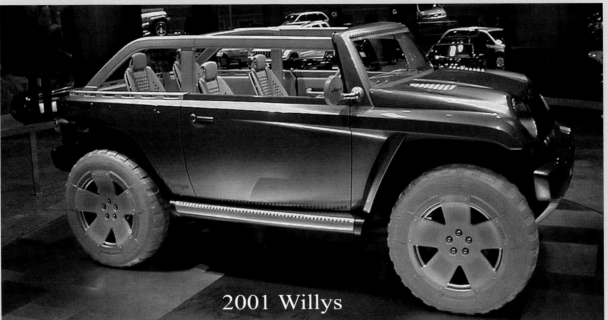

2001 Willys

2000 Varsity

2002 Compass

Independent/American Motors

1964 Rambler Tarpon

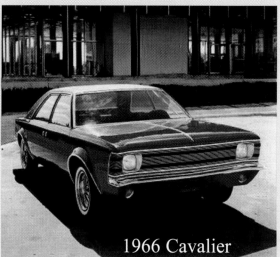

1966 Cavalier

1966 AMX

1969
AMX/2

1970 AMX/3

Independent/American Motors

In a time of crisis it is voluntary effort that makes the difference in a free society. What is not done voluntarily will be done by regulation. More regulation means more cost and less choice for the car buyers.

1978 Concept
AM VAN

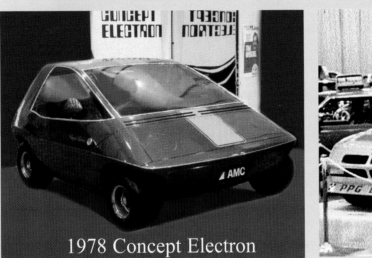

1978 Concept Electron

1981 PPG AMX Turbo

Independent/Hudson

1953 Super Jet/Italia

1968 Amitron

With much fanfare, American Motors and Gulton Industries announced the Amitron electric (above, left and top right) car in December of 1967. It was to be powered by batteries and controls from Gulton.

However, the Amitron was a roller with no batteries, motors, or controls therein.

Considering its 60-inch wheelbase and miniature 85-inch length, it's just as well batteries didn't have to be piled in.

Seating for three in the front (and only) seat would have made it crowded. The basis for the Amitron's design was a breakthrough in battery technology, which did not materialize.

Despite that, the Amitron returned 10 years later and became Concept Electron (right) as part of AMC's Concept 80 show vehicles. Little changed; it was still a roller.

1978 Concept Electron

1978 Concept AM VAN

Take all the gingerbread off the Concept 80's Concept AM VAN and you have a forerunner of the 1980s' craze, the minivan. Add the fact it was designed as a four-wheel-drive vehicle and there is a 20-some year advance look at today's crossover vehicles.

AMC did not see the market potential for the AM VAN and perhaps the market was not ready in 1978.

Pulling styling themes from the Pacer wagon and a driveline from a Jeep, the AM VAN came up with a unique body, loaded with custom touches.

Wheel flares, big wheels and tires, outside exhaust, road lights, small circular rear quarter windows and twin rear doors all were neat touches.

American Motors

1978 Crown Pacer

Trying to create a luxury image for its controversial wide small car, AMC put the Crown Pacer on the show circuit for 1978, starting with the fall 1977 Detroit Auto Show.

A two-section white padded vinyl roof helped offset the bubble styling, while a high and wide split grille with hidden headlights gave an alternative to the production Pacer front end.

It was painted pearlescent white with gold accents, including wire wheels with gold spokes. Inside, white leather seats, armrest, door panel trim, and steering wheel cover continued the theme.

1981 PPG AMX Turbo

Even though the AMX nameplate died midway through the 1980 model year, its last hurrah with American Motors was the 1981 AMX Turbo that was one of the pace cars for the CART PPG Indy Car World Series.

Under the wild (for AMC) fiberglass bodywork was a Spirit hatchback with a fuel injected, turbocharged 258-cubic-inch six-cylinder engine.

A beefed-up automatic transmission and heavy duty underpinnings handled the horses, reputed to be beyond the 400 mark. A special racing interior was suited for the race track duty the car would and did see.

In 1981, there was one pace car from each of the four domestic auto manufacturing corporations.

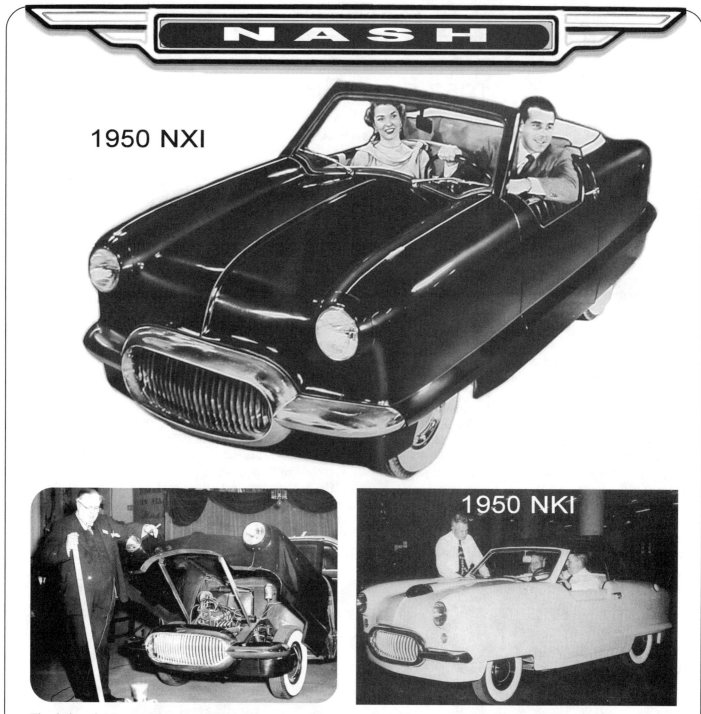

NASH

1950 NXI

1950 NKI

The beloved Metropolitan was sold by American Motors from mid-year 1954 through 1962, when leftover supplies ran out. Its development was far more public than most such vehicles that break into new markets.

The result of rotund Nash-Kelvinator President George W. Mason's belief in small cars, the NXI was first shown to the public at the Waldorf Astoria Hotel in New York in 1950. Mason is shown, top left, with the NXI as it was being prepared for the exhibit. A series of showings across the country followed and questionnaires were handed out to get the public's opinion.

The lines of the Metropolitan were pretty much down at that time and styling would prove a preview of the firm's all-new 1952 model big Nash line.

Reaction was generally favorable, save for the 18-horsepower 500 cc Fiat engine. Later in 1950, the NXI was followed up by the NKI (Nash-Kelvinator International), prototypes, including the two-door hardtop shown at right. The NKI was not shown to the public like the NXI. The NKI gained a front hood scoop, rear wheel cutout and a more powerful engine. Mason is at the wheel this time.

In 1952, it was announced that it would be produced-not in the U.S., but by Fisher & Ludlow, Ltd. in England. Power would come from an Austin-sourced driveline.

Several changes were made to the Metropolitan over the years, but the basic body remained little changed from the early examples, including not having an exterior trunk.

A trunk was finally added mid-year in 1959.

HUDSON

1953 Super Jet/Italia

Hudson, with its days as an independent manufacturer numbered, entered the dream car arena with a coupe, the Super Jet, above left, that eventually went into limited production under the Italia name.

Mounted on the unitized platform of its compact Jet and powered by a 202-cubic inch Jet engine, the Super Jet was full of styling gimmicks. An oval grille, triangle centered front bumper, bold headlight scoops, rounded sides with air scoops, wire wheels, and taillights mounted in three exhaust pipe-like tubes all broke with conservative Hudson styling - big time.

In front were individual bucket seats, a back seat, and modified Jet dashboard. When the decision was made to have Carrozzeria Touring of Italy, which built the prototype, construct a run of cars in 1954 under the Italia name, the prototype was renamed Italia and the badges on the front fenders changed.

At the time, Hudson was in the process of a merger with Nash-Kelvinator Corp. and only 25 production Italias were built.

The original Super Jet/Italia and the rest of the Italias differed in minor details, but all had the 114-horsepower Jet engine and three-speed manual transmissions. The Italia wasn't the only model to cease production in 1954, as the Jet and standard sized Hudson perished as well, being replaced by Kenosha, Wis.-built variations of Nash models.

The last production Hudson sold in the U.S. was the 1957 model. A four-door sedan prototype, the X-161, was constructed expanding Italia styling to a larger vehicle.

While the car was interesting, neither Hudson nor new partner Nash had the funds to further develop it.

1941 Phantom

Packard Motor Car Company boss Edward Macauley (second from left) was not the low profile sort, as he insisted on driving a Packard that stood out from the crowd of cars in general and Packards in particular. This creation, known as the Phantom, serviced him for several years and was updated several times.

Used as both personal transportation and a display car, it was the counterpart to Harley Earl's Buick Y-Job, which also was a specially built car driven regularly. The Phantom started life as a 1941 Packard One-Eighty Darrin Convertible Victoria and was modified with a fixed landau top, complete with irons. To keep the rain off, a removable clear plastic top fit between the windshield and the top.

The version shown here was as it appeared in early 1947. It had been fitted with a new grille, new sheet metal, and new bumpers.

1952 Pan American

Joining the dream/show car sweepstakes, the Packard Pan American appeared at the New York Auto Show in March of 1952.

Looking like a current convertible at first glance, the single seat sports model was lower than stock, featured a chopped windshield, front hood scoop, modified grille, spoke wheels, and continental rear spare.

It was designed by Richard Arbib and built by the Henney Co., Packard's specialty manufacturer.

Response from the public was positive, as the basic body was only in its second year and up to a half dozen were built with some being sold to the public.

Packard

1953 Balboa

Packard reaped more attention with a relatively simple move that yielded the Balboa hardtop. Starting with its custom built Caribbean, it added a chopped two-door hardtop roof with a reverse-slanted rear window under a canopy-like lid.

The window did not retract, as a similar design on future Mercurys and Lincolns would.

Spoke wheels, continental kit, and other details marked the car, built by Mitchell-Bentley, which had the contract for making Caribbeans.

Looking over the rear window, above, are, from left, William Graves, engineering vice president, and Edward Macauley, chief styling engineer.

1955 Request

Despite going back to production cars as a basis, Packard created one of its most memorable show cars, the 1955 Request.

With a 400 two-door hardtop to start with, a traditional pre-war Packard grille was fitted, along with split bumpers and modified front sheet metal.

Constructed by Creative Industries, it was rumored to be a preview of a future Packard. Such was not the case, as Detroit Packards stopped being built after the slightly face lifted 1956 models.

1954 Gray Wolf II/ Panther-Daytona

Not content with modified production show cars, Packard went all out with its 1954 entry, the Gray Wolf II, named after a 1903 Packard racer.

It featured a fiberglass body, with styling combining traditional Packard themes, and futuristic styling, wraparound windshield, and a single front seat.

Not just for looks, the Panther-Daytona, as it was renamed, got 275 horses out of its 359 cubic inch flathead straight eight, thanks to a McColloch supercharger.

To prove its mechanical prowess, it was entered in the speed trials at Daytona Beach, Florida. and Jim Rathmann turned in a 110-plus run officially and was clocked 20 mph faster unofficially.

Like the Pan American, multiple copies were made, with five constructed by Creative Industries. Two Panther-Daytonas were updated with 1955 styling cues and one was fitted with an experimental hardtop.

Packard

1956
Predictor

Belying the fact that operations in Detroit were in serious jeopardy, Packard's 1956 dream car, the Predictor, was easily the most impressive of the postwar period.

Designed by Richard Teague and built by Ghia of Italy, it borrowed styling from the stillborn prototypes for the 1957 models. It caught fire once it arrived in this country and had to be rebuilt by Creative Industries of Detroit, which turned out previous Packard show cars.

It appeared at the Chicago Auto Show and subsequent shows until the Packard balloon burst later in the year.

Features were many, including a front vertical grille bar which previewed the Edsel as much as anything, hidden headlights, wrap over windshield, retractable roof panels, reversed rear window, swivel seats, and expressive rear fins.

For the critics that felt Packard was too tied to the past and was still using its basic 1951 bodies, the Predictor showed a clear vision of future…styling.

Unfortunately, the future for Packard was considerably grimmer. Studebaker's South Bend, Indiana, plants produced the last Packards in 1957 and 1958, based on Studebaker designs.

1958 Studebaker-Packard Astral

Atomic energy provided the basis of several dream cars in the 1950s and beyond. One of the most radical was the Studebaker-Packard Corporation's Astral, first shown at the South Bend, Indiana, Art Center in 1958.

An open four-seater, it only had one wheel, a roll cage, and a receiver mounted on a single tail fin. The plan was for it to beam atomic power from a remote generator, which fueled its atomic engine and rendered it capable of running on one wheel, no wheels, flying, hovering, running in water or, if needed, on another planet…no, really, that was a claim.

The only problem was, all of the atomic stuff, including its engine, hadn't been invented yet, thus the Astral was a stationary model.

Brooks Stevens Prototypes

Technically, the Brooks Stevens prototypes for the 1964-66 Studebakers do not meet the dream/concept criteria of being shown to the public by the manufacturer, but after Studebaker's departure from automotive manufacturing in 1966, they have been seen by many. They have also been universally praised, as the talented designer not only proposed futuristic cars that could be produced at reasonable cost, but was involved in the construction of three cars.

They were built at Sibonia-Bassano of Milan, Italy.

A proposed 1964 four-door wagon, right, and 1965 four-door sedan, each with center opening doors and no B-pillar, and a 1966 two-door hardtop, the Sceptre, left, were built.

The wagon had a 1964-65 Studebaker-like grille, the sedan kind of a Hawk grille, and the Sceptre was distinguished by a full-width front light.

Stevens kept the wagon and the Sceptre hardtop at his museum in Mequon, Wis. for many years, until his death.

1965 Daytona Wagonaire Camper

Production of the remains of the Studebaker passenger car line continued only in Canada in 1964 and starting with the 1965 models, all were powered with General Motors (Chevrolet) engines.

To attract some attention at auto shows, a camper was fitted to the Daytona Wagonaire wagon, utilizing the sliding rear roof panel. Trim on the wagon more or less matched the unit.

Weighing some 800 pounds, it is likely the show vehicle was close to overloaded before any passengers or their gear got aboard.

Studebaker Canadian production ended mid-year in 1966.

TUCKER

1946 Torpedo Coupe

1946 Torpedo Coupe

Preston Tucker has been called everything from a visionary to a crook, but there is little question that he tried to take the automotive industry in new directions in style, engineering, and safety. His story of failure is well documented.

One of the earliest glimpses of what was coming from Tucker was the Torpedo coupe, shown to the public in early 1946. First drawings were released, above and right, that showed a streamlined vehicle with center steering, moveable front wheels, wrapover doors, and center front headlight.

That was followed later in the year by a quarter-scale model of the Torpedo, which now had a rear engine. The model was posed against an outdoor background, above, which made it look full-sized. No mention was made that it was a miniature.

A running Tucker was promised for 1947 and promise was fulfilled, but with a four-door sedan, rather than the Torpedo coupe. The rear engine sedan was more conventional than the drawings and the Torpedo model, but still full of different ideas.

Preston Tucker

KAISER

1951 Safari

1951 Explorer

To attract attention to its all-new 1951 models, Kaiser came up with a quartet of four-door sedan show cars for the Chicago Auto Show that year: the Explorer, Safari, South Seas, and Caballero. Each featured exotic interiors as part of the "Worldways in Motoring" exhibit. Animal rights' backers need read no further. The Explorer, shown above right, featured a polar bear fur interior, with bearskin on the outside. Zebra and lion fur got along in the Safari, (above left.

Not shown are the South Seas with Hawaiian pattern cloth, fish netting and grass mats, and the Caballero with horse hides and saddle bags. After the show, the cars were sold, some to celebrities and reportedly a few more Caballeros were built.

1953 DKF-161/KF-161

An early Kaiser Darrin prototype became a show car before it was approved to be a Kaiser, making one of the more interesting and complicated stories in dream/concept history. Howard "Dutch" Darrin, an internationally renowned stylist, decided to put a fiberglass sports-car body on a Henry J chassis not long after the Henry J bowed as a 1951 model compact.

Like most things Darrin put his hand to, it was striking, with a small grille, sliding and disappearing doors, and flowing lines. He proposed selling the design to Kaiser-Frazer, which was struggling in the marketplace and didn't have a sports-type car as its competitors like Nash were getting into.

Henry J. Kaiser and Edgar Frazer could not agree on taking action on the sports car, so Darrin displayed the car in a Los Angeles auto show in fall of 1952, without K-F knowledge.

Public reaction was favorable and so began a long-running relationship/feud that led to production of the Kaiser Darrin as a 1954 model. It only lasted that year and Darrin built his own versions for a couple of years after. The agreement between Darrin and K-F led to a number of prototypes being constructed with names DKF (Darrin Kaiser Frazer), DKF-161 (161 for the cubic inches of the Henry J six), and KF-161 (no Darrin). Changes and details before production could fill several pages, but the prototypes had two-piece windshields and the production versions got a one-piece job. Kaiser's marketing problems, production problems, and competition from the Chevrolet Corvette and others all cut the chances for the Kaiser Darrin to succeed. The photo is of the KF-161, which also was shown to the public prior to production starting in December of 1953.

Years of Automobile History At Your Fingertips

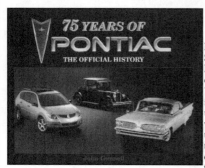

75 Years of Pontiac
The Official History
by John Gunnell
From the Chief of the Sixes and Silver Streaks to the famed GTO, Firebird and Trans Am, this full-color reference chronicles the rich 75-year history of Pontiac from its introduction in 1926 through today. Produced in full cooperation with Pontiac Motor Division, trace the development of the legend in this official hardcover anniversary edition featuring production figures for all models and 250 full-color photos.
Hardcover • 11-1/2 x 9 • 224 pages • 250 color photos
Item# SPONT • $29.95

Ultimate Truck & Van Spotter's Guide 1925-1990
by Tad Burness
This fun and informative guide will help you spot trucks and vans produced between 1920-1990. It's loaded with more than 3,000 side, front and rear photos and includes important technical information on model variations and modifications restorers and collectors need. Veteran author Tad Burness (*Ultimate Car Spotter's Guide 1946-1969*) comes through again with another winner all vehicle enthusiasts will treasure.
Softcover • 8-1/2 x 11 • 400 pages
3,000 b&w photos
Item# UTVG • $23.95

Classic Muscle Car Advertising
by MJ Frumkin
Strap yourself in for a powerful, historic ride through muscle car advertisements of the '50s, '60s, and '70s. You'll uncover hard-to-find factory facts and muscle car images from more than 160 near full size, restored-to-original-color advertisements. Includes popular models from American Motors, Buick, Chevrolet, Chrysler, Dodge, Ford, General Motors, Mercury, Oldsmobile, Plymouth, and Pontiac. Humorous text accompanies each advertisement for maximum enjoyment.
Softcover • 8-1/4 x 10-7/8 • 160 pages
160+ color photos
Item# CMCLC • $21.95

Ultimate Auto Album
An Illustrated History of the Automobile
by Tad Burness
Take a nostalgic trip with the classic cars you remember and discover some you've never seen before. As seen in a nationally syndicated newspaper feature across the country since 1966, Tad Burness' Auto Album, with hand drawn illustrations and accompanying text, offers glimpses of the time period, the featured car, or the manufacturer. Enjoy more than 490 classic domestic and import cars made from 1784 to 1985.
Softcover • 6 x 9 • 504 pages
496 b&w illustrations
Item# UAA • $16.95

Unusual Vintage Tractors
by C.H. Wendel
Here's a unique photographic look at American tractors with captions telling their amazing stories. Historian C.H. Wendel uncovers the companies who made big and small discoveries that led to some very unusual workhorses.
Softcover • 8-1/2 x 11 • 272 pages
250 b&w photos • 33 color photos
Item# UVT • $19.95

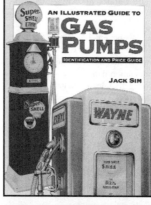

An Illustrated Guide to Gas Pumps
Identification and Price Guide
by Jack Sim
Identify and price gas pumps manufactured from 1885 to 1965 with the most comprehensive full-color gas pump resource available. More than 1,400 color images from original petroleum literature accurately identify the gas pumps. Listings provide current market value, company name, a brief description and history, years in production, original cost, and pump model number. Pump manufacturers include Acme Pump & Tank Company, Chicago Steel Tank Company, Erie Pump Company, United States Pump & Tank Company, and Wayne Tank & Pump Company.
Softcover • 8-1/4 x 10-7/8 • 352 pages
714 b&w illustrations & photos • 801 color illustrations & 41 color photos
Item# GSPP1 • $34.95

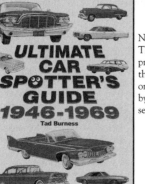

Ultimate Car Spotter's Guide 1946-1969
by Tad Burness
Name that American car every time. Thousands of detailed photographs and promotional illustrations along with thousands of fascinating marginal notes and original advertising slogans are all arranged by make of car and by year within each section.
Softcover • 8-1/2 x 11 • 384 pages
3,200 b&w photos • 1,200 illustrations
Item# UCSG • $21.95

GMC®
The First 100 Years
by John Gunnell
Celebrate 100 years of GMC trucks with this colorful hardcover reference covering the models of the company that "does one thing" and "does it well." This book is complete with photos, production figures, factory options, historical facts and advertisements. Read about the GMC trucks that helped shape America from the parlor-coach type buses of 1922 to the military "Ducks" of World War II to today's sport utility vehicles and pickup trucks.
Hardcover • 11 x 11 • 192 pages • 50+ b&w photos • 200+ color photos
Item# GMCHS • $29.95

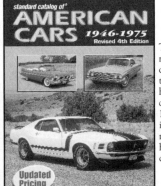

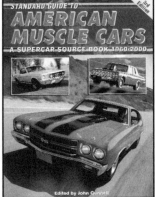
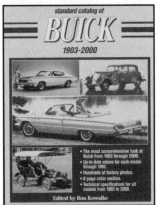